GED® Social Studies Test

FOR DUMMIES®

A Wiley Brand

by Murray Shukyn, BA, and
Achim K. Krull, BA, MAT

FOR DUMMIES®
A Wiley Brand

GED® Social Studies Test For Dummies®

Published by:
John Wiley & Sons, Inc.,
111 River Street, Hoboken, NJ 07030-5774,
www.wiley.com

Copyright © 2015 by John Wiley & Sons, Inc., Hoboken, New Jersey

Published simultaneously in Canada

For general information on our other products and services, please contact our Customer Care Department within the U.S. at 877-762-2974, outside the U.S. at 317-572-3993, or fax 317-572-4002. For technical support, please visit www.wiley.com/techsupport.

Wiley publishes in a variety of print and electronic formats and by print-on-demand. Some material included with standard print versions of this book may not be included in e-books or in print-on-demand. If this book refers to media such as a CD or DVD that is not included in the version you purchased, you may download this material at http://booksupport.wiley.com. For more information about Wiley products, visit www.wiley.com.

Library of Congress Control Number: 2015946682

ISBN 978-1-119-02983-0 (pbk); ISBN 978-1-119-02982-3 (ebk); ISBN 978-1-119-02984-7 (ebk)

Manufactured in the United States of America

10 9 8 7 6 5 4 3 2 1

Contents at a Glance

Table of Contents

Part II: Enhancing Your Social Studies Skills 65

Chapter 5: Reading and Understanding Social Studies Passages...........................67

Chapter 6: Understanding and Applying Key Social Studies Concepts 81

Chapter 7: Applying Mathematical Reasoning to Social Studies 99

Part III: Nurturing Your Knowledge: History, Civics, Economics, and Geography 111

Chapter 8: Brushing Up on Civics and Government 113

Introduction

You've decided to take the General Education Development (GED) test to earn the equivalent of a high school diploma. Congratulations! You're about to clear a major hurdle standing between you and your educational and professional goals. But now you realize that you need extra guidance to tackle the GED Social Studies test. Perhaps you took the test once or even twice and didn't do so well. Perhaps you've done an honest self-assessment and now realize that social studies was never your favorite or best subject. Whatever the reason, you need to quickly review the essentials and practice answering questions like those you'll encounter on the test. You want to know what to expect so you're not blindsided on test day.

Welcome to *GED Social Studies Test For Dummies* — your key to excelling on the GED Social Studies test. Here, you find everything you need to do well on the test, from guidance on how to improve reading speed and comprehension to whirlwind tours of civics, government, history, economics, and geography that get you up to speed on the basics. You also find out how to write a top-notch essay for the Extended Response portion of the test. Along the way, you get plenty of practice questions to cement your knowledge and skills.

About This Book

As we were writing *GED Test For Dummies*, 3rd Edition (Wiley), we didn't have the space to cover all four sections of the GED test in great detail. In that book, we provide a general overview of the GED test and two full-length practice tests that cover all four sections — Reasoning Through Language Arts (RLA), Mathematical Reasoning, Science, and Social Studies.

Knowing that test-takers can take each section of the GED test separately and that they probably need more guidance in some subject areas than in others, we decided to develop a separate workbook for each section — four workbooks, each with a balance of instruction and practice. In this book, the *GED Social Studies Test For Dummies,* we focus exclusively on the GED Social Studies test. Our goal is twofold: to prepare you to answer correctly any social studies question you're likely to encounter on the test so that you'll receive a high score and to help you do well on your Extended Response essay.

We begin by giving you a sneak peek at the test format and an overview of what's on the GED Social Studies test. We then provide a diagnostic test that presents you with Social Studies questions that challenge your reading, reasoning, and social studies skills and knowledge and identify your unique strengths and weaknesses. The diagnostic test and the self-assessment table following it guide you to specific skills and knowledge areas where you may need to focus your test-prep activities. When you feel ready, you can then tackle the full-length Social Studies practice test in Chapter 13 and turn to Chapter 14 for answers and explanations. Check the answers even for questions you answered correctly because the answers provide additional insight.

We wrap up with two Part of Tens chapters — one that presents ten study tips and another that reveals ten skills to develop prior to test day.

Foolish Assumptions

When we wrote this book, we made a few assumptions about you, dear reader. Here's who we think you are:

- You're serious about earning a GED as soon as possible.

- You're looking for additional instruction and guidance specifically to improve your score on the GED Social Studies test, not the Reasoning Through Language Arts (RLA), Math, or Science test. We have a separate workbook for each of those tests for when you're ready to tackle them.

- You've made earning your GED a priority in your life because you want to advance in the workplace or pursue higher learning that requires a GED or high-school diploma.

- You're willing to give up some activities so you have the time to prepare, always keeping in mind your other responsibilities.

- You meet your state's requirements regarding age, residency, and the length of time since leaving school that make you eligible to take the GED test. (See Chapter 1 for details.)

- You have sufficient English language skills to handle the test.

- You want a fun and friendly guide that helps you achieve your goal.

If any of these descriptions sounds like you, welcome aboard. You're about to embark on a journey that takes you from point A (where you are right now) to point B (passing the GED Social Studies test with flying colors).

Icons Used in This Book

Icons — little pictures you see in the margins of this book — highlight bits of text that you want to pay special attention to. Here's what each one means:

Whenever we want to tell you a special trick or technique that can help you succeed on the GED Social Studies test, we mark it with this icon. Keep an eye out for this guy.

This icon points out information you want to burn into your brain. Think of the text with this icon as the sort of stuff you'd tear out and put on a bulletin board or your refrigerator.

Take this icon seriously! Although the world won't end if you don't heed the advice next to this icon, the warnings are important to your success in preparing to take the Social Studies test.

We use this icon to flag example questions that are much like what you can expect on the actual GED Social Studies test. So if you just want to get familiar with the types of questions on the test, this icon is your guide.

Beyond the Book

In addition to the book content, you can find valuable free material online. We provide you with a Cheat Sheet that addresses things you need to know and consider when getting ready for the GED Social Studies test. You can access this material at www.dummies.com/cheatsheet/gedsocialstudiestest.

We also include additional articles at www.dummies.com/extras/gedsocialstudiestest that provide even more helpful tips and advice to help you score your best on the GED Social Studies test.

Where to Go from Here

Some people like to read books from beginning to end. Others prefer to read only the specific information they need to know now. Here we provide a road map so you can find your way around.

Chapter 1 starts off with an overview of the GED test and how to register for the exam. Chapter 2 brings you up to speed on what the Social Studies test covers. Chapter 3 is a must-read — a diagnostic test followed by a self-assessment to target areas where you need the most guidance and practice. Based on your self-assessment, you'll know which chapters to focus on in Parts II and III of this book, which divide instruction into two areas that the test evaluates:

- Part II focuses on social studies *skills,* which include reading comprehension; understanding data presented graphically in charts, tables, maps, political cartoons, and so on; and analyzing arguments and the evidence used to back them up. With these skills, you should be able to answer almost all the questions on the test.

- Part III focuses on social studies *knowledge* and breaks it down into subject areas — civics, government, history, economics, and geography.

When you're ready to dive into a full-length practice test that mimics the real GED Social Studies test, check out Part IV. After the test, you can check your answers with the detailed answer explanations we provide. (But be sure to wait until *after* you take the practice test to look at the answers!)

If you need a break, turn to the chapters in Part V, where you'll find ten study tips and ten skills you need to master.

Part I
Getting Started with the GED Social Studies Test

In this part . . .

✔ Get oriented to the test format, question types, test scheduling, and scoring, and find out what steps to take if English isn't your first language.

✔ Find out what's on the GED Social Studies test and the knowledge and skills you'll be required to demonstrate on the test.

✔ Take a diagnostic test to identify your strengths and weaknesses and highlight the areas where you may need additional practice.

✔ Find out what you should or shouldn't do on the day(s) before and the day of the test and during the exam.

Chapter 1

Taking a Quick Glance at the GED Social Studies Test

In This Chapter

▶ Warming up to the GED test format

▶ Checking out what's on the GED Social Studies test

▶ Registering for the test and choosing a test date

▶ Completing the GED test when English is your second language

▶ Understanding what your score means and how it's determined

The GED test offers high-school dropouts, people who leave school early, and people who were educated outside the United States an opportunity to earn the equivalent of a United States (U.S.) high-school diploma without the need for full-time attendance in either day or night school. The GED test is a recognized standard that makes securing a job or college placement easier.

The GED test complies with current 12th-grade standards in the United States and meets the College and Career Readiness Standards for Adult Education. The GED test also covers the Common Core Standards used in most states. These standards are based on the actual expectations stated by employers and postsecondary institutions.

The GED test measures whether you understand what high-school seniors across the country have studied before they graduate. Employers need better-educated employees. In addition, some colleges may be uncertain of the quality of foreign credentials. The GED provides those assurances. When you pass the GED test, you earn a high-school equivalency diploma. That can open many doors for you, perhaps doors that you don't even know exist at this point.

You're permitted to take the GED test in sections, so you can take the Reasoning Through Language Arts (RLA), Math, Science, and Social Studies tests in separate testing sessions. This flexibility enables you to focus your studies and practice on one section of the test at a time, and this book supports your efforts to do just that.

Ready to get started? This chapter gives you the basics of the GED Social Studies test: how the test is administered, what the Social Studies test section looks like, how to schedule the test (including whether you're eligible), and how your score is calculated (so you know what you need to focus on to pass).

Knowing What to Expect: The GED Test Format

A computer administers the GED test. That means that all the questions appear on a computer screen, and you enter all your answers into a computer with a keyboard and mouse. You read, evaluate, analyze, and write everything on the computer. Even when drafting an essay, you don't use paper. Instead, the test centers provide you with an erasable tablet. If you know how to use a computer and are comfortable with a keyboard and a mouse, you're ahead of the game. If not, practice your keyboarding. Also, practice reading from a computer screen, because reading from a screen is very different from reading printed materials. At the very least, you need to get more comfortable with computers, even if that means taking a short course at a local learning center. In the case of the GED test, the more familiar you are with computers, the more comfortable you'll feel taking the computerized test.

Under certain circumstances, the sections are available in booklet format as a special accommodation. Check with the GED Testing Service to see what exceptions are acceptable.

The computer-based GED test allows for speedy detailed feedback on your performance. When you pass (yes, we said *when* and not *if,* because we believe in you), the GED Testing Service provides both a diploma and a detailed transcript of your scores, similar to what high-school graduates receive. They're now available online at www.gedtestingservice. com within a day of completing the test. You can then send your transcript and diploma to an employer or college. Doing so allows employers and colleges access to a detailed outline of your scores, achievement, and demonstrated skills and abilities. This outline is also a useful tool for you to review your progress. It highlights those areas where you did well and areas where you need further work. If you want to (or have to) retake the test, these results will provide a detailed guide to what you should work on to improve your scores. Requests for additional copies of transcripts are handled online and also are available within a day.

Reviewing the GED Social Studies Test

The Social Studies test is scheduled for 90 minutes. You have 65 minutes to answer the multiple-choice and fill-in-the-blank questions and 25 minutes to write your Extended Response (an essay). You get no break between the two sections of the test and can't transfer time from one section to the other. Here's a breakdown of what you'll see on this test:

- **Multiple-choice, drag-and-drop, hot spot, and fill-in-the-blank questions:** The source text and data for these question types varies. For about half of the questions you get one source item, such as a graph or text, followed by a single question. Other items present a single source item as the basis for several questions. In either case, you need to analyze and evaluate the content presented to you as part of the question. The test items evaluate your ability to answer questions by using reasoning and analytical skills. The information for the source materials comes from primary and secondary sources, both text and visual. That means you need to be able to "read" charts, tables, maps, and graphs as well as standard text materials.

- **Extended Response:** In this part of the Social Studies test, you're presented with two source texts, usually a quote and a longer passage. You are required to analyze how the issues expressed represent an enduring issue in American history.

The content of the Social Studies test is drawn from these four areas:

- **Civics and government:** The largest part (about 50 percent of the test) focuses on civics and government. These items examine the development of democracy from ancient times to modern days. Other topics include how civilizations change over time and respond to crises.

- **American history:** American history makes up 20 percent of the test. It covers all topics from the pilgrims and early settlement to the American Revolution, the Civil War, World Wars I and II, the Vietnam War, and current history — all of which involve the United States in one way or another.

✔ **Economics:** Economics makes up about 15 percent of the test. The economics portion examines basic theories, such as supply and demand, the role of government policies in the economy, and macro- and microeconomic theory.

✔ **Geography and the world:** This area also makes up 15 percent of the test. The areas with which you need to become familiar are very topical: sustainability and environmental issues, population issues, and rural and urban settlement. Other topics include cultural diversity and migration and those issues that are of universal and not national concern.

You're not expected to be a historian or a civics professor. You won't be asked to identify state capitals, identify the key issues that triggered the Civil War, or name the ships that Christopher Columbus sailed to the New World. All the information you need to answer the questions is provided in the reading passages, maps, graphs, questions, and other material provided on the test. Only the Extended Response requires some prior outside knowledge. However, even on the rest of the test, knowing something about these topics and key historical events, terminology, and concepts helps a great deal in understanding the material presented on the test. That means you can answer the questions correctly and faster in the limited time you're given.

For more about what's covered on the GED Social Studies test, check out Chapter 2.

It's a Date: Scheduling the Test

To take the GED test, you schedule it based on the available testing dates. Each state or local testing center sets its own schedule for the GED test, which means that your state decides how and when you can take each section of the test. In some states, you're required to pass the GED Ready Test before taking the actual test; in others you're not. It also determines how often and how soon after failing a section you can retake it. Some states have a waiting period and additional charge for retakes. The GED Testing Service limits you to three retakes a year, but individual states may allow more. The fee for each retake varies by state. How different test centers administer the test also varies. Because the test is taken on a computer, many testing centers allow you to schedule an individual appointment. Your test starts when you start and ends when your allotted time expires. Other centers administer the test to groups on specific schedules. The test centers are small computer labs, often containing no more than 15 seats, and actual testing facilities are located in many communities in your state.

You book your appointment through the GED Testing Service (www.gedtestingservice. com). Your local GED test administrator can give you all the information you need about scheduling the test. In addition, local school districts and community colleges can provide information about local test centers in your area.

Sending a specific question or request to the GED Testing Service site may come with a charge for the service. To save money, you're better off asking a person at your local testing center. That way, you don't have to pay for the privilege of asking a question, and your answer will be based on rules and conditions specific to your area.

The following sections answer some questions you may have before you schedule your test date, including whether you're even eligible to take the test, when you can take the test, and how to sign up to take the test.

Determining whether you're eligible

Before you schedule your test, make sure you meet the requirements to take the GED test. You're eligible to apply to take the GED test only if

- ✔ **You're not currently enrolled in a high school.** If you're currently enrolled in a high school, you're expected to complete your diploma there. The purpose of the GED test is to give people who aren't in high school a chance to get an equivalent high-school diploma.

- ✔ **You're not a high-school graduate.** If you're a high-school graduate, you should have a diploma, which means you don't need to take the GED test. However, you can use the GED as proof of up-to-date skills and show that you're ready for further education and training.

- ✔ **You meet state requirements regarding age, residency, and the length of time since leaving high school.** Check with your local GED test administrator to determine your state's requirements concerning these criteria. Residency requirements are an issue, because you may have to take the test in a different jurisdiction, depending on how long you've lived at your present address.

Being aware of when you can take the test

If you're eligible, you can take the GED test whenever you're prepared. You can apply to take the GED test as soon as you want. Just contact your local testing center or www.gedtestingservice.com for a test schedule. Pick a day that works for you.

You can take all four sections of the GED test together, but that's seven hours of intense testing. To relieve the burden, the test is designed so that you can take each section separately, whenever you're ready. In most areas, you can take the test sections one at a time, even in the evening or on weekends, depending on the individual testing center. If you pass one test section, that section of the GED test is considered done no matter how you do on the other sections. If you fail one section, you can retake that section of the test. The scheduling and administration of the test and retakes vary from state to state, so check with the GED Testing Service site or your local high-school guidance office.

Because the test starts when you're ready and finishes when you've used up the allocated time, you should be able take it alone and not depend on other people. For you, that means you may be able to find locations that offer the testing in evenings or on weekends as well as during regular business hours. Even better, because you don't have to take the test with a group, you may be able to set an individual starting time that suits you.

If circumstances dictate that you must take the paper version of the test, you'll probably have to forgo the flexibility afforded by the computer. Check well in advance to see what the rules are for you.

You can also apply to take the test if you're not prepared, but if you do that, you don't stand a very good chance of passing. If you do need to retake any section of the test, use your time before your next test date to get ready. The GED Testing Service offers a discounted retake up to twice a year, but these promotions change. Some states include free retakes in the price of the test. Check with the GED Testing Service or your state about any special discounts that may be available. To save time and money, prepare well before you schedule the test. Refer to the later section "Knowing what to do if you score poorly on one or more tests" for details.

Are special accommodations available?

If you need to complete the test on paper or have a disability that makes it impossible for you to use the computer, your needs can be accommodated. However, other specifics apply: Your choice of times and testing locations may be much more restricted, but times to complete a test may be extended. Remember also that the GED testing centers will ask for documentation of the nature of the accommodation required.

The GED testing centers make every effort to ensure that all qualified people have access to the tests. If you have a disability, you may not be able to register for the tests and take them the same week, but, with some advanced planning, you can probably take the tests when you're ready. Here's what you need to do:

✔ Check with your local testing center or check out www.gedtestingservice.com/testers/accommodations-for-disability.

✔ Contact the GED Testing Service or your local GED test center and explain your disability.

✔ Request any forms that you have to fill out for your special circumstances.

✔ Ensure that you have a recent diagnosis by a physician or other qualified professional.

✔ Complete all the proper forms and submit them with medical or professional diagnosis.

✔ Start planning early so that you're able to take the tests when you're ready.

Note that, regardless of your disability, you still have to be able to handle the mental and emotional demands of the test.

The GED Testing Service in Washington, D.C., defines specific disabilities, such as the following, for which it may make special accommodations, provided the disability severely limits your ability to perform essential skills required to pass the GED test:

✔ Medical disabilities, such as cerebral palsy, epilepsy, or blindness

✔ Psychological disabilities, such as schizophrenia, major depression, attention deficit disorder, or Tourette's syndrome

✔ Specific learning disabilities, including perceptual handicaps, brain injury, minimal brain dysfunction, dyslexia, and developmental aphasia

Signing up

When you're actually ready to sign up for the test, follow these steps:

1. **Contact your local GED test administrator to make sure you're eligible.**

   Refer to the earlier section "Determining whether you're eligible" for some help.

2. **Ask the office for an application (if needed) or an appointment.**

3. **Complete the application (if needed).**

4. **Return the application to the proper office, with payment, if necessary.**

   The fees vary state by state, so contact your local administrator or testing site to find out what you have to pay to take the tests. In some states, low-income individuals may be eligible for financial assistance.

Note: You can also do all of this online, including submitting the payment, with your computer, tablet, or smartphone. Go to www.gedtestingservice.com to start the process.

Never send cash by mail to pay for the GED test. Most local administrators have payment rules and don't accept cash.

Working with unusual circumstances

If you feel that you may have a special circumstance that prevents you from taking the GED test on a given day, contact the GED test administrator in your area. If, for example, the test is going to be held on your Sabbath, the testing center may make special arrangements for you.

When applying for special circumstances, keep the following guidelines in mind:

- ✔ Document everything in your appeal for special consideration.
- ✔ Contact the GED test administrator in your area as early as you can.
- ✔ Be patient. Special arrangements can't be made overnight. The administrator often has to wait for a group with similar issues to gather so he can make arrangements for the entire group.
- ✔ Ask questions. Accommodations can be made if you ask. For example, special allowances include extended time for various disabilities, large print and Braille for visual impairments, and considerations for age (for individuals older than 60 who feel they may have a learning disability).

Taking the GED Test When English Isn't Your First Language

English doesn't have to be your first language for you to take the GED test. The GED test is offered in English, Spanish, and French. If you want to take the test in Spanish or French, contact your local GED test administrator to apply. Individuals who speak other languages as their first language, however, must do the test in English. If you're in that category, the GED Testing Service recommends that you take an English as a Second Language (ESL) competency test before taking the GED test.

If English, Spanish, or French isn't your first language, you must decide whether you can read and write English as well as or better than 40 percent of high-school graduates because you may be required to pass an English as a Second Language (ESL) placement test. If you write and read English well, prepare for and take the test (either in English or in Spanish or French). If you don't read or write English well, take additional classes to improve your language skills until you think you're ready. An English Language Proficiency Test (ELPT) is also available for people who completed their education in other countries. For more information about the language component of the GED test, check out www.gedtestingservice.com/testers/special-test-editions-spanish and www.gedtestingservice.com/testers/special-test-editions-french.

In many ways, the GED test is like the Test of English as a Foreign Language (TOEFL) comprehension test. If you've completed the TOEFL test with good grades, you're likely ready to take the GED test. If you haven't taken the TOEFL test, enroll in a GED test-preparation course to see whether you have difficulty understanding the subjects and skills assessed on the test. GED test courses provide you with some insight into your comprehension ability, along with a teacher to discuss your skills and struggles.

Websites that can help you plan to take the GED test

The Internet is a helpful and sometimes scary place. Some websites are there to help you in your GED test preparation, while others just want to sell you something. You have to know how to separate the good from the bad. Here are a couple of essential ones (most are accessible through www.gedtestingservice.com):

✔ `adulted.about.com/od/getting yourged/a/stateged.htm` is a website that links to the GED test eligibility requirements and testing locations in your state.

✔ `usaeducation.info/Tests/GED/ International-students.aspx` is a site that explains GED test eligibility for foreign students.

If you're curious and want to see what's out there, type "GED test" into any search engine and relax while you try to read about 22 million results, ranging from the helpful to the helpless. We suggest leaving this last activity until after you've passed the tests. As useful as the Internet can be, it still provides the opportunity to waste vast amounts of time. And right now, you need to spend your time preparing for the test — and leave the rest for after you get your diploma.

Taking Aim at Your Target Score

To pass the GED Social Studies test, you need to score a minimum of 150 on a scale of 100 to 200, and you must pass all other subjects of the test to earn your GED. If you achieve a passing score, congratulate yourself: You've scored better than at least 40 percent of today's high-school graduates, and you're now a graduate of the largest virtual school in the country. And if your marks are in the honors range (score of 170 or more), you're ready for college or career training.

Be aware that some colleges require scores higher than the minimum passing score. If you plan to apply to postsecondary schools or some other form of continuing education, check with their admissions offices for the minimum admission score requirements.

The following sections address a few more points you may want to know about how the GED test is scored and what you can do if you score poorly on one or more of the test sections.

Identifying how scores are determined

Correct answers may be worth one, two, or more points, depending on the item and the level of difficulty. The Extended Response (also known as the essay) is scored separately. However, the Extended Response is only part of the RLA and Social Studies sections. On each test section, you must accumulate a minimum of 150 points.

Because you don't lose points for incorrect answers, make sure you answer all the items on each test. After all, a guessed answer can get you a point. Leaving an answer blank, on the other hand, guarantees you a zero. The information and practice in this book provides you with the knowledge and skills you need to answer most questions on the Social Studies section with confidence and to narrow your choices when you're not quite sure which answer choice is correct.

Knowing what to do if you score poorly on one or more tests

If you discover that your score on the GED Social Studies test is less than 150, start planning to retake the test — and make sure you leave plenty of time for additional study and preparation.

As soon as possible after obtaining your results, contact your local GED test administrator to find out the rules for retaking the failed section of the test. Some states may ask that you wait a certain amount of time and/or limit the number of attempts each year. Some may ask that you attend a preparation course and show that you've completed it before you can retake the GED test. Some may charge you an additional fee. However, you need to retake only those sections of the test that you failed. Any sections you pass are completed and count toward your diploma. Furthermore, the detailed evaluation of your results will help you discover areas of weakness that need more work before repeating any section of the test.

One advantage of taking the GED test on a computer is that you can receive, within a day, detailed feedback on how you did, which includes some specific recommendations of what you need to do to improve your scores.

No matter what score you receive on your first round of the section, don't be afraid to retake any section that you didn't pass. After you've taken it once, you know what you need to work on, and you know exactly what to expect on test day.

Chapter 2

Preparing for the GED Social Studies Test

. . . .

In This Chapter

▶ Getting familiar with the Social Studies test's topics and components

▶ Surveying the types of questions and passages on the test

▶ Preparing for and writing the essay

▶ Optimizing your performance through proper preparation

▶ Budgeting your time

. . . .

The GED Social Studies test assesses your skills in understanding and interpreting concepts and principles in civics, history, geography, and economics. Consider this test as a kind of crash course in where you've been, where you are, and how you can continue living there. You can apply the types of skills tested on the Social Studies test to your experience in visual, academic, and workplace situations as a citizen, a consumer, or an employee.

This test includes questions drawn from a variety of written and visual passages taken from academic and workplace materials as well as from primary and secondary sources. The passages in this test are like the ones you read or see in most daily newspapers and news magazines. Reading either or both of these news sources regularly can help you become familiar with the style and vocabulary of the passages you find here.

In this chapter, we take a look at the skills required for the Social Studies section of the GED test, the format of the test, and what you can do to prepare.

Looking at the Skills the Social Studies Test Covers

The question-and-answer items of the Social Studies test evaluate several specific skills, including the ability to read and understand complex text, interpret graphs and relate graphs to text, and relate descriptive text to specific values in graphs. For example, an item may ask about the relationship between a description of unemployment in text and a graph of the unemployment rate over time.

You don't have to study a lot of new content to pass this test. Everything you need to know is presented to you with the questions. In each case, you see some content, either a passage or a visual; a question or direction to tell you what you're expected to do; and a series of answer options.

The questions do require you to draw on your previous knowledge of events, ideas, terms, and situations that may be related to social studies. From a big-picture perspective, you must demonstrate the ability to

✓ Identify information, events, problems, and ideas and interpret their significance or impact.

✓ Use the information and ideas in different ways to explore their meanings or solve a problem.

✓ Use the information or ideas to do the following:

- Distinguish between facts and opinions.

- Summarize major events, problems, solutions, and conflicts.

- Arrive at conclusions based on source material.

- Influence other people's attitudes.

- Find alternate meanings in a passage or mistakes in logic.

- Identify causes and their effects.

- Recognize how writers may have been influenced by the times in which they lived and a writer's historical point of view.

- Compare and contrast differing events and people and their views.

- Compare places, opinions, and concepts.

- Determine what impact views and opinions may have both at this time and in the future.

- Organize information to show relationships.

- Analyze similarities and differences in issues or problems.

- Give examples to illustrate ideas and concepts.

- Propose and evaluate solutions.

✓ Make judgments about the material's appropriateness, accuracy, and differences of opinion. Some questions will ask you to interpret the role information and ideas play in influencing current and future decision making. These questions ask you to think about issues and events that affect you every day. That fact alone is interesting and has the potential to make you a more informed citizen of the modern world. What a bonus for a test!

About one-third of the questions test your ability to read and write in a social studies context. That means you'll be tested on the following:

✓ Identifying and using information from sources

✓ Isolating central ideas or specific information

✓ Determining the meaning of words or phrases used in social studies

✓ Recognizing points of view, differentiating between fact and opinion, and identifying properly supported ideas

Another third of the questions ask you to apply mathematical reasoning to social studies. Much of that relates to the ability to do the following:

✓ Interpret graphs.

✓ Use charts and tables as source data and interpret the content.

✔ Interpret information presented visually.

✔ Differentiate between correlation and causation. Just because one event occurred after another (correlation) doesn't necessarily mean that the first event caused the second (causation).

The remaining third deals with applying social studies concepts. That includes the following:

✔ Using specific evidence to support conclusions

✔ Describing the connections between people, environments, and events

✔ Putting historical events into chronological order

✔ Analyzing documents to examine how ideas and events develop and interact, especially in a historical context

✔ Examining cause-and-effect relationships

✔ Identifying bias and evaluating validity of information, in both modern and historical documents

Being aware of what skills the Social Studies test covers can help you get a more accurate picture of the types of questions you'll encounter. The next section focuses more on the specific subject materials you'll face.

Understanding the Social Studies Test Format

You have a total of 90 minutes to complete the Social Studies test. That time is split between the two components of the test. You have 65 minutes to answer a variety of question-and-answer items and then 25 minutes to write an Extended Response (essay) of 250 to 500 words. You can't transfer time from one section to the other. The question-and-answer section consists mostly of multiple-choice questions with a few fill-in-the-blank questions. The multiple-choice questions come in various forms. Most are the standard multiple-choice you know from your school days. Other formats include drop-down menu, drag-and-drop, and hot-spot items. For more about responding to these different question types on the computerized version of the GED test, check out *GED Test For Dummies* (Wiley).

In the following sections, we explore the subject areas the Social Studies test covers, give you an overview of the types of passages you can expect to see, and take a look at what the Extended Response is all about.

Checking out the subject areas on the test

The question-and-answer section of the Social Studies test includes about 50 questions. The exact number varies from test to test because the difficulty level of the questions varies. Most of the information you need will be presented in the text or graphics accompanying the questions, so you need to read and analyze the materials carefully but quickly. The questions focus on the following subject areas:

✔ **Civics and government:** About 50 percent of the Social Studies test includes such topics as rights and responsibilities in democratic governance and the forms of governance.

✔ **American history:** About 20 percent of the test covers a broad outline of the history of the United States from precolonial days to the present, including such topics as the War of Independence, the Civil War, the Great Depression, and the challenges of the 20th century.

- ✔ **Economics:** Economics involves about 15 percent of the test and covers two broad areas — economic theory and basic principles. That includes topics such as how various economic systems work and the role of economics in conflicts.

- ✔ **Geography and the world:** In broad terms, the remaining 15 percent covers the relationships between the environment and societal development; the concepts of borders, region, and place and diversity; and human migration and population issues.

The test materials cover these four subject areas through two broad themes:

- ✔ **Development of modern liberties and democracy:** How did the modern ideas of democracy and human and civil rights develop? What major events have shaped democratic values, and what writings and philosophies underpin American views and expressions of democracy?

- ✔ **Dynamic systems:** How have institutions, people, and systems responded to events, geographic realities, national policies, and economics?

The Extended Response item (that is, the essay you write at the end of the test) is based on enduring issues, which cover issues of personal freedoms in conflict with societal interests and issues of governance — states' rights versus federal powers, checks and balances within government, and the role of government in society. These issues all require you to evaluate points of view or arguments and determine how such issues represent an enduring theme in American history. You need to be able to recognize false arguments, bias, and misleading comparisons.

If you're a little worried about all of these subject areas, relax. You're not expected to have detailed knowledge of all the topics listed. Although it helps if you have a general knowledge of these areas, most of the test is based on your ability to reason, interpret, and work with the information presented in each question. Knowing basic concepts such as checks and balances or representative democracy helps, but you don't need to know a detailed history of the United States.

Identifying the types of passages on the test

The passages in the Social Studies test are taken from two types of sources:

- ✔ **Academic material:** The type of material you find in a school — textbooks, maps, newspapers, magazines, software, and Internet material. This type of passage also includes extracts from speeches or historical documents.

- ✔ **Workplace material:** The type of material found on the job — manuals, documents, business plans, advertising and marketing materials, correspondence, and so on.

The material may be from *primary* sources (that is, the original documents, such as the Declaration of Independence) or *secondary* sources — material written about an event or person, such as someone's opinions or interpretation of original documents or historic events, sometimes long after the event takes place or the person dies.

Answering questions about text and visual materials

The source materials for the question-and-answer items facing you on the test fall into three broad categories. The materials require you to extract information, come to conclusions, and then determine the correct answer. These source materials consist of textual materials, something with which you're probably already quite familiar; visuals, like maps and diagrams; and statistical tables. Each of these categories requires careful reading, even the visuals, because the information you need to extract can be buried anywhere.

Questions about text passages

About half of the question-and-answer portion of the Social Studies test includes textual passages followed by a series of questions based on that passage. Your job is to read the passage and then answer questions about it.

When you're reading these passages on the test (or in any of the practice questions or tests in this book), read between the lines and look at the implications and assumptions in the passages. An *implication* is something you can understand from what's written, even though it isn't directly stated. An *assumption* is something you can accept as the truth, even though proof isn't directly presented in the text.

Be sure to read each item carefully so you know exactly what it's asking. Read the answer choices and go through the text again carefully. If the question asks for certain facts, you'll be able to find those right in the passage. If it asks for opinions, you may find that the text directly states those opinions or simply implies them. (And they may not match your own opinions, but you still have to answer with the best choice based on the material presented.)

If a question doesn't specifically tell you to use additional information beyond what is presented in the passage, use *only* the information given. An answer may be incorrect in your opinion but if it is correct according to the passage (or vice versa), you must go with the information presented, unless you're told otherwise. Always select the most correct answer choice, based on the information presented.

Questions about visual materials

To make sure you don't get bored, the other half of the question-and-answer portion of the Social Studies test is based on maps, graphs, tables, political cartoons, diagrams, photographs, and artistic works. Some items combine visual material and text. You need to be prepared to deal with all of these types of items.

If you're starting to feel overwhelmed about answering questions based on visual materials, consider the following:

- ✔ **Maps do more than show you the location of places.** They also give you information, and knowing how to decode that information is essential. A map may show you where Charleston is located, but it can also show you how the land around Charleston is used, what the climate in the area is, and whether the population there is growing or declining. Start by examining the print information with the map, the legend, title, and key to the colors or symbols on the map. Then look at what the question requires you to find. Now you can find that information quickly by relating the answer choices to what the map shows.

  For example, the map in Figure 2-1 shows you the following information:

  - The population of the United States for 2010
  - The population by state by size range

  Indirectly, the map also shows you much more. It allows you to compare the population of states with a quick glance. For example, you can see that Florida has a larger population than Montana, North Dakota, South Dakota, and Wyoming together. If you were asked what the relationship is between a state's size and population, you could argue, based on this map, that there isn't much relationship. You could also show that the states around Lakes Erie and Ontario have a higher population density than the states in the Midwest. This kind of conclusion-drawing is part of the skill of analyzing maps.

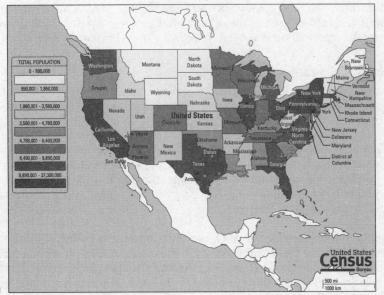

Figure 2-1:
Most populated states, 2010 census map.

✔ **Every time you turn around, someone in the media is trying to make a point with a graph.** The types of graphs you see in Figure 2-2 are very typical examples. The real reason people use graphs to explain themselves so often is because a graph can clearly show trends and relationships between different sets of information. The three graphs in Figure 2-2 are best suited for a particular use. For example, the bar graphs are great for comparing items over time, the line graphs show changes over time, and the pie chart shows you proportions. The next time you see a graph, such as the ones in Figure 2-2, study it. Be sure to look carefully at the scale of graphs; even visual information can fool you. A bar graph that shows a rapid rise of something may in fact show no such thing. It only looks that way because the bottom of the chart doesn't start with values of zero. Check carefully to make sure you understand what the information in the graph is telling you. (*Note:* Graphs are also called *charts.*)

✔ **Tables are everywhere.** If you've ever looked at the nutrition label on a food product, you've read a table. Study any table you can find, whether in a newspaper or on the back of a can of tuna. The population data table in Figure 2-3 is an example of the kinds of data you may see on the test. That table shows you a lot of information, but you can extract quite a bit more information that isn't stated. Just a quick look at the numbers tells you that nearly 1.6 million people are enlisted in the armed forces. How do you know that? Subtract the number in the Civilian Population column from the Resident Population Plus Armed Forces Overseas column. You can also calculate the change in the overall population, the rate of increase of both the population and the armed forces personnel, and even the size of the armed forces stationed in the United States compared to serving overseas.

Just like graphs, tables are also sometimes called "charts," which can be a little confusing. Regardless of what they're called, you need to be prepared to extract information, even if it isn't stated directly.

✔ **Political cartoons appear in the newspapers every day.** If you don't read political cartoons in the daily newspaper (usually located in the Editorial or Op-Ed pages), give them a try. Some days, they're the best entertainment in the paper. Political cartoons in the newspaper are usually based on an event in the last day or week. They can be nasty or funny and are always biased. If you want to get the most out of political cartoons, look for small details, facial expressions, and background clues. The cartoons on the test are obviously older than the ones in daily newspapers, so you may not get the context unless you've been reading the newspapers or watching the news for the past several weeks or months.

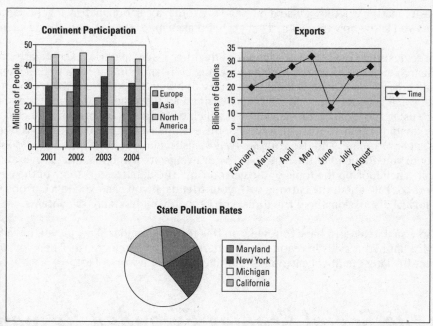

Figure 2-2:
Examples
of different
graphs.

John Wiley & Sons, Inc.

Monthly Population Estimates for the United States: April 1 to December 1, 2010			
Year and Month	Resident Population	Resident Population Plus Armed Forces Overseas	Civilian Population
2010			
April 1	308,747,508	309,180,459	307,517,564
May 1	308,937,636	309,361,879	307,702,883
June 1	309,122,451	309,544,899	307,889,928
July 1	309.326,225	309,745,660	308,091,141
August 1	309,540,608	309,956,285	308,313,027
September 1	309,768,270	310,173,518	308,531,330
October 1	309,994,453	310,395,556	308,761,399
November 1	310,179,397	310,589,914	308,957,140
December 1	310,353,742	310,774,403	309,141,425

Figure 2-3:
Population
data table.

Illustration courtesy of U.S. Census Bureau

✔ **You've no doubt seen countless photographs in your day.** Photos are all around you. All you need to do to prepare for the photograph-based questions on the test is to begin getting information from the photographs you see. Start with the newspapers or magazines, where photos are chosen to provide information that connects directly to a story. See whether you can determine what message the photograph carries with it and how it relates to the story it supports.

✔ **You probably like to look at works of art.** On the Social Studies test, you have a chance to "read" works of art. You look at a work of art and gather information you can use to answer the item. To get yourself ready to gather information from works of art on the test, take a look at art galleries, the Internet, and library books. Lucky for you, some books even give some background or other explanation for these works.

It doesn't matter whether a visual passage is a table, a cartoon, a drawing, or a graph — as long as you know how to read it. That's what makes maps, tables, and charts such fun.

If you're unsure of how to read a map (or any other visual material except cartoon), go to any search engine and search for "map reading help" or a similar term to find sites that explain how to read those elements. If you try to follow the same procedure for political cartoons, you'll get a lot of actual cartoons but not a lot of explanations about them. Instead, search using "political cartoons analysis," which will find lots of cartoons but also some help understanding them. Afterward, look at some examples of political cartoons (either in the newspaper or online) and use your analysis skills to understand what the cartoonist is saying to you. Remember the figures in the drawings are symbolic and exaggerated to make a point. Then look up the topic of the cartoon and the date to read some of the news stories it refers to. Talk about the cartoon with your friends. If you can explain a cartoon or carry on a logical discussion about the topic, you probably understand its contents.

All the visual items you have to review on this test are familiar. Now all you have to do is practice until your skills in reading and understanding them increase. Then you, too, can discuss the latest political cartoon or pontificate about a work of art.

Writing the Social Studies Extended Response

The Social Studies Extended Response requires you to relate materials to key issues in American economic, political, and social history. Although you don't need a detailed knowledge of American history, you must have a broad sense of key issues because your answer needs to go beyond just the facts and attitudes presented in the text. In the following sections, we offer guidance in how to prepare for and write your Extended Response.

Gearing up for the Extended Response

For the Social Studies Extend Response item, you're given a quotation and a passage. Your assignment is to write a 250-to-500-word essay in 25 minutes, based on your analysis of each source text. You're asked to discuss how these materials present an enduring issue in American history and society. You must use quotes from the source documents to support your argument. You should also use your own personal knowledge to support your arguments. Read the instructions carefully. Write the key words down on your tablet to ensure you don't misread. As you prepare your answer, go back to the basic question and make sure you're staying on topic and that all of your answering points relate strictly to that topic.

Because the GED test is now administered on the computer, you'll use the computer's word processor to write your response. The word processor has all the functions you'd expect — copy, paste, undo, and redo — but it doesn't include either a grammar-checker or a spell-checker. That's part of your job.

The evaluation looks at three specific areas of essay writing:

✔ **Creation of argument and use of evidence:**

- Your argument must show that you understand not only the arguments being presented but also the relationship between the ideas presented and their historical or social context.

- You must effectively use relevant ideas from the source text to back your arguments.

✔ **Development of ideas and organizational structure:**

- Your arguments develop logically and clearly.

- You connect details and main ideas.

- You explain details as required to further your argument.

✔ **Clarity and command of Standard English:**

- You use proper English.

- You demonstrate a command of proper writing conventions.

- You show correct usage of subject-verb agreement, homonyms, capitalization, punctuation, and proper word order.

To prepare for the Extended Response item, we say read, read, and then read some more. Look for magazine and newspaper editorials. Look for documentaries on television, DVD, or even online about controversial issues in American history. For example, look for a documentary on school busing in the 1950s. List the issues surrounding the decision to bus pupils in one area to schools in another area. Consider the issues of personal freedom, the rights to choose, and civil liberties in a larger community sense. Look at the changing views on the role of government in our daily lives. What forces drove decision making at that time? How were those decisions a reflection of their times, and to what extent do similar views and decisions still apply today?

Writing your Extended Response: A sample prompt

Here's a sample Extended Response prompt, like you may see on the Social Studies test.

Stimulus: The following statements were made about slavery sometime before the Civil War. The Jay letter, written almost a hundred years before the Civil War, reflects the views of abolitionists, common right up to the Civil War. Hammond's speech reflects the continuing justification of, and for, slavery. In what way is this an enduring issue to this day?

It is much to be wished that slavery may be abolished. The honour of the States, as well as justice and humanity, in my opinion, loudly call upon them to emancipate these unhappy people. To contend for our own liberty, and to deny that blessing to others, involves an inconsistency not to be excused. (John Jay, letter to R. Lushington, March 15, 1786.)

In all social systems there must be a class to do the menial duties, to perform the drudgery of life. That is, a class requiring but a low order of intellect and but little skill. Its requisites are vigor, docility, fidelity. Such a class you must have, or you would not have that other class which leads progress, civilization, and refinement. It constitutes the very mud-sill of society and of political government; and you might as well attempt to build a house in the air, as to build either the one or the other, except on this mud-sill. Fortunately for the South, she found a race adapted to that purpose to her hand. A race inferior to her own, but eminently qualified in temper, in vigor, in docility, in capacity to stand the climate, to answer all her purposes. We use them for our purpose, and call them slaves. We found them slaves by the common "consent of mankind," which, according to Cicero, "lex naturae est." The highest proof of what is Nature's law. (The "Mudsill Theory," James Henry Hammond, speech to the U.S. Senate, March 4, 1858.)

Prompt: Isolate the main issue presented in these two quotes, identify the points of view of the authors, consider how these positions reflect an enduring issue in American history, and use your own knowledge of the issue to show how this continues to be one of the enduring issues.

To start drafting your response, first make a list of key points each author uses to support his position. List them as pro and con, and relate them to the enduring issue you've identified. Now think back to your own general knowledge of the issue and consider what other information you can bring to the essay to explain how and why this is an enduring issue. For example, you may consider why the founding fathers argued nonwhites should count as only three-fifths of a person. You may consider that there will always be people at the bottom of the food chain, regardless of race, and there will always have to be people who do the drudge work. Go beyond the idea of racial discrimination and consider the idea of equality of opportunity. Whatever points you choose to use, you need to go beyond the text and build on your own knowledge of American history and issues.

When composing your response, you should select a few key statements. In the Jay letter, the most significant statement is "To contend for our own liberty, and to deny that blessing to others, involves an inconsistency not to be excused." How can society argue that it's acceptable to have some deprived of freedom when regarding freedom essential for itself? The Hammond speech is more practical. In essence, he states that in order for some to be wealthy, others must be poor. Now, you have the enduring issue. You can discuss it in several ways: the dissonance between slavery and freedom, or the necessity of poverty's existence for wealth's existence. In modern terms, you may argue about the 99 percent and the 1 percent. That then allows you to develop an argument about the enduring issue. You need to use quotes from these two source documents to show that it's indeed an enduring issue and add your own information to those quotations to back the argument.

Examining Preparation Strategies That Work

To improve your skills and get better results, we suggest you try the following strategies when preparing for the Social Studies test:

- ✔ **Take as many practice tests as you can get your hands on.** The best way to prepare is to answer all the sample Social Studies test questions you can find. Work through the diagnostic test in Chapter 3, the full-length practice test in Chapter 13, and practice questions in the chapters in Part II of this book. Search online for additional practice questions, such as those at www.gedtestingservice.com/educators/freepracticetest. (**Note:** This site is intended for educators teaching the GED test prep courses. Because you're your own educator while using this book, try it. If you're in a prep class, check with your teacher.)

  You will find a few more free practice questions at www.gedtestingservice.com/testers/sample-questions.

  Consider taking a preparation class to get access to even more sample Social Studies test questions, but remember that your task is to pass the test — not to collect every question ever written.

- ✔ **Practice reading a variety of documents.** The documents you need to focus on include historic passages from original sources (such as the Declaration of Independence and U.S. Constitution) as well as practical information for consumers (such as voters' guides, atlases, budget graphs, political speeches, almanacs, and tax forms). Read about the evolution of democratic forms of government. Read about climate change and migration, about food and population, and about American politics in the post-9/11 world. Read newspapers and news magazines about current issues, especially those related to civics and government, and social and economic issues.

- ✔ **Summarize the passages you read in your own words.** After you read these passages, write a summary of what you read. Doing so can help you identify the main points of the passages, which is an important part of succeeding on the Social Studies test. Ask yourself the following two questions when you read a passage or something more visual like a graph:

- **What's the passage about?** The answer is usually in the first and last paragraphs of the passage. The rest is usually explanation. If you don't see the answer there, you may have to look carefully through the rest of the passage.

- **What's the visual material about?** Look for the answer in the title, labels, captions, and any other information that's included.

After you get an initial grasp of the main idea, determine what to do with it. Some questions ask you to apply information you gain from one situation to another similar situation. If you know the main idea of the passage, you'll have an easier time applying it to another situation.

✔ **Draft a series of your own test questions that draw on the information contained in the passages you read.** Doing so can help you become familiar with social studies–based questions. Look in newspapers and magazines for articles that fit into the general passage types that appear on the Social Studies test. Find a good summary paragraph and develop a question that gets to the point of the summary.

✔ **Compose answers for each of your test questions.** Write down four answers to each of your test questions, only one of which is correct based on the passage. Creating your own questions and answers helps reduce your stress level by showing you how answers are related to questions. It also encourages you to read and think about material that may be on the test. Finally, it gives you some idea of where to look for answers in a passage.

✔ **Discuss questions and answers with friends and family to make sure you've achieved an understanding and proper use of the material.** If your friends and family understand the question, you know it's a good one. Discussing your questions and answers with others gives you a chance to explain social studies topics and concepts, which is an important skill to have as you get ready to take this test.

✔ **Don't assume.** Be critical of visual material and read it carefully. You want to be able to read visual material as accurately as you read text material, and doing so takes practice. Don't assume something is true just because it looks that way in a diagram, chart, or map. Visual materials can be precise drawings with legends and scales, or they can be drawn in such a way that the information appears to be different at first glance than it really is. Manipulating the scale for graphs is one way to skew the information. Even visuals can be biased, so "read" them carefully to determine their purposes. Verify what you think you see by making sure the information looks correct and realistic. Finally, before coming to any conclusions, check the scale and legend to make sure the graph is really showing what you think it does.

✔ **Be familiar with general graphical conventions.** Maps and graphs have conventions. The top of a map is almost always north. The horizontal axis is always the x-axis, and the vertical axis (the y-axis) is dependent on the x-axis. Looking at the horizontal axis first usually makes the information clearer and easier to understand. Practice reading charts and tables in an atlas or check out government websites where information is displayed in tables, charts, and maps.

Managing Your Time for the Social Studies Test

You have a total of 65 minutes to answer about 50 question-and-answer items and then an additional 25 minutes to write your Extended Response. The exact number of questions varies from test to test, but the time remains the same. That means you have less than 90 seconds for each question-and-answer item. Answering those items that you find easy first should allow you to progress faster, leaving you a little more time per item at the end so you can come back to work on the harder ones.

The questions on the Social Studies test are based on both regular textual passages and visual materials, so when you plan your time for answering the questions, consider the amount of time you need to read both types of materials. (See the "Questions about visual materials" section earlier in this chapter for advice on how you can get more comfortable with questions based on graphs, charts, and the like.)

When you come to a prose passage, read the questions first and then skim the passage to find the answers. If this method doesn't work, read the passage carefully, looking for the answers. This way, you take more time only when needed.

Because you have such little time to gather all the information you can from a visual material and answer questions about it, you can't study the map, chart, or cartoon for long. You have to skim it the way you skim a paragraph. Reading the questions that relate to a particular visual first helps you figure out what you need to look for as you skim the material.

If you're unsure of how quickly you can answer questions based on visual materials, time yourself on a few and see. If your time comes out to be more than 1.5 minutes, you need more practice.

Realistically, you have about 20 seconds to read the question and the possible answers, 50 seconds to look for the answer, and 10 seconds to select the correct answer. Dividing your time in this way leaves you less than 20 seconds for review or for time at the end of the test to spend on difficult items. To finish the Social Studies test completely, you really have to be organized and watch the clock.

You have 25 minutes to finish your essay for the Extended Response on the Social Studies test, and in that time you have four main tasks:

- ✔ Plan
- ✔ Draft
- ✔ Edit and revise
- ✔ Rewrite

A good plan for action is to spend 4 minutes planning, 12 minutes drafting, 4 minutes editing and revising, and 5 minutes rewriting (remembering that the computer doesn't have a spell-checker). Keep in mind that this schedule is a tight one, though, so if your keyboarding is slow, consider allowing more time for rewriting. No one but you will see anything but the final version.

Chapter 3

Taking a Social Studies Diagnostic Test

- -

In This Chapter

▶ Diagnosing areas of strength and weakness with a sample Social Studies test

▶ Checking your answers and reading explanations to gain additional insight

▶ Noting areas you need to work on

▶ Knowing where to go from here

- -

*B*efore committing to any serious training regimen for the GED Social Studies test, take the diagnostic test in this chapter and check the answers and explanations in order to identify the skills you need to work on most. This approach enables you to focus your efforts on your weakest areas so you don't waste a lot of time on what you already know.

Tackling the Diagnostic Test

The diagnostic test is a little shorter than the full-scale Social Studies test. You have 65 minutes to complete the question-and-answer section, then another 25 minutes to write the Extended Response (the essay). The Social Studies test doesn't allow any break in between sections, nor can you transfer unused time from one section to another.

The answers and explanations to this test's questions are at the end of this chapter. Review the explanations to all the questions, as well as the skills table. Reviewing questions and answers on this diagnostic test is a good study technique.

Practice tests work best when you take them under the same conditions as the real test. We can't provide a computer along with the test, but you can simulate the test-taking experience in other ways. Take this test in a room with no distractions, no music, no telephone, no munchies, and no interruptions. Tell family and friends you've left town for the day and do the diagnostic test in one sitting.

Unless you have a specific medical condition requiring accommodations, you'll be taking the GED test on a computer. You'll see all the questions on a computer screen and use a keyboard or mouse to indicate your answers. We formatted the questions and answer choices in this book to make them visually as similar as possible to the real GED test. We retained the same multiple choice format with A, B, C, D choices for marking your answers. However, rather than clicking on a computer screen, you'll be marking your answers on the answer sheet we provide. The Extended Response follows the question and answer items. You'll also have paper there on which to write your response.

Answer Sheet for the Social Studies Diagnostic Test

1.	Ⓐ Ⓑ Ⓒ Ⓓ	21.	Ⓐ Ⓑ Ⓒ Ⓓ
2.	Ⓐ Ⓑ Ⓒ Ⓓ	22.	Ⓐ Ⓑ Ⓒ Ⓓ
3.	Ⓐ Ⓑ Ⓒ Ⓓ	23.	Ⓐ Ⓑ Ⓒ Ⓓ
4.	Ⓐ Ⓑ Ⓒ Ⓓ	24.	Ⓐ Ⓑ Ⓒ Ⓓ
5.	Ⓐ Ⓑ Ⓒ Ⓓ	25.	Ⓐ Ⓑ Ⓒ Ⓓ
6.	Ⓐ Ⓑ Ⓒ Ⓓ	26.	Ⓐ Ⓑ Ⓒ Ⓓ
7.	Ⓐ Ⓑ Ⓒ Ⓓ	27.	Ⓐ Ⓑ Ⓒ Ⓓ
8.	Ⓐ Ⓑ Ⓒ Ⓓ	28.	Ⓐ Ⓑ Ⓒ Ⓓ
9.	Ⓐ Ⓑ Ⓒ Ⓓ	29.	Ⓐ Ⓑ Ⓒ Ⓓ
10.	Ⓐ Ⓑ Ⓒ Ⓓ	30.	Ⓐ Ⓑ Ⓒ Ⓓ
11.	Ⓐ Ⓑ Ⓒ Ⓓ	31.	Ⓐ Ⓑ Ⓒ Ⓓ
12.	Ⓐ Ⓑ Ⓒ Ⓓ	32.	Ⓐ Ⓑ Ⓒ Ⓓ
13.	Ⓐ Ⓑ Ⓒ Ⓓ	33.	Ⓐ Ⓑ Ⓒ Ⓓ
14.	Ⓐ Ⓑ Ⓒ Ⓓ	34.	Ⓐ Ⓑ Ⓒ Ⓓ
15.	Ⓐ Ⓑ Ⓒ Ⓓ	35.	Ⓐ Ⓑ Ⓒ Ⓓ
16.	Ⓐ Ⓑ Ⓒ Ⓓ	36.	Ⓐ Ⓑ Ⓒ Ⓓ
17.	Ⓐ Ⓑ Ⓒ Ⓓ	37.	Ⓐ Ⓑ Ⓒ Ⓓ
18.	Ⓐ Ⓑ Ⓒ Ⓓ	38.	[ ]
19.	Ⓐ Ⓑ Ⓒ Ⓓ	39.	Ⓐ Ⓑ Ⓒ Ⓓ
20.	Ⓐ Ⓑ Ⓒ Ⓓ	40.	Ⓐ Ⓑ Ⓒ Ⓓ

Social Studies Diagnostic Test

Time: 65 minutes for 40 questions

Directions: Choose the best answer for each question.

Questions 1–3 refer to the following passage from CliffsQuickReview U.S. History I *by P. Soifer and A. Hoffman (Wiley).*

The First Inhabitants of the Western Hemisphere

In telling the history of the United States and also of the nations of the Western Hemisphere in general, historians have wrestled with the problem of what to call the hemisphere's first inhabitants. Under the mistaken impression he had reached the "Indies," explorer Christopher Columbus called the people he met "Indians." This was an error in identification that has persisted for more than five hundred years, for the inhabitants of North and South America had no collective name by which they called themselves.

Historians, anthropologists, and political activists have offered various names, none fully satisfactory. Anthropologists have used "aborigine," but the term suggests a primitive level of existence inconsistent with the cultural level of many tribes. Another term, "Amerindian," which combines Columbus's error with the name of another Italian explorer, Amerigo Vespucci (whose name was the source of "America"), lacks any historical context. Since the 1960s, "Native American" has come into popular favor, though some activists prefer "American Indian." In the absence of a truly representative term, descriptive references such as "native peoples" or "indigenous peoples," though vague, avoid European influence. In recent years, some argument has developed over whether to refer to tribes in the singular or plural — Apache or Apaches — with supporters on both sides demanding political correctness.

1. Why was the term *Amerindian* not accepted by historians and others?

    (A) It still contains Columbus's *India* error.

    (B) Native Americans rejected it.

    (C) It ignored Columbus's role.

    (D) It had no connection with native people.

2. Why was the term *aborigine* rejected?

    (A) It did not encompass all native people.

    (B) Political activists were opposed.

    (C) It incorrectly suggested all native people were primitives.

    (D) The term *First Nations* was a better fit.

3. The French, British, Germans, and others all agree to call each other "Europeans." Why is finding a collective name for Native Americans so difficult?

    (A) There was no collective name for all native people.

    (B) Native people prefer tribal names.

    (C) Many of the options have a European influence.

    (D) Historians and anthropologists can't agree.

Questions 4–6 refer to the following passage from U.S. History For Dummies *by Steve Wiegand (Wiley).*

Starting in the 1470s, Columbus and his brother began making the rounds of European capitals, looking for ships and financial backing for his idea. His demands were exorbitant. In return for his services, Columbus wanted the title of Admiral of the Oceans, 10 percent of all the loot he found, and the ability to pass governorship of every country he discovered to his heirs.

The rulers of England and France said no thanks, as did some of the city-states that made up Italy. The king of Portugal also told him to take a hike. So in 1486, Columbus went to Spain. Queen Isabella listened to his pitch, and she, like the other European rulers, said no. But she did appoint a commission to look into the idea and decided to put Columbus on the payroll in the meantime.

The meantime stretched out for six years. Finally, convinced she wasn't really risking much because chances were that he wouldn't return, Isabella gave her approval in January 1492. Columbus was on his way. Partly because of error and partly because of wishful thinking, Columbus estimated the distance to the Indies at approximately 2,500 miles, which was about 7,500 miles short. But after a voyage of about five weeks, he and his crews, totaling 90 men, did find land at around 2 a.m. on October 12, 1492.

It was an island in the Bahamas, which he called San Salvador. The timing of the discovery was good; it came even as the crews of the *Nina, Pinta,* and *Santa Maria* were muttering about a mutiny.

4. By how much was Columbus's estimate of the distance to the Indies wrong?

    (A) He overestimated by a third.

    (B) He underestimated by more than half.

    (C) He was almost completely correct.

    (D) He used Vespucci's estimate.

5. Why did Isabella of Spain finally agree to sponsor Columbus's exploration?

    (A) The British were competing with Spain for new colonies.

    (B) He was already on the payroll anyway.

    (C) She thought she would never have to honor Columbus's contract.

    (D) She was worried Portugal might back him.

6. In what way was the timing of landfall lucky for Columbus?

    (A) He had no other way to raise money.

    (B) His crew was ready to mutiny.

    (C) Isabella was impatient for his return.

    (D) All of the above.

Questions 7–9 are based on the following passage from U.S. History For Dummies *by Steve Wiegand (Wiley).*

One of the earliest cultures to emerge in what's now the United States was the *Anasazi.* The group's name comes from a Navajo word that has been translated to mean "ancient people" or "ancient enemies." Although they were around the southwestern United States for hundreds of years, they flourished from about AD 1100 to 1300.

At their peak, the Anasazi built adobe-walled towns in nearly inaccessible areas, which made the communities easy to defend. The towns featured apartment houses, community courts, and buildings for religious ceremonies. The Anasazi made highly artistic pottery and tightly woven baskets. The baskets were so good that the culture is sometimes referred to as the *Basket Makers.*

Because of the region's arid conditions, the Anasazi people couldn't support a large population and were never numerous. But just why their culture died out so suddenly around the beginning of the 14th century is a puzzle to archaeologists. One theory is that a prolonged drought simply made life unsustainable in the region. A more controversial theory is that marauding Indians from Mexico conquered the Anasazi or drove them off. However the Anasazi's demise came about, their culture was developed enough to continue, in many ways unchanged, and is evident in some of the Southwest tribes of today....

Arid conditions made life tougher for tribes in the Southwest. Tribes such as the Apache were foragers, scrounging for everything from bison to grasshoppers, while tribes such as the Hopi scratched out an existence as farmers. In what's now California, most of the scores of different tribes were pretty laid-back. They lived in villages, as hunters and gatherers.

7. Why is the disappearance of the Anasazi mysterious?

(A) They had a highly developed culture.

(B) They were ancient enemies of the Navajo.

(C) Archaeologists have not yet found a clear explanation.

(D) All of the above.

8. What suggests that the Anasazi were attacked by hostile tribes from time to time?

(A) Their towns had high, easily-defended walls.

(B) They lived in that area for at least 200 years.

(C) There were many competing tribes in the area.

(D) All of the above.

9. What evidence supports the statement that the tribes in what is now California were "pretty laid-back"?

(A) No evidence supports that claim.

(B) They lived as hunters and gatherers.

(C) They were not farmers.

(D) It was California.

Questions 10–12 refer to the following graph.

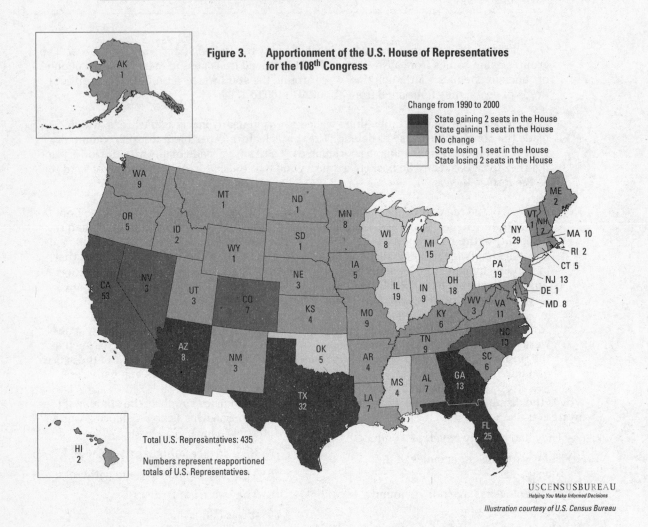

Figure 3.   Apportionment of the U.S. House of Representatives for the 108th Congress

Change from 1990 to 2000
- State gaining 2 seats in the House
- State gaining 1 seat in the House
- No change
- State losing 1 seat in the House
- State losing 2 seats in the House

Total U.S. Representatives: 435

Numbers represent reapportioned totals of U.S. Representatives.

USCENSUSBUREAU
Helping You Make Informed Decisions

Illustration courtesy of U.S. Census Bureau

10. Which state shows the greatest gains in seats in the House of Representatives?

   (A) Washington (WA)

   (B) New York (NY)

   (C) Oklahoma (OK)

   (D) Texas (TX)

11. Which state lost the most representatives?

   (A) Washington (WA)

   (B) New York (NY)

   (C) Oklahoma (OK)

   (D) Texas (TX)

12. What is the underlying population shift leading to this reapportionment of seats?

   (A) The western population is growing compared to the rest of the country.

   (B) The eastern population is growing compared to the rest of the country.

   (C) The states around the Great Lakes are losing population compared to the rest of the country.

   (D) Texas has had a significant increase in population.

Questions 13–14 refer to the following graph.

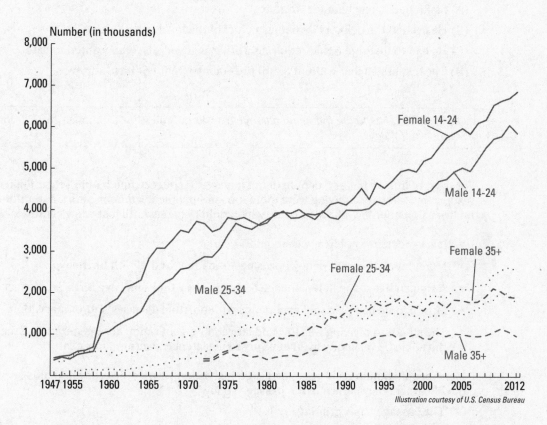

Number (in thousands)

Illustration courtesy of U.S. Census Bureau

13. Which group shows the fastest increase in college enrollment?

(A) Male 14–24

(B) Female 14–24

(C) Male 35+

(D) Female 25–34

14. What was the approximate overall enrollment of men 14–24 in college in 2012?

(A) 5,800

(B) 5,800,000

(C) 5,000,000

(D) 6,800,000

Question 15 refers to the following passage from U.S. History For Dummies *by Steve Wiegand (Wiley).*

An experienced and courageous adventurer, [John] Smith was also a shameless self-promoter and a world-class liar, with a knack for getting into trouble. On the voyage over, for example, he was charged with mutiny, although he was eventually acquitted.

But whatever his faults, Smith was both gutsy and diplomatic. He managed to make friends with Powhatan, the chief of the local Native Americans, and the tribe provided the colonists with enough food to hold on. Smith provided much-needed leadership, declaring, "He that will not work neither shall he eat." Without Smith, the colony may not have survived.

15. What statement in this passage suggests a problem with colonists who were not working hard enough?

    (A) Smith had a penchant for trouble.

    (B) He needed the help of Powhatan, a chief of the local tribe.

    (C) He had to institute a rule requiring work from everyone who wanted to eat.

    (D) The text states that without Smith the colony might not have survived.

Question 16 refers to the following passage from Economics For Dummies, 2nd Edition, *by Sean Flynn (Wiley).*

For most of human history, people didn't manage to squeeze much out of their limited resources. Standards of living were quite low, and people lived poor, short, and rather painful lives. Consider the following facts, which didn't change until just a few centuries ago:

- Life expectancy at birth was about 25 years.
- More than 30 percent of newborns never made it to their 5th birthdays.
- A woman had a one in ten chance of dying every time she gave birth.
- Most people had personal experience with horrible diseases and/or starvation.
- The standard of living was low and stayed low, generation after generation. Except for the nobles, everybody lived at or near subsistence, century after century.

16. Many people hundreds of years ago lived just as long as people today. If that is so, why is the life expectancy shown in the passage so low?

    (A) The passage has a printing error

    (B) The 25 years is an average. The large numbers of children who died very young offset the number of long-lived people.

    (C) It is only an estimate.

    (D) It does not include the nobles.

Questions 17–19 refer to the following passage from the Declaration of Independence, 1776.

Declaration of Independence

We hold these truths to be self-evident: that all men are created equal; that they are endowed by their Creator with certain inalienable rights; that among these are life, liberty, and the pursuit of happiness. That to secure these rights, governments are instituted among men, deriving their just powers from the consent of the governed; that whenever any form of government becomes destructive of these ends it is the right of the people to alter or to abolish it, and to institute a new government, laying its foundation on such principles, and organizing its powers in such form, as to them shall seem most likely to effect their safety and happiness. Prudence, indeed, will dictate that governments long established should not be changed for light and transient causes; and accordingly, all experience hath shown, that mankind are more disposed to suffer, while evils are sufferable, than to right themselves by abolishing the forms to which they are accustomed. But when a long train of abuses and usurpations, pursuing invariably the same object, evinces a design to reduce them under absolute despotism, it is their right, it is their duty, to throw off such government, and to provide new guards for their future security. Such has been the patient sufferance of these colonies; and such is now the necessity which constrains them to alter their former system of government. The history of the present king of Great Britain is a history of repeated injuries and usurpations, all having in direct object the establishment of an absolute tyranny over these states. To prove this, let facts be submitted to a candid world.

17. What does *self-evident* mean?

    (A) All men are not created equal.

    (B) Men don't have rights.

    (C) These points are so obvious they need no explanation.

    (D) There is evidence to support the concept that men have certain rights.

18. When should people rebel against an unjust government?

    (A) whenever a government becomes unjust

    (B) only when government tries to reduce the people under absolute rule

    (C) whenever they feel subjugated

    (D) never

19. According to the Declaration of Independence, what did King George do wrong?

    (A) He abused his powers.

    (B) He tried to usurp people's rights.

    (C) He resorted to absolute despotism.

    (D) All of the above.

Questions 20–21 refer to the following political cartoon. The figure represents the kaiser during World War I.

THE GRAVES OF ALL HIS HOPES

Source: http://www.gutenberg.org/files/37846/37846-h/
37846-h.htm#GERMAN_CHIVALRY_ON_THE_SEA

20. What do these tombstones for revolutions represent?

   (A) pending strategies that might turn the war around

   (B) strategies that never worked out

   (C) revolutions that the Germans inspired but that failed

   (D) none of the above

21. What point is the cartoon making?

   (A) The Germans have had heavy losses in the war.

   (B) Germans are responsible for causing heavy casualties among their enemies.

   (C) The war is almost over.

   (D) German strategies have failed again and again.

Question 22 is based on the following image from the Library of Congress (`www.loc.gov/pictures/item/2005696251/`).

LANDING NEGROES AT JAMESTOWN
FROM DUTCH MAN-OF-WAR. 1619.

22. Name one country, according to this image, involved in the slave trade in the 1600s.

   (A) France

   (B) England

   (C) the Netherlands

   (D) Spain

> *Questions 23–24 refer to the following passage from* CliffsQuickReview U.S. History I *by P. Soifer and A. Hoffman (Wiley).*

Resistance to Slavery

Resistance to slavery took several forms. Slaves would pretend to be ill, refuse to work, do their jobs poorly, destroy farm equipment, set fire to buildings, and steal food. These were all individual acts rather than part of an organized plan for revolt, but the objective was to upset the routine of the plantation in any way possible. On some plantations, slaves could bring grievances about harsh treatment from an overseer to their master and hope that he would intercede on their behalf. Although many slaves tried to run away, few succeeded for more than a few days, and they often returned on their own. Such escapes were more a protest — a demonstration that it could be done — than a dash for freedom. As advertisements in southern newspapers seeking the return of runaway slaves made clear, the goal of most runaways was to find their wives or children who had been sold to another planter. The fabled Underground Railroad, a series of safe houses for runaways organized by abolitionists and run by former slaves like Harriet Tubman, actually helped only about a thousand slaves reach the North.

23. What was one of the main reasons slaves ran away from their masters?

    (A) They were ill.

    (B) They were poorly paid.

    (C) They wanted to find wives or children that had been sold to others.

    (D) They longed to be free.

24. How successful was the fabled Underground Railroad?

    (A) It wasn't very successful, based on the numbers it helped.

    (B) It was important mainly because it offered hope to all slaves of permanent escape.

    (C) It funded slave rebellions.

    (D) It helped end slavery.

> *Question 25 refers to the following passage from* U.S. History For Dummies *by Steve Wiegand (Wiley).*

Although the total population of slaves was relatively low through most of the 1600s, colonial governments took steps to institutionalize slavery. In 1662, Virginia passed a law that automatically made slaves of slaves' children. In 1664, Maryland's assembly declared that all black people in the colony were slaves for life, whether they converted to Christianity or not. And in 1684, New York's legislators recognized slavery as a legitimate practice.

As the 17th century closed, it was clear that African slaves were a much better bargain, in terms of costs, than European servants, and the numbers of slaves began to swell. In 1670, Virginia had a population of about 2,000 slaves. By 1708, the number was 12,000. Slavery had not only taken root; it was sprouting.

25. What does the phrase *institutionalize slavery* mean?

    (A) establish laws defining and controlling slavery

    (B) turning slavery into an institution

    (C) replacing European servants with slaves

    (D) making laws that automatically enslaved children of slaves

> *Question 26 refers to the following passage from* Economics For Dummies, 2nd Edition, *by Sean Flynn (Wiley).*

The obvious reason for higher living standards, which continue to rise, is that human beings have recently figured out lots of new technologies, and people keep inventing more. But if you dig a little deeper, you have to wonder why a technologically innovative society didn't happen earlier.

The Ancient Greeks invented a simple steam engine and the coin-operated vending machine. They even developed the basic idea behind the programmable computer. But they never quite got around to having an industrial revolution and entering on a path of sustained economic growth.

And despite the fact that there have always been really smart people in every society on earth, it wasn't until the late 18th century, in England, that the Industrial Revolution actually got started and living standards in many nations rose substantially and kept on rising, year after year.

26. Why did the Greeks not make use of the ideas of steam engines or vending machines?

    (A) They never developed sufficient technology to apply these ideas.

    (B) They didn't realize what they had invented.

    (C) They saw no need for these inventions.

    (D) impossible to say based on the text

> *Questions 27–28 are based on the following report.*

Weather and Traffic Report

Good morning, and welcome to America's weather and traffic on WAWT, the voice of the world in the ear of the nation. Today is going to be hot. That's H-O-T, and we all know what that means. The big P is coming back for a visit. We are going to have pollution today for sure with our record heat on each coast. If you think it's hot here, it's even hotter up higher. And that means unhealthy air, leading to unhealthy people. I can hear the coughs and sneezes coast to coast. I think I hear a whole series of gasps from our nation's capital, good ol' Washington, D.C., and it's not Congress that is producing all that hot air. And out in western California, it's just as bad. Just the other day, I looked up "poor air quality" in the dictionary, and it said "see California." Lots of luck breathing out there.

This morning, once again, there's a layer of hot air just above ground level. That's where we live — ground level. This temperature inversion acts like a closed gate, keeping the surface air from rising and mixing. Of course, we are all going to drive our cars all day in heavy traffic, and some of us will go to work in factories. And, surprise: By afternoon, all those pollutants from the cars mix with the emissions from the factories and get trapped by the layer of hot air, and it's try-to-catch-your-breath time. Unhealthy air is here again. Tomorrow and every day after, we'll probably have more of the same until we learn to take care of our environment.

Well, I'll see you tomorrow, if the air's not too thick to see through.

27. What is the big P?

   (A) the president

   (B) pollution

   (C) record heat

   (D) smog

28. What is a temperature inversion?

   (A) hot air holding down cooler air, trapping pollution

   (B) colder air higher in the atmosphere

   (C) an unexpected cold front

   (D) ground level pollution

Questions 29–30 are based on the following passage from Geography For Dummies *by Charles A. Heatwole.*

In the third century BC, the Greek scholar Eratosthenes made a remarkably accurate measurement of Earth's circumference. At Syene (near Aswan, Egypt), the sun illuminated the bottom of a well only one day every year. Eratosthenes inferred correctly this could only happen if the sun were directly overhead the well — that is, 90 degrees above the horizon. By comparing that sun angle with another one measured in Alexandria, Egypt, on the same day the sun was directly overhead at Syene, Eratosthenes deduced that the distance between the two locations was one-fiftieth (1/50th) of Earth's circumference. Thus, if he could measure the distance from Syene to Alexandria and multiply that number times 50, the answer would be the distance around the entire Earth.

There are diverse accounts of the method of measurement. Some say Eratosthenes had his assistants count camel strides (yes, camel strides) that they measured in *stade,* the Greek unit of measurement. In any event, he came up with a distance of 500 miles between Syene and Alexandria. That meant Earth was about 25,000 miles around. ("About" because the relationship between stade and miles is not exactly known.) The actual average circumference is 24,680 miles, so Eratosthenes was very close.

29. How long ago did the Greek scholar Eratosthenes calculate the Earth's circumference?

   (A) about 300 years ago

   (B) about 2,000 years ago

   (C) about 2,300 years ago

   (D) not enough information given

30. What information did Eratosthenes have with which to calculate the Earth's circumference?

   (A) two angles and the distance between two points

   (B) two angles and one side of a triangle

   (C) one 90-degree angle and a distance

   (D) not enough information given

Questions 31–32 refer to the following passage from CliffsQuickReview U.S. History II *by P. Soifer and A. Hoffman (Wiley).*

The End of the Cold War

In July 1989, Gorbachev repudiated the Brezhnev Doctrine, which had justified the intervention of the Soviet Union in the affairs of communist countries. Within a few months of his statement, the Communist regimes in Eastern Europe collapsed — Poland, Hungary, and Czechoslovakia, followed by Bulgaria and Romania. The Berlin Wall came down in November 1989, and East and West Germany were reunited within the year. Czechoslovakia eventually split into the Czech Republic and Slovakia with little trouble, but the end of the Yugoslav Federation in 1991 led to years of violence and ethnic cleansing (the expulsion of an ethnic population from a geographic area), particularly in Bosnia-Herzegovina. The Soviet Union also broke up, not long after an attempted coup against Gorbachev in August 1991, and the Baltic states of Latvia, Estonia, and Lithuania were the first to gain their independence. That December, Gorbachev stepped down, and the old Soviet Union became the Commonwealth of Independent States (CIS). The CIS quickly disappeared, and the republics that had once made up the Soviet Union were recognized as sovereign nations. The end of the Cold War led directly to major nuclear weapons reduction agreements between President Bush and the Russian leaders as well as significant cutbacks in the number of troops the United States committed to the defense of NATO.

31. Which of these statements is true?

(A) Gorbachev accepted the Brezhnev doctrine.

(B) Brezhnev ended the Cold War in 1991.

(C) Gorbachev stepped down in 1989.

(D) None of the above.

32. What was the effect of the end of the Yugoslav Federation?

(A) years of violence and ethnic cleansing

(B) the reunification of East and West Germany

(C) major arms reductions in Europe

(D) the independence of Latvia

Question 33 refers to the following passage from Geography For Dummies *by Charles A. Heatwole (Wiley).*

A *region* is an area of Earth, large or small, that has one or more things in common. So when you say "I'm going to the mountains" or "I'm heading for the shore," you refer to an area — a region — that has a certain set of characteristics over a broad area. . . .

Regions make it easier to comprehend our Earthly home. After all, Earth consists of gazillions of locations, each of which has its own particular and peculiar characteristics. Knowing every last one of them would be impossible. But we can simplify the challenge by grouping together contiguous locations that have one or more things in common — Gobi Desert, Islamic realm, tropical rainforest, Chinatown, the Great Lakes, suburbia. Each of these is a region. Some are big and some are small. Some refer to physical characteristics. Some refer to human characteristics. Some do both. But each facilitates the task of understanding the world.

33. What process do geographers use when they divide the Earth into regions for easier study?

(A) simplification

(B) generalization

(C) classification

(D) approximation

> *Question 34 refers to the following passage from* Economics For Dummies, 2nd Edition, *by Sean Flynn (Wiley).*

A firm that has no competitors in its industry is called a *monopoly*. Monopolies are much maligned because their profit incentive leads them to raise prices and lower output in order to squeeze more money out of consumers. As a result, governments typically go out of their way to break up monopolies and replace them with competitive industries that generate lower prices and higher output.

At the same time, however, governments also very intentionally create monopolies in other situations. For instance, governments issue patents, which give monopoly rights to inventors to sell and market their inventions. Similarly, in many places, local services such as natural gas delivery and trash collection are also monopolies created and enforced by local government.

34. Under what circumstances are monopolies encouraged?

    (A) for local services

    (B) to protect inventors

    (C) both of the above

    (D) neither of the above

> *Question 35 is based on the following passage from* www.loc.gov/teachers/ classroommaterials/presentationsandactivities/presentations/ elections/voters6.html.

Alice Paul, leader of the National Women's Party, brought attention-grabbing protest tactics from British suffragists to the United States. In 1917, ten suffragists were arrested for picketing the White House. Their crime, obstructing sidewalk traffic. Their presence, noted by President Wilson and his wife, was soon forgotten as clouds of war gathered over the United States.

The suffrage movement slowed during World War I, but women continued to assert their status as full and independent members of society. During World War II, women began entering the work force in support of the war effort.

Since 1878, a women's suffrage amendment had been proposed each year in Congress. In 1919, the suffrage movement had finally gained enough support, and Congress, grateful for women's help during the war, passed the Nineteenth Amendment on June 5. With these words, Congress at last enfranchised half of the American population:

The right of citizens of the United States to vote shall not be denied or abridged by the United States or by any state on account of sex.

35. When did women receive the right to vote?

    (A) 1878

    (B) 1917

    (C) 1919

    (D) During World War II

> *Questions 36–37 refer to the following passage* CliffsQuickReview U.S. History I *by P. Soifer and A. Hoffman (Wiley)*

The Panic of 1873

In 1873, over-speculation in railroad stocks led to a major economic panic. The failure of Jay Cooke's investment bank was followed by the collapse of the stock market and the bankruptcy of thousands of businesses; crop prices plummeted and unemployment soared. Much of the problem was related to the use of greenbacks for currency. Hard-money advocates insisted that paper money had to be backed by gold to curb inflation and level price fluctuations, but farmers and manufacturers, who needed easy credit, wanted even more greenbacks put in circulation, a policy that Grant ultimately opposed. He recommended and the Congress enacted legislation in 1875 providing for the redemption of greenbacks in gold. Because the Treasury needed time to build up its gold reserves, redemption did not go into effect for another four years, by which time the longest depression in American history had come to an end.

36. What was the role of paper money in the economic collapse in 1873?

(A) It triggered the collapse.

(B) It led to easy credit.

(C) It caused crop prices to plummet.

(D) It had no effect.

37. What was Grant's position on paper money?

(A) He favored it.

(B) He was opposed.

(C) He took no official position.

(D) insufficient information in the passage

> *Question 38 is based on the following passage from* www.loc.gov/teachers/
> classroommaterials/presentationsandactivities/presentations/
> elections/voters6.html.

In 1963 and 1964, Dr. Martin Luther King Jr. brought hundreds of black people to the courthouse in Selma, Alabama to register [to vote]. When they were turned away, Dr. King organized and led protests that finally turned the tide of American political opinion. In 1964, the Twenty-Fourth Amendment prohibited the use of poll taxes. In 1965, the Voting Rights Act put federal teeth into enforcing the right to vote for African Americans.

The 1965 Voting Rights Act created a significant change in the status of African Americans throughout the South. The Voting Rights Act prohibited the states from using literacy tests . . . and other methods of excluding African Americans from voting. Prior to this, only an estimated twenty-three percent of voting-age blacks were registered nationally, but by 1969 the number had jumped to sixty-one percent.

38. What were some of the requirements used by local authorities to stop African Americans from voting? Write the correct letter(s) in these boxes: ☐☐ ☐☐ ☐☐ ☐☐

(A) poll taxes

(B) literacy tests

(C) photo identification

(D) passports

Questions 39–40 are based on the following chart for 2014–2015 from www.bea.gov/newsreleases/regional/gdp_state/gsp_glance.htm.

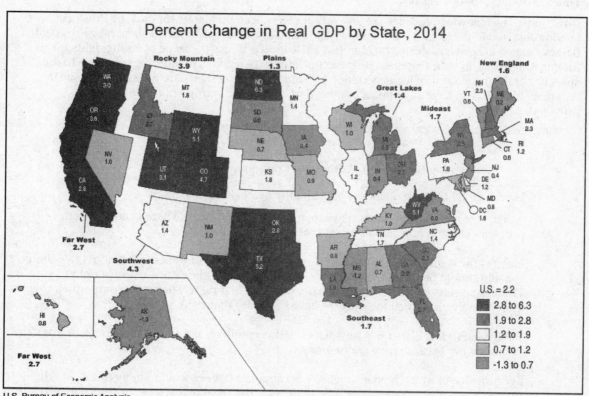

Percent Change in Real GDP by State, 2014

U.S. Bureau of Economic Analysis

39. Which state experienced the greatest decrease on real GDP in 2013?

(A) Texas

(B) Alaska

(C) New England

(D) Georgia

40. Which region among those listed showed the greatest increase in GDP?

(A) Far West

(B) Southwest

(C) Great Lakes

(D) New England

The Extended Response

Time: 25 minutes for one essay

Directions: The following passages are an excerpt of a speech on March 15, 1965, by President Lyndon Johnson to Congress on the Voting Rights Act, and an excerpt from a speech by President Barack Obama in Selma, Alabama, on March 7, 2015. Both address the issue of voting rights for African Americans. In your response, discuss this information and, with specific reference to the speeches and using your own life experience, explain why voting rights are an enduring issue in American history. You have 25 minutes to plan, draft, and write your response in the space provided.

Lyndon B. Johnson, Address to Congress, March 15, 1965

I speak tonight for the dignity of man and the destiny of democracy.

. . .There is no Negro problem. There is no Southern problem. There is no Northern problem. There is only an American problem. . . .

Many of the issues of civil rights are very complex and most difficult. But about this there can and should be no argument. Every American citizen must have an equal right to vote. There is no reason which can excuse the denial of that right. There is no duty which weighs more heavily on us than the duty we have to ensure that right.

Yet the harsh fact is that in many places in this country, men and women are kept from voting simply because they are Negroes.

Every device of which human ingenuity is capable has been used to deny this right. The Negro citizen may go to register only to be told that the day is wrong, or the hour is late, or the official in charge is absent. And if he persists, and if he manages to present himself to the registrar, he may be disqualified because he did not spell out his middle name or because he abbreviated a word on the application. . . .

For the fact is that the only way to pass these barriers is to show a white skin.

Experience has clearly shown that the existing process of law cannot overcome systematic and ingenuous discrimination. No law that we now have on the books — and I have helped to put three of them there — can ensure the right to vote when local officials are determined to deny it.

In such a case our duty must be clear to all of us. The Constitution says that no person shall be kept from voting because of his race or his color. . . .

Wednesday I will send to Congress a law designed to eliminate illegal barriers to the right to vote. . . .

This bill will strike down restrictions to voting in all elections: federal, state, and local; which have been used to deny Negroes the right to vote. . . .

To those who seek to avoid action by their National Government in their own communities; who want to and who seek to maintain purely local control over elections, the answer is simple: Open your polling places to all your people.

Allow men and women to register and vote whatever the color of their skin.

Extend the rights of citizenship to every citizen of this land. . . . We have already waited a hundred years and more, and the time for waiting is gone. . . .

Their cause must be our cause too. Because it's not just Negroes, but really it's all of us, who must overcome the crippling legacy of bigotry and injustice.

And we shall overcome. . . .

The time of justice has now come. And I tell you that I believe sincerely that no force can hold it back. It is right, in the eyes of man and God, that it should come. And when it does, I think that day will brighten the lives of every American. . . .

Barack Obama, Speech in Selma, March 7, 2015

. . . It's the idea held by generations of citizens who believed that America is a constant work in progress; who believed that loving this country requires more than singing its praises or avoiding uncomfortable truths. It requires the occasional disruption, the willingness to speak out for what is right, to shake up the status quo. That's America. . . .

Right now, in 2015, fifty years after Selma, there are laws across this country designed to make it harder for people to vote. As we speak, more of such laws are being proposed. Meanwhile, the Voting Rights Act, the culmination of so much blood and sweat and tears, the product of so much sacrifice in the face of wanton violence, stands weakened, its future subject to partisan rancor.

How can that be? The Voting Rights Act was one of the crowning achievements of our democracy, the result of Republican and Democratic effort. President Reagan signed its renewal when he was in office. President Bush signed its renewal when he was in office. One hundred Members of Congress have come here today to honor people who were willing to die for the right it protects. If we want to honor this day, let these hundred go back to Washington, and gather four hundred more, and together, pledge to make it their mission to restore the law this year. . . .

Answers and Explanations

Review the detailed answer explanations to help you discover areas which you understand well and where you may need to do more work. Reading the explanations, even for the questions you answered correctly, helps you understand how these question-and-answer items are set up.

The GED Testing Service notes on its website that students don't need to do extensive studying of possible content to do well on the Social Studies test. However, it also states that any additional reading you do will contribute to your understanding of the content and help you find answers more quickly.

Ready to find out how you did? Here are the answers and explanations.

1. **D. It had no connection with native people.** The term derived from a combination of American and Indian. Choice (A) is partially correct. The passage mentions no native people input, so you can ignore Choice (B). Columbus made the original error of assuming he had arrived in India, so Choice (C) is wrong.

2. **C. It incorrectly suggested all native people were primitive.** Political activists may have been opposed, and debates raged about whether the term was all encompassing, but according to the passage, this name was rejected because not all tribes were primitive. Choice (D) doesn't apply because that term was never discussed.

3. **A. There was no collective name for all native people.** According to the passage, Native Americans had no collective name for themselves. Columbus named them in error, and no one since has been able to agree on one single name. In many instances, historians and anthropologists simply use tribal names or the term *Native Americans*. Other nations in America have developed other conventions. In Canada, the proper name for Eskimo is Inuit, while Native Indians are referred to as First Nations people.

4. **B. He underestimated by more than half.** The total distance, according to the text, is 10,000 miles. Columbus estimated 2,500 miles, or about one quarter of the distance. That means he underestimated by three-quarters, so the best answer is Choice (B). The other answers are incorrect according to the passage.

5. **C. She thought she would never have to honor Columbus's contract.** Choice (A) is wrong because the English told Columbus to get lost. Spain already had Columbus on the payroll, but that's not the key point in the passage. Portugal also had turned down Columbus, so Choice (D) isn't a consideration. Your best choice is Choice (C), which is backed by a direct statement in the text.

6. **B. His crew was ready to mutiny.** According to the passage, Columbus's crew was ready to mutiny, Choice (B). Nothing in the passage relates the landing and money, and other areas of the text suggest Isabella wasn't waiting for Columbus's return.

7. **C. Archaeologists have not yet found a clear explanation.** The text suggests two possible explanations, with some support for the drought explanation but no proof for the second possible explanation. Choices (A) and (B) are in the text but don't relate to the question. That also makes Choice (D) irrelevant.

8. **A. Their towns had high, easily defended walls.** The text states that the area is arid and that it couldn't support a large population. The text also notes that the theory of Indian attacks from what is now Mexico is controversial, meaning it's disputed. However, the high walls suggest a threat of attack from some source; otherwise, the Anasazi would not have expended the energy and resources to build such a wall. Choice (B) has no bearing on the question. Choice (C) is interesting, but no evidence suggests that these other tribes did attack.

9. **A. No evidence supports that claim.** There is no link between the laid-back description and hunting or gathering as a lifestyle, nor is merely living in California a valid explanation (although it's the beginning of a great joke). Your only feasible answer is Choice (A).

10. **D. Texas (TX).** The labels indicate the greatest gains are made in the darkest shaded areas. Only one state is among the choices in the darkest shade, Texas. Choice (D) is the correct answer.

11. **B. New York (NY).** The states losing representatives are in the lightest shades. White indicates the greatest loss. The only state shaded white from among the choices is New York.

12. **C. The states around the Great Lakes are losing population compared to the rest of the country.** The two shades that represent loss of representatives, the white and the lightest gray, are found only around the Great Lakes. Though the western population (Choice (A)) and Texas (Choice (D)) are growing, those are incomplete answers.

13. **B. Female 14–24.** The graph shows that the overall increase in enrollment is highest for women. The line rises more steeply at either end and is the same as that for men 14–24 in the middle years. It also rises higher by 2012. The line for men 14–24 is also high but not as high as that for women of the same age group. The other lines all rise more slowly and are at lower levels. Choice (B) is your only option.

14. **B. 5,800,000.** The graph indicates enrollment for men in the 5,800,000 range. Choice (A) is wrong because the scale indicates that the numbers are in thousands. That means, for example, that 5,000 on the scale is really 5,000,000. The scale may be difficult to read, but it's clear enough that you can tell that the only number close to the correct choice is Choice (B).

15. **C. He had to institute a rule requiring work from everyone who wanted to eat.** Choices (D) and (B) hint that trouble was brewing, but only Choice (C) gives an answer. That answer is supported by the text, while the other choices have no direct link to the question.

16. **B. The 25 years is an average. The large numbers of children who died very young offset the number of long-lived people.** Several reasons for the low life expectancy are in the text: One woman in ten died in childbirth, and 30 percent of children died before their fifth birthday. Further, this type of statistic is always an average. If nearly one third of the young die that early, then others must live a lot longer for the average to work out. Choice (A) isn't a reasonable assumption, and the text doesn't support Choice (D). Choice (C) may be true, but it isn't the best answer.

17. **C. These points are so obvious they need no explanation.** The term *self-evident* means that an idea is so apparent that it needs no further evidence. Choices (A) and (B) are wrong, while Choice (D) contradicts the definition of *self-evident.*

18. **B. only when government tries to reduce the people under absolute rule.** According to the passage, people are prone to tolerate abuses for a long time and indeed should, rebelling only when the government seems intent on reducing them through absolute despotism. Choices (A) and (C) aren't strong enough reasons, according to the text, and Choice (D) is contradicted by the passage.

19. **D. All of the above.** The Declaration of Independence lists many grievances the colonists had against King George and his colonial government. Choices (A), (B), and (C) are all correct.

20. **B. strategies that never worked out.** The German government tried to stir up revolutions in various British possessions, but they failed. Choice (C) is close; the British experienced some trouble in these territories, but these events never became revolutions. Choices (A) and (D) are wrong.

21. **D. German strategies have failed again and again.** The tombstones each represent either a strategy the German government tried to undermine the Allied war effort or a major battle defeat. The other choices are all partially correct, but only Choice (D) is a complete answer. Remember, you must choose the most correct answer from the choices offered.

22. **C. the Netherlands.** The caption beneath the drawing states that the ship landing slaves was a Dutch man-of-war; the nationality *Dutch* refers to the Netherlands.

23. **C. They wanted to find wives or children that had been sold to others.** The text makes no mention of illness, Choice (A), as a cause for running away. Slaves weren't paid, so Choice (B) isn't valid. Slaves wanted to be free, but that's not the best answer based on the text. The text quotes newspaper ads stating that reunification with family was one of the main reasons for running away.

24. **B. It was important mainly because it offered hope to all slaves of permanent escape.** The Underground Railroad actually succeeded in helping only about 1,000 slaves escape to Canada. However, you can infer that its importance lay in that it gave hope. The text doesn't support the idea that it was the most successful escape method nor that it funded slave rebellions or helped end slavery.

25. **A. establish laws defining and controlling slavery.** The term *institutionalize* refers to creating a set of laws and regulations that define and regulate slavery. Choice (B) merely restates the question and isn't a valid answer. Choices (C) and (D) are correct but incomplete answers.

26. **A. They never developed sufficient technology to apply these ideas.** The text states that the Greeks never got around to having an industrial revolution. That implies they never developed the technology to make use of these ideas. You can infer that Choice (A) is the correct answer. Choices (B) and (C) may be partially correct but aren't supported by the text. Choice (D) is wrong.

27. **B. pollution.** The whole discussion is about pollution. The forecast specifically mentions smog and record heat, but they're a subset of pollution. The president isn't mentioned in the text.

28. **A. hot air holding down cooler air, trapping pollution.** *Temperature inversions* occur when the normal sequence of air mass temperatures is reversed. Normally, air cools as it rises, which allows warm air at ground level to rise and disperse ground-level pollution. Choice (B) is reversed, and Choices (C) and (D) have nothing to do with the question.

29. **C. about 2,300 years ago.** The calculations were made in 300 BC, which is about 2,300 years ago. Choice (B) is the only answer that's close. Choice (A) confuses the date of 300 BC with the length of time. (**Note:** Common practice now replaces BC [Before Christ] with BCE [Before Common Era], and AD [Anno Domini] with CE [Common Era], so don't be confused if you see those abbreviations. The actual year numbers remain the same either way.)

30. **A. two angles and the distance between two points.** He had two angles — the 90-degree angle when the sun was directly overhead Syene, and the sun angle measured in Alexandria, Egypt, on the same day — and the distance from Syene to Alexandria.

31. **D. None of the above.** None of these statements is correct. Gorbachev rejected the Brezhnev Doctrine. No date is given for the end of the Cold War, so Choice (B) isn't acceptable, and Gorbachev stepped down in 1991, not 1989.

32. **A. years of violence and ethnic cleansing.** According to the passage, the end of the federation led to conflicts and ethnic cleansing. The other events listed happened but had nothing to do with the collapse of the Yugoslav Federation.

33. **B. generalization.** The process of dividing the Earth into areas that have something in common is a form of generalization. It does simplify studying the Earth (Choice (A)), and classification of features is part of that process (Choice (C)), these are incomplete answers. Choice (D), approximation, doesn't make sense in this context.

34. **C. both of the above.** Both Choices (A) and (B) are correct according to the text.

35. **C. 1919.** The text states all the dates and times mentioned in the answer choices, but only the 1919 date is correct. The other answers are incorrect based on the passage.

36. **A. It triggered the collapse.** The text indicates that the *greenback,* the paper money, wasn't backed by gold. That meant the government could print as much as it wanted. The easy credit led to speculation and economic collapse. Choice (B) is partially correct but not the best answer. Choices (C) and (D) are wrong.

37. **B. He was opposed.** Grant "ultimately opposed" the printing of greenbacks and putting more paper money into circulation. The text directly contradicts Choices (A) and (C).

38. **A and B.** The states used poll taxes and literacy tests to discourage African American voters. The passage also mentions "other methods," but it never clarifies what they are or whether they involve the other answer options.

39. **B. Alaska.** According to the chart, Alaska's GDP declined by 2.5 percent. Choice (C) is wrong because New England is a region, not a state. The other answer choices are wrong because in both cases the GDP increased.

40. **B. Southwest.** This question is somewhat tricky. According to the chart, the greatest increase in GDP was 4.1 percent in the Rocky Mountain area. However, the question asks you to choose from among the answer choices listed, and the Rocky Mountain region isn't one of those. The best answer among the listed choices is Choice (B), the Southwest Region. The other answers are simply incorrect according to the graphs.

Sample Extended Response

The following sample essay would receive a reasonable mark. It isn't perfect, but it meets the criteria for an acceptable essay. It explains the issue, shows why it's an enduring issue, and links the essay directly back to the source material. It uses quotes from the source material and interprets the data. It (mostly) uses correct spelling and grammar and has topic sentences. It also shows that the writer had existing knowledge on the topic. (***Remember:*** Your time is restricted. You're not expected to write a fabulous research paper in 25 minutes, only a good, draft-quality one.)

Compare the following sample to the response you wrote.

Both presidents in their speeches point to voting rights as one of the defining issues in the civil rights movement. The fact that 50 years has elapsed between these two speeches and that both speeches point to continuing difficulties for blacks to exercise the right to vote clearly shows that this is indeed an enduring issue.

In the first passage, President Johnson outlines the need for the new voter registration legislation. He discusses the difficulties blacks endured, and the obstacles placed in their way, when they tried to vote. He reminds the listeners that blacks were granted the right to vote after the Civil War. He shows how unjustly some states were still using various methods to exclude black voters, from poll taxes to literacy tests. He tells of three separate pieces of legislation that were passed to address these problematic laws. All three efforts were subverted by various states responsible for the implementation of these laws. He concludes with the argument that the time has come, that Congress must take action.

Comparing Johnson's speech to President Obama's in Selma 50 years later shows how little has actually changed. Obama talks about the fact that there are once again state voter registration laws whose sole aim to make voting access for blacks more difficult. He also points out how voting rights have become a partisan issue dividing Congress when under Lyndon Johnson the Voting Rights Act had been an example of bipartisan unity.

In addition, events surrounding the last election certainly support President Obama's comments. Voters' lists in various states were purged without giving people an opportunity to appeal. Reviews of the purge lists show that many on lists had every legal right to vote. Some states ignored or voided absentee ballots. Strangely, the preponderance of purged voters were black or Hispanic.

Both President Johnson and President Obama make the point that voting rights are the very foundation of American liberty. If people cannot have a say in choosing their representatives in government, they are not living in a democracy. Obama concludes his speech by asking people to let Congress know that any weakening of voters' rights laws is unacceptable, that the spirit of Selma has not faded.

This essay isn't a perfect response; it's a short essay written to first-draft standards. However, the more important skill to pick up is how to evaluate your own extended response. If you know how to mark an essay, you'll know what to watch for when writing one. Answer these questions to evaluate your own response:

✔ **Content**

- Do you clearly state the ongoing issue presented in these passages?

- Do you give clear evidence, using multiple points from the passages to support your position?

- Do you explain how you arrived at your conclusion? (You don't have to agree with the position.)

- Have you used evidence from the passages and your own knowledge?

✔ **Style and organization**

- Does your introduction clearly state your position?

- Is your evidence presented in a logical order to build your case?

- Does your conclusion contain an appropriate summary of the evidence and why you took the stand you did?

- Does your essay stay on point?

- Do you use proper linking and transition words and phrases between paragraphs?

- Do you use varied and clear sentences and sentence structure?

✔ **Writing mechanics**

- Is your essay written in a clear, concise manner?

- Do you use grammar and spelling correctly?

- Do you use vocabulary appropriately?

Diagnostic Grid

The diagnostic grid has no option for close reading or careful reading. All questions require that skill. Other skills highlighted in the diagnostic grid relate to map reading, chart and table interpretation, and other skills the GED test requires of students. For guidance on how to improve your reading and comprehension skills, turn to Chapter 5. Turn to Chapter 6 for more about analyzing what you read, including evaluating cause-and-effect relationships and drawing inferences from evidence provided. If you struggled with questions involving math, maps, charts, or tables, turn to Chapter 7. If you struggled with the Extended Response item, head to Chapter 12. Chapters 8 through 11 are designed to make you more comfortable reading and answering questions in specific social studies content areas: civics and government, U.S. history, economics, and geography.

Question	Use evidence	Validate	Interpret graphics	Read charts and tables	Understand words in context	Evaluate cause and effect	Perform calculations	Analyze	Deduce
1	X	X						X	
2	X							X	
3	X							X	
4	X						X		
5	X							X	
6	X							X	
7	X	X						X	
8	X	X				X		X	X
9	X	X							
10	X		X						
11	X		X						
12	X		X						
13	X		X						
14	X		X				X		
15	X							X	
16		X						X	
17					X				
18	X							X	
19	X							X	
20			X					X	
21			X					X	
22			X						
23	X							X	
24	X	X						X	X
25	X				X			X	X
26	X								X
27	X							X	X
28	X					X			X
29							X	X	
30	X							X	
31	X							X	X
32	X							X	X
33	X								
34	X								X
35	X								
36	X							X	X
37	X				X				
38	X								
39			X	X				X	
40	X		X	X					

Chapter 4

Succeeding on the GED Social Studies Test

*Y*ou may never have taken a standardized test before. Or if you have, you may wake up sweating in the middle of the night from nightmares about your past experiences. Whether you've experienced the joys or sorrows of standardized tests, you must know how to perform well on them to succeed on the GED Social Studies test, which consists mostly of multiple-choice questions.

The good news is that you've come to the right spot to find out more about this type of test. This chapter explains some important pointers on how to prepare on the days and nights before the test, what to do on the morning of the test, and what to do during the test to be successful. You also discover some important test-taking strategies to build your confidence.

Gearing Up for Test Time

Doing well on the GED Social Studies test involves more than walking into the test site and answering the questions. You need to be prepared for the challenges in the test. To ensure that you're ready to tackle the test head-on, do the following leading up to the test:

✔ **Get enough sleep.** We're sorry if we sound like your parents, but it's true; you shouldn't take tests when you're approaching exhaustion. Plan your time so you can get a good night's sleep for several days before the test and avoid excess caffeine. If you prepare ahead of time, you'll be ready, and sleep will come easier.

✔ **Eat a good breakfast.** A healthy breakfast fuels your mind and body. You have to spend several hours taking the test, and you definitely don't want to falter during that time. Eat some protein, such as eggs, bacon, or sausage with toast for breakfast. Avoid sugars (doughnuts, jelly, fruit, and so on) because they can cause you to tire easily. You don't want your empty stomach fighting with your full brain.

✔ **Take some deep breaths.** During your trip to the testing site, prepare yourself mentally for the test. Clear your head of all distractions, practice deep breathing, and imagine yourself acing the test. Don't panic.

✔ **Start at the beginning, not the end.** Remember that the day of the test is the end of a long journey of preparation and not the beginning. It takes time to build mental muscles.

✔ **Be on time.** Make sure you know what time the test begins and the exact location of your test site. Arrive early. If necessary, take a practice run to make sure you have enough time to get from your home or workplace to the testing center. You don't need the added pressure of worrying about whether you can make it to the test on time. In fact, this added pressure can create industrial-strength panic in the calmest of people.

Traffic congestion happens. No one can plan for it, but you can leave extra time to make sure it doesn't ruin your day. Plan your route and practice it. Then leave extra time in case a meteor crashes into the street and the crowd that gathers around it stalls your progress. Even though the GED test is now administered on a computer and not everyone has to start at the same time, test centers are open only for certain hours, and if they close before you finish, you won't get any sympathy. Check the times the test center is open. Examiners won't show you a lot of consideration if you show up too late to complete the test because you didn't check the times. They have even less sympathy if you show up on the wrong date.

Using the Diagnostic and Practice Tests to Your Advantage

Taking diagnostic and practice GED Social Studies tests is important for a few reasons, including the following:

✔ **They help you prepare for the test.** Practice tests, the diagnostic test in particular (Chapter 3), shed light on knowledge and skills you need to focus on leading up to the actual test.

✔ **They give you an indication of how well you know the material.** One or two tests won't give you a definitive answer to how you'll do on the actual test, because you need to do four or five tests to cover all possible topics, but they do give you an indication of where you stand.

✔ **They confirm whether you know how to use the computer to answer the questions.** You don't get this benefit by taking the practice tests in the book, but you can go online at www.gedtestingservice.com/educators/freepracticetest to take a computer-based practice test.

✔ **They familiarize you with the test format.** You can read about test questions, but you can't actually understand them until you've worked through several.

✔ **They can ease your stress.** A successful run-through on a practice test allows you to feel more comfortable and confident in your own abilities to take the GED test successfully and alleviate your overall anxiety.

Turn to Chapter 3 to take the diagnostic test or to Chapter 13 to take the practice test. These tests are an important part of any preparation program. They're the feedback mechanism that you may normally get from a private tutor. To get the most out of any practice test, be sure to check your answers after each test and read the answer explanations. If possible, take the additional GED Testing Service practice tests mentioned earlier in this section and a few more sample questions you can find at www.gedtestingservice.com/testers/sample-questions. Use your favorite Internet search engine to find more practice tests online. The GED Testing Service also offers GED Ready tests that you can purchase through authorized outlets.

Packing for Test Day

The GED test may be the most important exam you ever take. Treat it seriously and come prepared. Make sure you bring the following items with you on test day:

- **You:** The most important thing to bring to the GED test is obviously you. If you enroll to take the test, you have to show up; otherwise, you'll receive a big fat zero and lose your testing fee. If something unfortunate happens after you enroll, contact the test center and explain your situation to the test administrators. They may reschedule the test with no additional charge.

- **Correct identification:** Before test officials let you into the room to take the test, they want to make sure you're you. Bring the approved photo ID — your state GED office can tell you what's an approved form of photo ID. Have your ID in a place where you can reach it easily. And when asked to identify yourself, don't pull out a mirror and say, "Yep, that's me."

- **Registration receipt and any fees you still owe:** Check with your local administrator to confirm when and where the fee has to be paid and how to pay it. The same people don't run all test centers. With some, you may have to pay in advance when booking the test. In that case, bring your receipt to avoid any misunderstandings. Others may allow you to pay at the door. Find out whether you can use cash, check, debit, or credit card. The amount of the GED test registration fee also varies from state to state. If you don't pay, you can't play, or in this case, take the test.

  If needed, you may be able to get financial assistance to help with the testing fees. Further, if you do the test one section at a time (which we recommend), you can probably pay for each test section separately. Check with your state or local education authorities.

- **Registration confirmation:** The registration confirmation is your proof that you did register. If you're taking the test in an area where everybody knows you and everything you do, you may not need the confirmation, but we suggest you take it anyway. It's light and doesn't take up much room in your pocket.

- **Other miscellaneous items:** In the instructions you receive after you register for the test, you get a list of what you need to bring with you. Besides yourself and the items we list previously, other items you want to bring or wear include the following:

  - **Comfortable clothes and shoes:** When you're taking the test, you want to be as relaxed as possible. Uncomfortable clothes and shoes may distract you from doing your best. You're taking the GED test, not modeling the most recent fashions. Consider dressing in layers; you don't want to be too hot or too cold.

  - **Reading glasses:** If you need glasses to read a computer monitor, don't forget to bring them to the test. Bring a spare pair, if you have one. You can't do the test if you can't read the screen. And before you go, make sure your reading glasses work with a computer screen. The focal distance for reading print materials and computer screens is different, depending on your prescription.

  - **Calculator:** You're provided with an onscreen calculator. You can bring your own handheld calculator, but it must be a specific make and model. Visit www.gedtestingservice.com/testers/calculator to find out more about the onscreen calculator and which handheld make and model you're allowed to bring. In either case, be sure to familiarize yourself with that model calculator before the test.

The rules about what enters the testing room are strict. Don't take any chances. If something isn't on the list of acceptable items and isn't normal clothing, leave it at home. Laptops, cellphones, and other electronic devices will most likely be banned from the testing area. Leave them at home or locked in your car. The last place on earth to discuss whether you can bring something into the test site is at the door on test day. If you have questions, contact the test center in advance. Check out the GED Testing Service website to start the registration process and find a list of sites close to your home with their addresses and phone numbers. You can also call 877-EXAM-GED (877-392-6433) to have real people answer your questions.

Whatever you do, be sure not to bring the following with you to the GED testing center:

- ✔ Books
- ✔ Notes or scratch paper
- ✔ MP3 players or tablets
- ✔ Cellphone (leave it at home or in your car)
- ✔ Anything valuable, like a laptop computer, that you don't feel comfortable leaving outside the room while you take the test

Getting Comfortable Before the Test Begins

You usually take the GED Social Studies test in an examination room with at least one official (sometimes called a *proctor* or *examiner*) who's in charge of monitoring you while you take the test. (Some locations have smaller test centers that have space for no more than 15 test-takers at a time.) In either case, the test is the same.

As soon as you sit down to take the GED Social Studies test, spend a few moments before the test actually starts to relax and get comfortable. You're going to be in the chair for quite some time, so settle in. Keep these few tips in mind before you begin:

- ✔ **Make sure that the screen is at a comfortable height and adjust your chair to a height that suits you.** Unlike a pencil-and-paper test, you'll be working with a monitor and keyboard. Although you can shift the keyboard around and maybe adjust the angle of the monitor, generally you're stuck in that position for the duration of the test. If you need to make any adjustments, make them before you start. You want to feel as physically comfortable as possible.
- ✔ **Find out whether you can have something to drink at your computer station.** You may depend on that second cup of coffee to keep you upright and thinking. Even a bottle of water may make your life easier.
- ✔ **Go to the bathroom before you start.** This may sound like a silly suggestion, but it all contributes to being comfortable. You don't need distractions. Even if permitted during the test, bathroom breaks take time away from the test.

The proctor reads the test instructions to you and lets you log into the computer to start the test. Listen carefully to these instructions so you know how much time you have to take the test as well as any other important information.

Brushing Up on Test-Taking Strategies

You can increase your score by mastering a few smart test-taking strategies. To help you do so, we give you some tips in these sections on how to

- ✔ Plan your time.
- ✔ Determine the question type.

✔ Figure out how to answer the different types of questions.

✔ Guess intelligently.

✔ Review your work.

Watching the clock: Using your time wisely

When you start the computerized version of the GED Social Studies test, you may feel pressed for time and have the urge to rush through the questions. We strongly advise that you don't. You have sufficient time to do the test at a reasonable pace. You have only a certain amount of time for each section in the GED exam, so time management is an important part of succeeding on the test. You need to plan ahead and use your time wisely.

You don't get a break on the Social Studies GED test; you're required to complete it in a single sitting. Only the RLA (Reasoning Through Language Arts) test offers students a break.

During the test, the computer keeps you constantly aware of the time with a clock in the upper right-hand corner. Pay attention to the clock. When the test begins, check that time, and be sure to monitor how much time you have left as you work your way through the test. The GED Social Studies test is 90 minutes long. You have 65 minutes to answer a variety of question-and-answer items and then 25 minutes to write an Extended Response (essay) of 250 to 500 words.

As you start on the question-and-answer items, scroll through the test and find out how many questions you have to answer. (Not all GED Social Studies tests have the same number of questions.) Quickly divide the time by the number of questions. Doing so can give you a rough idea of how much time to spend on each question. For example, suppose that you see you have 50 questions to answer in 65 minutes. Divide the time by the number of questions to find out how much time you have for each item: 65/50 = 1.3, which is about 1 minute and 20 seconds per question. As you progress, repeat the calculation to see how you're doing. And remember that you can do questions in any order, except for the Extended Response item. Do the easiest questions first. If you get stuck on a question, leave it and come back to it later if you have time. Keeping to that schedule and answering as many questions as possible are essential.

If you don't monitor the time for each question, you won't have time to answer all the questions on the test. Keep in mind the following general time-management tips to help you complete each exam on time:

✔ **Tackle questions in groups.** For example, calculate how much time you have for each item on each test. Multiply the answer by 5 to give you a time slot for any five test items. Then try to answer each group of five items within the time you calculated. Doing so helps you complete all the questions and leaves you several minutes for review.

✔ **Keep calm and don't panic.** The time you spend panicking is better spent answering questions.

✔ **Practice using the diagnostic and practice tests in this book.** The more you practice timed sample test questions, the easier managing a timed test becomes. You can get used to doing something in a limited amount of time if you practice. Refer to the earlier section "Using the Diagnostic and Practice Tests to Your Advantage" for more information.

When time is up, immediately stop and breathe a sigh of relief. The examiner will give you a log-off procedure. Listen for instructions on what to do or where to go next.

Evaluating the different questions

Although you don't have to know much about how the test questions were developed to answer them correctly, you do need some understanding of how they're constructed. Knowing the types of items you're dealing with can make answering them easier — and you'll face fewer surprises.

To evaluate the types of questions that you have to answer, keep these tips in mind:

- ✔ **As soon as the computer signals that the test is running, start by skimming the questions.** Don't spend a lot of time doing so — just enough to spot the questions you absolutely know and the ones you think you'll need more time to answer.

- ✔ **Rely on the Previous and Next buttons on the bottom of the screen to scroll through the questions.** After you finish skimming, answer all the questions you know first; that way, you leave yourself much more time for the difficult questions. Check out the later section "Addressing and answering questions" for tips on how to answer questions.

- ✔ **Answer the easiest questions first.** You don't have to answer questions in order. Nobody except you will ever know, or care, in which order you answer the questions, so do the easiest questions first. You'll be able to answer them the most quickly, leaving more time for the other, harder questions.

- ✔ **Answer all questions.** No points are deducted for wrong answers. Look at the answer choices. You can discard some as obviously wrong. That may leave you to guess among a few choices rather than all four options. Guessing may mean getting the right answer; leaving the answer blank means a definite zero. And don't forget to go back to any questions you skipped.

Knowing the question type can shape the way you think about the answer. Some questions ask you to analyze a passage or extract from a document, which means the information you need is in the source text. Others ask you to infer from the passage, which means that not all of the information is in the passage. Although none of the tests are labeled with the following titles, the GED test questions assess your skills in these areas.

You use three basic skills on the Social Studies test: analysis, application of concepts, and interpretation. Some questions require you to break down information in source text materials and make inferences or draw conclusions. Analyzing information requires you to

- ✔ **Separate facts from opinions:** Unless the text you're reading gives evidence or "proof" to support statements, treat them as opinion. You also need to identify biases and propaganda and opinions shaped by particular times and events.

- ✔ **Extract data from reading passages, tables, and charts:** You need to be able to understand data presented in various ways.

- ✔ **Identify a cause-and-effect relationship:** Events in history, economics, and politics are often the results of a sequence of events. Understand how society got here from there.

- ✔ **Infer:** You may be asked to reach a conclusion based on evidence presented in the question. *Inferring* is a fancy way of saying that you'll draw a conclusion from the details presented.

- ✔ **Compare:** Consider the similarities and differences between ideas or issues from history, economics, geography, or politics, to evaluate and explain their significance or impact.

- ✔ **Contrast:** If you consider the differences between ideas or issues, you're *contrasting* them. You may contrast the events leading to strengthening the union movement under FDR to current antiunion movements and attitudes.

✔ **Understand:** When analyzing primary and secondary sources, you must show how history, politics, social issues, or the environment shape human actions.

✔ **Evaluate:** You need to weigh the materials presented for validity and evaluate the credibility of the author(s) of the sources.

Relating to other people in social situations exposes most people to these skills. For example, in most sports-related conversations between friends (or rivals), you quickly figure out how to separate fact from opinion and how to infer, compare, contrast, and identify cause-and-effect relationships. In other social situations, you come to realize when an assumption isn't stated. For example, you assume that your best friend going to join you for a late coffee the night before an important test, but, in reality, your friend may be planning to go to bed early. Unstated assumptions you make can get you into trouble, both in life and on the GED test.

Addressing and answering questions

When you start the test, you want to have a game plan in place for how to answer the questions. Keep the following pointers in mind to help you address each question:

✔ **Whenever you read a question, ask yourself, "What am I being asked?"** Doing so helps you stay focused on what you need to find out to answer the question. You may even want to decide quickly what skills are required to answer the question (see the preceding section for more on these skills). Then try to answer it.

✔ **Try to eliminate some answers.** Even if you don't really know the answer, guessing can help. When you're offered four answer choices, some will be obviously wrong. Eliminate those choices, and you've already improved your odds of guessing a correct answer.

✔ **Don't overthink.** Because all the questions are straightforward, don't look for hidden or sneaky questions. The questions ask for an answer based on the information given.

✔ **Find the answer choice you think is best and quickly verify that it answers the question.** If it does, click on that choice and move on. If it doesn't, leave it and come back to it if you have time after you answer all the other questions. *Remember:* You need to pick the *most* correct answer from the choices offered even if it's not the perfect answer.

Guess for success: Using intelligent guessing

The multiple-choice questions, regardless of the on-screen format, provide you with four possible answers. You get between one and three points for every correct answer. Nothing is subtracted for incorrect answers. That means you can guess on the items you don't know for sure without fear that you'll lose points if your guess is incorrect. Make educated guesses by eliminating as many obviously wrong choices as possible and choosing from the remaining choices.

When the question gives you four possible answers and you randomly choose one, you have a 25 percent chance of guessing the correct answer without even reading the question. Of course, we don't recommend using this method during the test.

If you know that one of the answers is definitely wrong, you now have just three answers to choose from and have a 33 percent chance (one in three) of choosing the correct answer. If you know that two of the answers are wrong, you leave yourself only two possible answers to choose from, giving you a 50 percent (one in two) chance of guessing right — much better than 25 percent! Removing one or two choices you know are wrong makes choosing the correct answer much easier.

If you don't know the answer to a particular question, try to spot the wrong choices by following these tips:

✔ **Make sure your answer really answers the question.** Wrong choices usually don't answer the question — that is, they may sound good, but they answer a different question than the one the test asks.

✔ **When two answers seem very close, consider both answers carefully because they both can't be right — but they both *can* be wrong.** Some answer choices may be very close, and all seem correct, but there's a fine line between completely correct and nearly correct. Be careful. These answer choices are sometimes given to see whether you really understand the material.

✔ **Look for opposite answers in the hopes that you can eliminate one.** If two answers contradict each other, both can't be right, but both can be wrong.

✔ **Trust your instincts.** Some wrong choices may just strike you as wrong when you first read them. If you spend time preparing for these exams, you probably know more than you think.

Leaving time for review

Having a few minutes at the end of a test to check your work is a great way to set your mind at ease. These few minutes give you a chance to look at any questions that may be troubling. If you've chosen an answer for every question, enjoy the last few minutes before time is called — without any panic. Keep the following tips in mind as you review your answers:

✔ **After you know how much time you have per item, try to answer each item in a little less than that time.** The extra seconds you don't use the first time through the test add up to time at the end of the test for review. Some questions require more thought and decision making than others. Use your extra seconds to answer those questions.

✔ **Don't try to change a lot of answers at the last minute.** Second-guessing yourself can lead to trouble. Often, second-guessing leads you to changing correct answers to incorrect ones. If you've prepared well and worked numerous sample questions, then you're likely to get the correct answers the first time. Ignoring all your preparation and knowledge to play a hunch isn't a good idea, either at the race track or on a test.

✔ **If you have time left after writing your Extended Response essay, use any extra time to reread and review the essay.** You may have written a good essay, but you always need to check for typos and grammar mistakes. The essay is evaluated for style, content, and proper English. That includes spelling and grammar.

Sharpening Your Mental Focus

To succeed in taking the GED Social Studies test, you need to be prepared. In addition to studying the content and honing the skills required, you also want to be mentally prepared. Although you may be nervous, you can't let your nerves get the best of you. Stay calm and take a deep breath. Here are a few pointers to help you stay focused on the task at hand:

✔ **Take time to rest and relax.** Rest and relaxation are restorative, revitalizing your body and providing your brain with the downtime it needs to digest all the information you've been feeding it.

✔ **Make sure you know the rules of the room before you begin.** If you have questions about using the bathroom during the test or what to do if you finish early, ask the proctor before you begin. If you don't want to ask these questions in public, call the GED office in your area before test day and ask your questions over the telephone. For general GED questions, call 877-392-6433 or check out www.gedtestingservice.com. This site has many pages, but the FAQ page is always a good place to start.

✔ **Keep your eyes on your computer screen.** Everybody knows not to look at other people's work during the test, but to be on the safe side, don't stretch, roll your eyes, or do anything else that may be mistaken for looking at another test. Most of the tests will be different on the various computers, so looking around is futile, but doing so can get you into a lot of trouble.

✔ **Stay calm.** Your nerves can use up a lot of energy needed for the test. Concentrate on the job at hand. You can always be nervous or panicky some other time.

Because taking standardized tests probably isn't a usual situation for you, you may feel nervous. This feeling is perfectly normal. Just try to focus on answering one question at a time and push any other thoughts to the back of your mind. Sometimes taking a few deep breaths can clear your mind, but don't spend a lot of time focusing on your breath. After all, your main job is to pass this test.

Part II
Enhancing Your Social Studies Skills

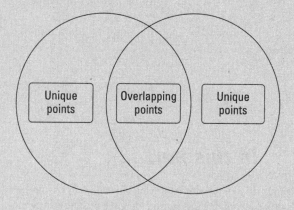

In this part . . .

✔ Discover techniques for improving your reading comprehension, including identifying the central idea in a passage, drawing conclusions from details, analyzing claims and supporting evidence, and comparing and contrasting two passages.

✔ Hone your social studies analysis skills by finding out how to make evidence-based inferences, analyze interactions among various factors, trace a sequence of events, examine causes and their effects, and evaluate arguments.

✔ Develop crucial skills for answering social studies questions, including the ability to extract information from graphs and tables, interpret maps and other images, formulate predictions based on data, and recognize the difference between independent and dependent variables.

Chapter 5

Reading and Understanding Social Studies Passages

In This Chapter

▶ Catching the central idea and the author's point of view

▶ Drawing conclusions from details

▶ Analyzing claims and supporting evidence

▶ Noting similarities and differences in two passages

▶ Construing a word's meaning based on how it's used

The GED Social Studies test doesn't require a great deal of specific knowledge about social studies topics. You don't have to name the U.S. presidents or the capitals of each state, identify the steps required to pass a bill, or recite the preamble to the U.S Constitution. In fact, nearly all the information you need to answer the questions is provided on the test itself. The key to answering the question correctly is an ability to read and understand the information provided and then apply your powers of reason.

Many questions involve short reading passages. Others present data graphically in charts, tables, photos, or illustrations. Some questions provide a combination of the two. In this chapter and Chapters 6 and 7, you find out how to extract and use the information presented in questions and your reasoning abilities to choose or enter the correct answers. This chapter focuses on reading and understanding the reading passages.

Recognizing the Central Idea and Thesis

Every passage has a *central idea* — what the passage is about. Some passages also contain a *thesis* — a claim, the point the author is trying to establish. Identifying the central idea and, in some passages, the thesis is important because it helps you understand the passage and provides a context for understanding the rest of the details or evidence provided in the passage. Unfortunately some of the passages on the Social Studies test are densely packed, making it quite a challenge to identify the central idea and thesis.

Fortunately, passages contain clues to help you isolate both. The author wants you to "get it," so the central idea and thesis typically appear early in the passage, often in the first sentence or second sentence. If the passage consists of several paragraphs, the very first paragraph is key because it spells out the central idea of the remaining text and contains the thesis if necessary. It also outlines the basic evidence to support that thesis. The other sentences in the first paragraph usually show some of the evidence that the writer intends to use to support the thesis. The first sentences of subsequent paragraphs also link back to the thesis statement in the first paragraph.

Single paragraph passages follow a similar pattern. The first sentence states the thesis or central idea, and subsequent sentences expand on that by presenting supporting details. Shorter passages are commonly used with short answer questions, such as multiple-choice items.

Some writers use what is called the *inverted pyramid* model. In that case, they present the supporting details first and end the paragraph with a thesis statement or a sentence that summarizes or encapsulates the details. In either case, one or two sentences spell out the intent of the passage.

Here's an example of a relatively long passage like those you may encounter on the Social Studies test.

Statement by the President on Armenian Remembrance Day

```
www.whitehouse.gov/the-press-office/2015/04/23/statement-president-
armenian-remembrance-day
```

This year we mark the centennial of the Meds Yeghern, the first mass atrocity of the 20th century. Beginning in 1915, the Armenian people of the Ottoman Empire were deported, massacred, and marched to their deaths. Their culture and heritage in their ancient homeland were erased. Amid horrific violence that saw suffering on all sides, one and a half million Armenians perished.

As the horrors of 1915 unfolded, U.S. Ambassador Henry Morgenthau, Sr. sounded the alarm inside the U.S. government and confronted Ottoman leaders. Because of efforts like his, the truth of the Meds Yeghern emerged and came to influence the later work of human rights champions like Raphael Lemkin, who helped bring about the first United Nations human rights treaty.

Against this backdrop of terrible carnage, the American and Armenian peoples came together in a bond of common humanity. Ordinary American citizens raised millions of dollars to support suffering Armenian children, and the U.S. Congress chartered the Near East Relief organization, a pioneer in the field of international humanitarian relief. Thousands of Armenian refugees began new lives in the United States, where they formed a strong and vibrant community and became pillars of American society. Rising to great distinction as businesspeople, doctors, scholars, artists, and athletes, they made immeasurable contributions to their new home.

This centennial is a solemn moment. It calls on us to reflect on the importance of historical remembrance, and the difficult but necessary work of reckoning with the past. I have consistently stated my own view of what occurred in 1915, and my view has not changed. A full, frank, and just acknowledgement of the facts is in all our interests. Peoples and nations grow stronger, and build a foundation for a more just and tolerant future, by acknowledging and reckoning with painful elements of the past. We welcome the expression of views by Pope Francis, Turkish and Armenian historians, and the many others who have sought to shed light on this dark chapter of history.

On this solemn centennial, we stand with the Armenian people in remembering that which was lost. We pledge that those who suffered will not be forgotten. And we commit ourselves to learn from this painful legacy, so that future generations may not repeat it.

This statement is a typical example of a well-structured essay. The first paragraph contains the central idea of the passage, and the first sentence specifies that key idea: The murder of Armenians in 1915 is the first mass atrocity of the 20th century. The next two paragraphs reinforce the key idea with the phrases "backdrop of terrible carnage" and "solemn moment." The summary in the last paragraph also refers to the key idea, although in indirect language, especially the phrase "painful legacy."

Passages consisting of a single paragraph have a similar structure. The first sentence and the last sentence contain the central idea of the paragraph, while the details in the middle explain or support it. The second to last paragraph is a good example. The paragraph is framed by these sentences: "This centennial is a solemn moment. . . . We welcome the expression of views by Pope Francis, Turkish and Armenian historians, and the many others who have sought to shed light on this dark chapter of history." They focus on the central idea — the need to reflect on the importance of remembering history. The middle of the paragraph explains why people need to remember.

As you read a *source,* a passage on which questions are based, do a quick analysis similar to the one in the preceding paragraph. Analyzing the passage clarifies its meaning and enables you to use the information in the passage more effectively to answer questions.

Extracting Details to Make Inferences and Claims

Well-written passages contain details or evidence, information that fleshes out the central idea or supports the thesis. In long passages, the central idea or thesis is broken down into smaller components. For example, if the author is presenting and supporting a specific point of view, she may state her thesis and then present one or more premises (claims) on which that thesis is based, supporting each with evidence. Likewise, a central idea may be broken down into subtopics, each of which is developed with additional details.

In some cases, however, authors don't come right out and say what they're getting at. They may simply present the details and rely on the reader to draw his own conclusions. More importantly, in terms of the test, you may be presented with a passage and asked to make inferences (draw conclusions) or identify claims (a thesis or premise) that can be drawn from the details provided in a passage. To answer such questions, take the following approach:

1. **Read the passage.**

2. **Test each answer choice by comparing it to the evidence in the passage.**

3. **Eliminate answer choices that are obviously not supported by the evidence in the passage.**

4. **Choose the answer that has the most supporting evidence.**

Here's a sample question based on the passage on Armenian Remembrance Day in the preceding section:

Which of the following conclusions can be drawn from the evidence presented in this passage?

(A) In Meds Yeghern, over 1 million Armenians perished.

(B) We must forget the past and look to the future.

(C) Those who committed this atrocity must be punished.

(D) A free society benefits from diversity.

To choose the correct answer, test each answer choice against the evidence provided in the passage. Choice (A) is true, but it's stated in the passage, so it's not a conclusion that can be drawn from the evidence; it is the evidence. The passage contradicts Choice (B) because the thesis of the passage is that people must remember history in order to learn from it and not repeat past mistakes. Nothing in the passage supports Choice (C). That leaves Choice (D) as the only option, and it is, in fact, supported in the passage:

> Thousands of Armenian refugees began new lives in the United States, where they formed a strong and vibrant community and became pillars of American society. Rising to great distinction as businesspeople, doctors, scholars, artists, and athletes, they made immeasurable contributions to their new home.

Here's another question, based on the same passage, that requires you to draw conclusions from on the evidence presented:

Which of the following conclusions can be drawn from the evidence presented in this passage?

(A) No good can come from such atrocities.

(B) People can transcend evil with good.

(C) Atrocities such as Meds Yeghern are unavoidable.

(D) Human beings are condemned to repeat history.

Again, test each answer choice against the details presented in the passage. Some good has come as a result of the Meds Yeghern genocide, as detailed in the first and second paragraphs of the passage, so you can eliminate Choice (A). Choice (B) is correct for the same reasons you eliminated Choice (A). The passage explains that people can learn from history to prevent repeating mistakes, so you can eliminate Choices (C) and (D). Choice (B) is the only correct answer.

Identifying the Author's Point of View in Historical Documents

The author's *point of view* is the position or attitude toward the issue or information he's presenting. Knowing the author's point of view is important in determining the point he's trying to convey. Authors bring with them their own priorities, beliefs, and values, and that can influence how they select and present the information.

Start by identifying the intended audience and purpose of the passage:

- ✔ **Audience:** The *audience* is comprised of the people the author is addressing. Do you think the author is addressing the general public, his peers, people who oppose his views, those who support his views, or some other group?

- ✔ **Purpose:** The *purpose* is the reason the author wrote the passage. Is the passage intended to inform, tell a story, describe a situation, or persuade the audience to believe or do something?

After sizing up the audience and purpose, you should have a fairly clear idea of the author's point of view. If the author is trying to convince the audience to believe or do something, for example, he probably believes in it himself.

You can also pick up clues about the author's point of view from the evidence presented in the passage and the author's word choice:

✔ List the information and supporting evidence presented. Has the author omitted facts? What authorities does the author use to back up the argument or evidence? Are these authorities themselves reliable and unbiased? If an author omits certain facts or draws evidence from biased sources, it clues you in that the author's point of view is firmly on one side of an issue.

If an author uses quotations or refers to other sources, ask yourself whether these sources are accepted and knowledgeable ones. A pattern in the selective use of supporting evidence or authorities may indicate that the author is going to present information with a particular, possibly biased, point of view.

✔ Look at the vocabulary used. Use of "loaded" words or inflammatory terms is a strong signal that the author is biased. For example, if a passage refers to opponents as fascists or bureaucrats, the author is using emotionally charged language to cast his opponents in the worst possible light.

This extract from the Declaration of Independence is a good example of a passage that expresses a strong author point of view with plenty of loaded words:

Extract from the Declaration of Independence

Prudence, indeed, will dictate that Governments long established should not be changed for light and transient causes; and accordingly all experience hath shewn, that mankind are more disposed to suffer, while evils are sufferable, than to right themselves by abolishing the forms to which they are accustomed. But when a long train of abuses and usurpations, pursuing invariably the same Object evinces a design to reduce them under absolute Despotism, it is their right, it is their duty, to throw off such Government, and to provide new Guards for their future security. Such has been the patient sufferance of these Colonies; and such is now the necessity which constrains them to alter their former Systems of Government. The history of the present King of Great Britain is a history of repeated injuries and usurpations, all having in direct object the establishment of an absolute Tyranny over these States.

Here's a sample question based on this passage that requires an ability to identify the author's point of view:

The author of this passage believes which of the following?

(A) Citizens should overthrow rulers they disagree with.

(B) Rulers are tyrants.

(C) Overthrowing an established government is likely to cause people to suffer.

(D) Absolute tyranny and despotism are characteristics of any governing body.

Although the passage presents a very strong emotional argument defending the right and obligation of the people to overthrow tyrannical rulers, the passage begins with a statement that "mankind are more disposed to suffer . . . by abolishing the forms to which they are accustomed," as stated in Choice (C), which is the correct answer. Choice (A) is wrong because the passage states that the people should rise up only when the rulers are guilty of long-term tyranny and despotism that "reduces" the people. Although the passage acknowledges that rulers can be tyrants and points to the example of the current king, Choice (B) is an overgeneralization not made in the passage. Likewise, Choice (D) is much broader than what the passage suggests.

The authors' intent is to convince the reader that secession and creation of an independent United States is a justified action. The audience is both American and British people, both contemporary and future generations. First the document raises the obvious objection to overthrowing existing rule: "it should not be done," but then modifies it by stating "lightly." That implies that this decision was carefully considered. The rest of the passage is a justification for revolution. The words chosen reinforce the perception of injustices suffered by the people. In addition to their dictionary meaning, the words *despotism, usurpations,* and *tyranny* have strong emotional overtones. By the end of the passage, you have no doubt that the authors believe revolution is not only justified but obligatory.

Distinguishing Fact from Opinion

Certain questions on the GED Social Studies test challenge your ability to distinguish factual statements from opinions:

✔ **Fact:** A verifiable truth. You can look it up. Facts are incidents that occurred, statistics, test results, measurements, and anything else that can be verified or quantified in some way.

✔ **Opinion:** A view, judgment, or feeling that may or may not be based on facts. An opinion may be supported by facts, but it can't be proven by facts. Opinions often speculate on the future.

In the following sections, we offer guidance and practice in distinguishing fact from opinion in statements, short passages, and longer passages that you're likely to encounter in the Extended Response portion of the test.

Identifying fact and opinion in statements

To determine whether a statement is fact or opinion, ask whether whatever it's claiming can be verified by looking it up, examining past events, reviewing statistical data, or considering other hard evidence. If a claim can't be verified, it's a statement of opinion. Practice by identifying the following as statements of fact or opinion:

1. Unless the United States and the United Kingdom maintain their "special relationship," untold destruction will result.

   ❑ Fact

   ❑ Opinion

2. Illegal international fishing practices are decimating fisheries.

   ❑ Fact

   ❑ Opinion

3. More than a billion people eat fish for their primary source of protein.

   ❑ Fact

   ❑ Opinion

4. U.S. exports to Russia represent less than 1 percent of its global exports.

   ❑ Fact

   ❑ Opinion

5. U.S.–Russian bilateral trade isn't reaching anything close to its full potential today.

   ❑ Fact

   ❑ Opinion

Here are the correct answers.

1. **Opinion.** This statement is speculative. Nobody can tell the future, so there is no way to verify the claim as a statement of fact.

2. **Opinion.** Although this statement may be true, without evidence to back it up it's just an opinion. To prove it, you need to prove first that fisheries are decimated and second that the cause is illegal international fishing practices and not something else.

3. **Fact.** You could verify this statement through statistical evidence. It's quantifiable; that is, measurable.

4. **Fact.** You could verify this statement by looking at data regarding U.S. exports to Russia and other countries.

5. **Opinion.** This statement may be true, but you need evidence to determine what the current trade amounts look like and could look like in the future. You can only conjecture what "full potential" is.

Dealing with a mixture of fact and opinion

Here's a passage that contains a combination of fact and opinion, (from "Stopping the Flow of Corruption," a State Department press release by Tom Malinowski, Assistant Secretary, Bureau of Democracy, Human Rights, and Labor, December 26, 2014), followed by a question that requires you to distinguish between fact and opinion:

When Viktor Yanukovych fled Kiev in February, the Ukrainian leader left behind a spectacular Swiss chalet-style mansion, a golf course, dozens of antique cars and a private zoo boasting $10,000 nameplates for the animal pens. Even the Ukrainian public, painfully familiar with the corruption of its leaders, was shocked. Yanukovych had managed to keep the chalet hidden because it was owned not by him but by an anonymous shell company registered in Britain. Other corrupt leaders have used the same trick to hide billions of dollars offshore, including through companies registered in the United States. . . .

Fighting corruption by improving financial transparency may be one of the most effective ways of promoting liberty around the world. Members of Congress who believe in that cause and who want us to do better should embrace the president's proposal to strengthen those laws by closing the shell company loophole that enables dictators to conceal their criminality from their people and the world.

Which of the following phrases reflects the author's opinion?

(A) left behind a spectacular Swiss chalet-style mansion

(B) used the same trick to hide billions of dollars offshore

(C) most effective ways of promoting liberty

(D) Yanukovych had managed to keep the chalet hidden

To answer this question, ask yourself which answer choices can and can't be verified. The only statement that can't be verified is the statement in Choice (C), indicating that something is or may be one of the most effective ways to promote liberty. "Most effective" is a judgment call. Although the other answer choices all include loaded language, including the words *spectacular, trick,* and *managed to keep,* they're all verifiable by examining events from the past.

Evaluating claims in Extended Response passages

The Extended Response passages are also likely to contain both facts and opinions. Writers present information in order to convince readers of their particular point of view. Start by establishing the author's point of view and then review the facts in the passage. After identifying the central idea or thesis and the author's point of view, separate fact from opinion:

- ✔ **Look for claims (premises), which are often statements of opinion.** Authors commonly state an opinion and then provide supporting evidence (facts) to back up each claim. If the author backs up an opinion with more opinions rather than facts, you may have uncovered a weakness in the argument.

- ✔ **Look for loaded words or vocabulary that suggests bias.** Such words may be woven into factual statements, and although they're not reason enough to dismiss the facts, they indicate that the author isn't neutral and may be prone to presenting only one side of the issue.

- ✔ **Isolate points that have no supporting evidence.** Look for overgeneralizations that go beyond what the facts support or for claims made without supporting evidence.

- ✔ **Ask whether evidence presented as facts can be verified.** Evidence that can't be verified constitutes opinion. Facts can be verified by examining events, research data, statistics, and other forms of hard data.

Distinguishing between Hypotheses and Unsupported Claims

To perform well on the Social Studies test, you must be able to distinguish between hypotheses and unsupported claims. A *hypothesis* is an educated or informed guess or belief that's typically proposed and then supported with evidence. An *unsupported claim* is a statement of opinion, often presented as factual or generally accepted, without evidenced to support it. Here's an example of an argument backed by evidence from a NASA page (`climate.nasa.gov/evidence`) introducing climate change.

The current warming trend is of particular significance because most of it is very likely human-induced and proceeding at a rate that is unprecedented in the past 1,300 years.

Earth-orbiting satellites and other technological advances have enabled scientists to see the big picture, collecting many different types of information about our planet and its climate on a global scale. This body of data, collected over many years, reveals the signals of a changing climate.

The heat-trapping nature of carbon dioxide and other gases was demonstrated in the mid-19th century. Their ability to affect the transfer of infrared energy through the atmosphere is the scientific basis of many instruments flown by NASA. There is no question that increased levels of greenhouse gases must cause the Earth to warm in response.

Ice cores drawn from Greenland, Antarctica, and tropical mountain glaciers show that the Earth's climate responds to changes in greenhouse gas levels. They also show that in the past, large changes in climate have happened very quickly, geologically speaking: in tens of years, not in millions or even thousands.

Although this passage begins with a hypothesis — an assumption that global warming is occurring and the claim that human activities are the cause — the hypothesis is backed by a series of facts that link climate change to human activities. The increase in atmospheric carbon dioxide is an accepted fact, and the cause for that increase, industrialization, is also accepted. The other evidence, from ice cores and the rate of climate change, is a secondary level of evidence that further supports the role of human activity in climate change. Thus all the other materials presented form a cogent, supported, picture. Even if the source were not given, the manner of presentation lends a degree of credibility to the material. Knowing the source adds to the validity of the information because NASA is considered an authority. Finally, the material is presented in a straightforward manner without emotional or manipulative language, which also enhances the credibility.

In contrast, here's a passage that presents an argument against human-induced climate change that's not supported by verifiable evidence:

The concern over climate change and the belief that it is caused by humans are speculative. The fact that we have just had the coldest winter on record should be enough to make scientists question whether global warming is actually occurring. Moreover, the climate has changed several times throughout Earth's existence, long before human beings began burning fossil fuels. Blaming global warming entirely on human activities is ridiculous.

This passage provides very little evidence to attack the opposing view about climate change. It presents one example of a very cold winter on one part of the planet to question whether the planet is really warming, and although there is evidence that climate change has occurred in the past before humans existed, that doesn't mean that the current warming trend isn't linked to human activities.

Which of the following is the best evidence that the current warming trend is most likely human induced?

(A) Ice cores show that the Earth's climate responds to changes in greenhouse gas levels.

(B) Earth-orbiting satellites have enabled scientists to see the big picture.

(C) Ice cores show that large changes in climate have happened very quickly.

(D) The current warming trend is unprecedented in the past 1,300 years.

Each of these statements is a fact, but only one provides the best evidence linking global warming to human activities. Choice (A) merely shows that increases in greenhouse gas levels, not necessarily related to human activities, have been linked to global warming. Choice (B) suggests that satellites have enabled scientists to confirm that global warming is occurring but not that it's related to human activities. Choice (C) indicates the ice cores show that global warming can occur rapidly, a statement that can be used to support or refute a connection to human activities. Choice (D) is best because it suggests a link to industrialization, a distinctly human activity, and global warming.

When a hypothesis has plenty of verifiable evidence to back it up, often the best way to disprove the hypothesis is to call the evidence into question by providing conflicting evidence or questioning the methods used to obtain the evidence. Questions on the Social Studies test may challenge your ability to evaluate evidence, as in the following sample question.

Which of the following statements, if true, would most effectively challenge the hypothesis that human activities are responsible for global warming?

(A) Earth's average temperature did not change from 1940 to 1970.

(B) Five million years ago, the Canadian Arctic islands were completely forested.

(C) A warmer planet would be far better for humans than a colder one.

(D) Oceans absorb much of the heat, limiting global warming's effect on surface temperatures.

If Choice (A) were true, it would indicate a lull in global warming, which would be difficult to explain without a corresponding cessation of the human activities that would contribute to global warming. The other choices are interesting but don't suggest a connection between human activities and global warming.

Comparing Two Sources and Identifying Their Differences

In both the questions on the test and in the Extended Response, you may be asked to compare two sources on the same topic and identify or explain how they differ. Start assessing the passages by sorting the materials into primary and secondary sources:

- ✔ **Primary sources** are the original materials, written at the time in question or by the individuals involved. Government statistics on unemployment in 1930 would be an excellent primary source on the Great Depression. The Declaration of Independence is a great example of a historical document and primary source, written at a specific moment in history, by the individuals involved in the independence movement.

- ✔ **Secondary sources** are those that are written about, reference, or are based on one or more primary sources. Examples of secondary sources are papers written about the Declaration of Independence or unemployment in the Great Depression.

After noting whether a passage is a primary or secondary source, identify the central idea or thesis in each passage, all the claims presented, and all of the evidence or details used to support each claim. You can then use a Venn diagram, shown in Figure 5-1, to determine the similarities and differences between the two passages.

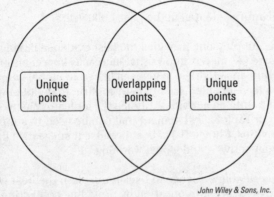

Figure 5-1:
Use a Venn diagram to identify similarities and differences in sources.

Unique points | Overlapping points | Unique points

John Wiley & Sons, Inc.

Following are two passages from a Webster-Hayne debate over the government policy on public lands followed by a question that challenges you to identify the difference between the two.

Excerpt from speech of Senator Robert Y. Hayne of South Carolina, January 19, 1830

I am opposed, therefore, in any shape, to all unnecessary extension of the powers, or the influence of the Legislature or Executive of the Union over the States, or the people of the States; and, most of all, I am opposed to those partial distributions of favors, whether by legislation or appropriation, which has a direct and powerful tendency to spread corruption through the land; to create an abject spirit of dependence; to sow the seeds of dissolution;

to produce jealousy among the different portions of the Union, and finally to sap the very foundations of the Government itself.

Excerpt from speech of Senator Daniel Webster of Massachusetts, January 20, 1830

I deem far otherwise of the Union of the States; and so did the framers of the constitution themselves. What they said I believe; fully and sincerely believe, that the Union of the States is essential to the prosperity and safety of the States. I am a Unionist, and in this sense a National Republican. I would strengthen the ties that hold us together.

Which of the following statements best summarizes the differences between the views expressed in these two passages?

(A) The first passage favors a strong federation, whereas the second favors states' rights.

(B) The first passage promotes states' rights, whereas the second promotes a strong federation.

(C) The first opposes the partial distribution of favors, whereas the second supports the partial distribution of favors.

(D) The second favors a strong union, whereas the first favors an extension of powers or influence of the union over the states.

In this example, the correct answer choice must highlight a difference between the two passages, and both the first and second part of the statement must accurately describe what's being stated in each passage. You can rule out Choices (A) and (D) because the first passage does not support a strong federation or union as these statements claim. You can also rule out Choice (C) because although the first passage opposes the partial distribution of favors, nothing in the second passage suggests support for such a thing. Choice (B) is correct because the first passage opposes any extension of union powers over the states, and the second supports a stronger union.

Knowing a Word's Meaning from Its Context

When reading passages on the Social Studies test, you're likely to encounter unfamiliar terms and phrases. You don't necessarily need to know the exact definition of a term or phrase to understand the passage. You can often determine a word's meaning from how it's used in a sentence. Here are some suggestions for determining the meaning of a word in context:

✔ **Look for a definition immediately following the term.** Sometimes, an unfamiliar word is followed by a phrase that explains its meaning, as in this example: "He was a connoisseur, a real expert and lover, of fine wines and cigars." From the sentence, you know that *connoisseur* means someone who is knowledgeable and appreciative of fine things — in this case, wine and cigars.

✔ **Break the word down.** Many words are made up of several parts. Breaking the word down into its component parts may reveal its meaning. For example, if you know that *contra* means "against," you know that *contravene* means "against [something]." So if a judge contravenes the system's due process, you know that the judge did something against the system's due process even if you don't know what *contravene* means. (Actually, *vene* is from the Latin verb *venire,* which means "to go," so *contravene* means "to go against.")

Brush up on the meanings of prefixes and suffixes added to the beginning and ending of root words to change their meanings, such as *con-* (with), *anti-* (against), *inter-* (between), *pre-* (before), *-ible* and *-able* (can), *-less* (without), *-ion* and *-tion* (act or process), and *-y* and *-ly* (state of). Knowing some Latin roots is also very useful.

> ✔ **Consider the context in which a word is used.** In the Declaration of Independence, for example, one of the charges against King George was the forced *quartering* of troops in private homes. You know that this quartering has nothing to do with fractions or cutting troops into pieces. You may also remember that military people refer to their residences as quarters. Combining that information, you can make a pretty accurate guess that *quartering* is a verb version of the word and means "housing" or "providing shelter."

Here are a few questions to help you practice determining the meanings of words in context. Choose the best definition for the underlined word.

1. Christopher Hitchens was well known for his <u>acerbic</u> wit, which was just as apt to entertain as to offend.

   (A) sharp, biting

   (B) assertive

   (C) benign

   (D) breezy

2. The <u>appellate</u> court granted the defense a retrial.

   (A) attractive

   (B) having the power to appeal

   (C) having the authority to permit requests

   (D) criminal in nature

3. The <u>suffrage</u> movement did have some early successes. New Zealand is recognized as the first country in the world to grant women the right to vote.

   (A) the right to suffer

   (B) the right not to suffer

   (C) the right to pray

   (D) the right to vote

4. As more businesses hire part-time employees, workers are increasingly reliant on <u>ancillary</u> income from side jobs to pay their living expenses.

   (A) principal

   (B) undependable

   (C) supplemental

   (D) unpredictable

5. To counteract efforts to <u>disenfranchise</u> voters, some politicians promote a system for automatically registering voters on their 18th birthdays.

   (A) incarcerate

   (B) liberate

   (C) emancipate

   (D) deprive

Now check your answers.

1. You probably know what *acid* means, and the sentence ends by implying that Christopher Hitchens's wit could be offensive, so you should be able to select the correct answer as Choice (A), sharp, biting.

2. From context you can work out that *appellate* must have something to do with *appeal*. You can be certain from the context that it does not mean "attraction," so it must refer to appealing in a legal sense. That lets you conclude that *appellate* court must refer to a court where individuals can appeal a court decision, so Choice (B) is the correct answer.

3. From the second sentence, you can surmise that the suffrage movement was one whose goal was to achieve voting rights for women and that *suffrage* means "the right to vote," making Choice (D) the correct answer.

4. *Ancillary* means "subsidiary" or "supplemental," Choice (C). Principal income would come from workers' main jobs, ruling out Choice (A). Although ancillary income may be undependable (Choice (B)) and unpredictable (Choice (C)), the phrase "from side jobs" clues you into the fact that the income is supplemental and not from the person's main job.

5. If politicians are promoting a system that enables more people to vote and it counter-acts (acts against) something, that something must be disabling people from voting. Choice (D) is the only correct answer.

Chapter 6

Understanding and Applying Key Social Studies Concepts

In This Chapter

▶ Making inferences based on evidence presented in a reading passage

▶ Studying relationships and interactions among different factors

▶ Tracing a sequence of events

▶ Examining causes and their effects

▶ Inspecting arguments by comparing the ideas expressed in each

Many of the questions on the GED Social Studies test are based on short reading passages. To do well on the test, you need to grasp some basic social studies concepts, including inferences, relationships, interactions, sequence of events, cause-and-effect, and argumentation. Don't be concerned if you don't recognize these concepts. By the end of this chapter, you will.

A *social studies concept* is an abstract idea or general notion used to explain or understand ideas or events in the context of social studies. In practical terms, people who write the passages on the test apply these concepts when determining how to present information in written passages. You apply the concepts to more fully extract meaning and understanding from the passages — that is, to "decode" the passages so you can answer questions on the test.

In this chapter, we present the various social studies concepts and provide practice so you get hands-on experience applying these concepts to reading passages like those you'll encounter on the test.

Extracting Evidence to Support Inferences and Analyses

The question-and-answer items on the GED Social Studies test require extracting evidence from passages to support inferences and analyses. All passages contain details or evidence that present supporting information. The trick is finding it.

The questions themselves typically tell you what you need to find in the passage. The question may ask you to choose which option from a list of inferences and conclusions most accurately reflects the details presented in the passage. Or it may present you with an inference or claim made in the passage and ask you to identify which piece of evidence from the passage supports it.

To answer questions such as these, take the following steps:

1. **Start reading the passage to identify the main idea or thesis.**

   The main idea or thesis typically is stated in the first paragraph, often in the first sentence.

   If the passage has a title, take note of it. A title tells you what the passage is about.

2. **Continue reading the passage to identify any sub-claims that support the main idea and evidence that supports the sub-claims or main idea.**

   You're scoping out the passage at this point to find out where claims and supporting evidence are located so you can quickly dip back into the passage to find information to answer specific questions.

3. **Read the question and any and all answer choices.**

   The question tells you which information you need from the passage to answer it. If the question contains answer choices (most do), you have the answer right in front of you.

4. **Determine whether you know the answer.**

   If you do, identify the correct answer. If you have multiple choices, return to the passage and find the piece of evidence that answers the question *and* matches one of the answer choices.

5. **Select or enter the correct answer.**

Here's a sample passage from *Economics For Dummies* by Sean Flynn (Wiley).

Market economies are simply collections of billions of small, face-to-face transactions between buyers and sellers. Economists use the term *market production* to capture what happens when one individual offers to make or sell something to another individual at a price agreeable to both.

In markets, the allocation of resources is facilitated by the fact that each resource has a price, and whoever is willing to pay the price gets the resource. In fact, market economies are often called *price systems* because prices serve as the signals that direct resources. Holding supply constant, products in high demand have high prices, and products in low demand have low prices. Because businesses like to make money, they follow the price signals and produce more of what has a high price and less of what has a low price. In this way, markets tend to take limited resources and use them to produce what people most want — or at least, what people are most willing to pay for.

For instance, the guy who sells you a TV at the local store has no idea about the total demand for TVs in the world, how many tons of steel or plastic are needed to produce them, or how many other things weren't produced because the steel and plastic needed to make the TVs was used for TVs rather than other things. All he knows is that you're willing to pay him for a TV. And if he's making a profit selling TVs, he orders more TVs from the factory. The factory, in turn, increases production, taking resources away from the production of other things.

The first step is to identify the main idea or thesis statement. The first sentence of the first paragraph is the thesis statement: "Market economies are simply collections of billions of small, face-to-face transactions between buyers and sellers."

The next step is to analyze the passage for supporting evidence — evidence that fleshes out the main idea or supports the thesis statement. The second sentence in the passage defines the term *market production,* and the rest of the passage explains the concept. You can summarize the supporting evidence by outlining it:

✔ Every resource has a price.

✔ She who pays the price gets the resource.

✔ Prices are established by supply and demand.

- Constant supply causes prices of better selling goods (higher demand) to rise.

- Constant supply causes prices of slower selling goods (low demand) to drop.

✔ Business responds to price signals.

- Produce more of high-priced products.

- Produce less of low-priced products.

✔ Resources are allocated to produce high-demand products.

✔ Extended example, indicated by "for instance."

By summarizing the supporting details in the passage, you're essentially extracting evidence from the passage that supports claims made in the passage or inferences that can be drawn from the supporting evidence.

Here are a few questions based on the passage in this section that test your ability to identify the main idea or thesis and extract evidence from the passage to answer questions about claims made in the passage or inferences that can be drawn from the supporting evidence.

1. What point does the author make in this passage?

(A) The economy is a price system.

(B) The market economy is the sum of all transactions, large and small.

(C) Factories set production levels based on sales volume.

(D) Sales volumes determine prices of goods.

2. What determines the price of goods?

(A) a constant volume of goods

(B) high demand

(C) low demand

(D) sales volume

3. What will make prices for televisions drop?

(A) increase in sales

(B) decrease in sales

(C) stable sales volume

(D) fewer sellers

Now check your answers.

1. All the choices are at least partially true. Choice (A) is implied in the opening paragraph, Choice (C) is implied in the last sentence, and Choice (D) is the argument in the middle paragraph. However, only one of the answer choices encompasses the entire point in one statement: Choice (B), which is stated explicitly in the first sentence.

2. The choices offered here are all true; you need to determine which is the most complete answer. Test the choices against the passage. Choice (A) has an effect on prices, but only as a starting point in deciding how prices will develop. Choices (B) and (C) are true, but only in specific cases: Prices drop if demand is low; prices rise if demand is high. The only complete answer is Choice (D), sales volume. That choice encompasses all other choices and is the best, most complete, answer.

3. Answering this question requires you to make a deduction based on the information presented. The answer isn't directly stated in the passage. The passage notes that increasing demand, reflected by increasing sales, will cause prices to rise, so Choices (A) and (C) are wrong. You can guess accurately that having fewer outlets (Choice (D)) will allow the remaining outlets to raise prices to meet the same demand. The only mechanism that causes a price drop according to the passage is a drop in demand. That means Choice (B) is the best answer.

Describing Relationships among People, Places, Environments, and Development

Passages on the Social Studies test may focus on how people, places, environments, and development correlate and interact. In a social studies context, these passages and the questions related to them look at how personal identities, beliefs, and behaviors are influenced by where a person lives, the institutions and belief systems predominant in those locations, the environment (for example, jungle or desert, city, or country), how people support their existence (for instance, hunting and gathering, agriculture, manufacturing, or technology), shared life experiences, and so on.

Here's a sample passage followed by several questions to give you a preview of what you're likely to encounter on the test.

People live where they can access the necessities of life. For the most basic cultures, that means food, water, and shelter. Depending on a society's level of development, such a setup may have been as simple as campsites near water surrounded by hospitable land (areas where people could hunt, fish, or gather food and have access to drinking water and materials to build shelter and cook their food). If the resources in an area were sufficient, individuals prospered and tribes expanded. When local resources ran out or growth outpaced resources, they moved on, spread out to include new areas, or gradually faded away.

The development of agriculture changed how cultures and society developed. The earliest form of agriculture was nomadic herding, which developed more than 12,000 years ago. Sedentary farming, growing crops in one location rather than migrating with herds of food animals, first developed about 8,000 to 10,000 years ago. Growing crops developed independently in several parts of the world. The oldest sites are in the Yangtze Basin and along the Yellow River in China and in the Fertile Crescent in the Middle East. Somewhat later, crop farming developed in sub-Saharan Africa, in Mexico, and in northern South America.

All these areas had commonalities: fertile soils, access to fresh water, and reasonable but varied precipitation. In each case, the domestication of crops varied with available native species, the soils, and the climate. Most farming developed along rivers on flood plains where soils were fertile and annual flooding replenished soil nutrients. The Mediterranean climate of the Middle East has long dry seasons and only moderate precipitation. Cereal crops such as wheat and barley grow better in that climate. In areas with heavier precipitation, crops such as rice were domesticated. In dryer areas of Mexico and southwestern United States, farmers concentrated on corn, beans, and squash, while farmers in South America had domesticated potatoes.

The development of sedentary civilization had consequences. Among nomad herders, the size of the herd indicated the wealth of the individual. However, there were limits on surpluses because herds supplied the raw materials on which the herders survived. That included hides for clothing and tents, bones for tools, and of course meat and milk for food. Though one group of herders may have had a bigger herd than another, and some therefore were wealthier than others, the degree of difference in wealth was limited. The grazing land available, the need to move as the pastures ran out, and the need for the raw materials that the herd provided all set practical limits on the size of any herd.

Farmers, on the other hand, learned how to produce more food than they needed and were able to trade that surplus for other goods. They also learned how to store surplus food, which became a source of wealth. Societies changed as the concept of private ownership replaced communal property. That allowed some to become significantly richer than others. The concentration of people also required people to cooperate with one another. Towns and cities developed, necessitating some form of government, more than just tribal leadership. Surplus wealth also led to both trade and specialization of skills. No longer were most people able to perform most jobs the tribe required. Now some could concentrate on specialized jobs, from weaving to pottery, metal working to building. The old tribal leadership structure was gradually replaced by monarchs and by military and religious leaders.

1. Which of the following enabled humans to adopt a more sedentary lifestyle?

   (A) herding

   (B) fishing

   (C) hunting and gathering

   (D) farming

2. Why did farming and sedentary living lead to government?

   (A) Life became more complicated.

   (B) People were tired of arbitrary chiefs.

   (C) There was a demand for democracy.

   (D) Competition between nomads and farmers had killed off tribal leaders.

3. The earliest societies could be classified as

   (A) hunting and gathering

   (B) nomadic herders

   (C) sedentary crop farmers

   (D) fishers and seafarers

Now check out the correct answers.

1. Farming, Choice (D), enabled people to stay in one place longer because it was a way for them to gain more control over food production, which is mentioned in the second paragraph.

2. The last paragraph explains that sedentary living allowed specialization and the accumulation of wealth (at least by some), Choice (A). The growing settlements also required more governance than tribal systems were able to offer. Choices (B), (C), and (D) are never mentioned in the passage and are thus wrong.

3. The passage begins with the comment that the most basic cultures hunted and gathered food, and Choice (A) is correct. It mentions Choices (B) and (C), but as later manifestations; although it brings up fishing, the passage never refers to seafaring, so Choice (D) is wrong as well.

Grasping the Sequence of Events and of Steps in Social Studies Processes

History is a chronology. It consists of events that happened in *chronological* (time-based) order and the people who make these events happen. To understand history, you need to understand who did what to whom, as well as when and why. In geography, a sequence of events, such as the discovery of gold, often leads to the movement of people to exploit the resource, which in turn may lead to settlement and a developing economy. One event triggers a sequence of others. Situations have an impact on later decisions and events. Without some earlier events, later events may never have happened or may have occurred differently. Some events form a pattern. Understanding that pattern helps clarify events. Knowing the sequence of the who, what, when, where, and why — the 5 *W*s — is often key to understanding.

In the following sections, we look at questions like those you may encounter on the test that involve a sequence of historical events or the steps in a social studies process that are often repeated — for example, the stages a civilization undergoes through its rise and fall.

Gaining insight through a chronology of events

Historians record many events chronologically. They list events by date, forming a sequence of events. Such a chronology of events often sheds light on history to show, for example, how modern societies transitioned from being hunter-gatherers to manufacturing, how conflict escalated to all-out war, and how developments in technology influenced the course of history.

Table 6-1 presents a chronology of events that led up to the point in time when the United States entered into World War II. This chronology helps explain the conditions, events, and decisions that convinced U.S. leaders that, after two years of remaining relatively neutral, the country needed to become an active participant in the war efforts.

Here are a few questions about the chronology of events presented in Table 6-1 that are similar to questions you're likely to encounter on the test.

Table 6-1	U.S. Chronology of Events Leading Up to WWII
Date	*Event*
September 5, 1939	World War II starts. The United States declares neutrality.
June 22, 1940	National Defense Tax bills passed.
July 20, 1940	FDR signs bill to build a "two oceans" navy.
September 16, 1940	The Selective Training and Service Act passed, leading to the military draft.
March 11, 1941	Congress passes the Lend-Lease Act, allowing for the provision of military goods to Great Britain.
August 14, 1941	FDR and Churchill announce the Atlantic Charter, outlining their peace goals.

Date	Event
August 18, 1941	Congress extends the service period for military personnel by 18 months.
December 7, 1941	Japan attacks the United States in Hawaii, the Philippines, Guam, and elsewhere.
December 8, 1941	The United States declares war on Japan.
December 11, 1941	Germany and Italy declare war on the United States.

1. What evidence does the chronology show to support the idea that the United States actually supported the Allied side?

   (A) the building of a two oceans navy

   (B) the introduction of the draft

   (C) the Lend-Lease Act

   (D) all of the above

2. When did the United States declare war on Germany?

   (A) 1939

   (B) 1941, after Japan attacked the United States

   (C) December 11, 1941

   (D) It did not; Germany and Italy declared war on the United States.

3. What in the sequence of events shows that the United States, despite declaring neutrality, was preparing for the eventuality of war?

   (A) a pattern of defense preparations

   (B) the provision of military goods by the United States to Great Britain (Lend-Lease Act)

   (C) the Atlantic Charter

   (D) all of the above

Here are the answers.

1. Though all the choices indicate preparations for war, only the Lend-Lease Act, Choice (C), shows specific support for the Allied side.

2. Nowhere in the timeline does the United States declare war on Germany. A closer reading shows that Germany declared war on the United States after the United States declared war on Japan, so the correct answer is Choice (D).

3. Choice (C) is wrong because the Lend-Lease Act didn't involve American preparations for joining the war. Rather, it helped the Allies to fight the war on their own. And if Choice (C) is incorrect, Choice (D) doesn't work either. The Atlantic Charter stated peace aims but didn't involve the United States in the war. The only supported choice is Choice (A), the pattern of preparations for war.

Understanding the order of steps in social studies processes

One key skill in social studies is understanding the sequence of events required to achieve certain ends. Before the president can sign a law into effect, it has to go through a variety of steps. The Constitution requires specific steps be taken to bring someone to court. Before a company decides to build a new plant, it does financial projections and needs assessments, transportation, and site studies. Choosing a candidate for election follows a process set out in local, state, or federal legislation. Economic systems have an impact on how people live; studying how various systems achieve their social goals is part of this process.

The Social Studies portion of the GED test may require you to extract a sequence of events from a passage or explain the effects of such a process. Examine this passage from USA Elections in Brief (`photos.state.gov/libraries/amgov/30145/publications-english/USA_Elections_InBrief.pdf`):

Most states now hold primary elections. Depending on the laws of the state, primary voters may cast a ballot for a party's presidential nominee and a slate of "pledged" delegates, may vote for the presidential candidate with delegates to be chosen later to reflect the vote, or may indirectly vote for a candidate in a caucus by choosing convention delegates who are "pledged" to one or another candidate. Under the caucus system, partisans who live within a relatively small geographic area — a local precinct — get together and vote for delegates who are pledged to support specific candidates for president. Those delegates, in turn, represent their precinct at a county convention, which chooses delegates to attend the congressional district and state conventions. The delegates to these conventions ultimately elect delegates to represent the state at the national convention. Although this system takes place over several months, the candidate preferences are essentially determined in the first round of voting.

The actual size of any state's delegation to the national nominating convention is calculated on the basis of a formula established by each party that includes such considerations as the state's population, its past support for the party's national candidates and the number of elected officials and party leaders currently serving in public office from that state. The allocation formula that the Democrats use results in national conventions that have about twice as many delegates as those of the Republicans.

As a result of these reforming tendencies since World War II, two important trends stand out. First, more states have moved their presidential primaries and caucuses earlier on the calendar toward the decisive early stage of the nominating season, a trend known as "front-loading." Being an early primary or caucus state may allow voters in the state to exercise more influence over the ultimate selection of the nominees. In addition, it may encourage the candidates to address the needs and interests of the state early on, and may force candidates to organize within the state, spending money on staff, media, and hotels to try to obtain a decisive psychological victory early in the party nomination process.

In addition, in some parts of the country, states have cooperated with one another to organize "regional primaries" by holding their primaries and caucuses on the same date to maximize the influence of a region. Both of these trends have forced candidates to begin their campaigns earlier to gain a foothold in the increasing number of states that hold the early contests.

Here are a few practice questions related to the passage you just read.

1. What is the effect of the caucus system on individual voters' ability to elect their party's candidate for president?

   (A) Voters directly elect the presidential candidate.

   (B) Voters elect delegates to attend a state convention that elects the presidential candidate.

   (C) Voters elect precinct delegates, who are the first step in electing a series of delegates to wider assemblies who will eventually select the presidential candidate.

   (D) Voters elect candidates to attend the national convention to select the presidential candidate.

2. In what way does the primary process affect the way candidates campaign for election?

   (A) Candidates are more likely to try to appeal to delegates rather than to the voters themselves.

   (B) Candidates are likely to invest more resources in states that hold their primaries early in the election cycle.

   (C) Candidates tend to focus their efforts on individual precincts rather than on entire states.

   (D) Candidates pour more campaign money into states with a larger number of delegates.

3. The purpose of front-loading is to

   (A) enable candidates who win early primaries to have greater success in later primaries

   (B) enable candidates to more effectively address the needs of voters in early primary states

   (C) enable states to hold regional primaries to increase their influence in the region

   (D) give voters in early primary states more influence over national elections

How did you do? Compare your answers to these explanations.

1. The correct answer is Choice (C). Voters make up only the initial stage of the selection process. Voters in each precinct elect delegates to represent them at a county convention. These delegates choose other delegates, who represent the voters' wishes at the congressional district and state conventions. These delegates then elect other delegates that represent the state at the national convention.

2. Look to the last sentence of the third paragraph for the answer. Candidates are highly motivated to win the early primaries because success in those primaries is likely to influence success in later primaries, Choice (B).

3. Front-loading is described in the third paragraph as a way to give voters more influence over the ultimate selection of candidates. That matches Choice (D).

Analyzing Development of and Interactions among Events, Processes, and Ideas

Historical events, such as the American Revolution, don't occur in a vacuum. This particular war may have started with the Boston Tea Party, as a protest against the high taxes being levied by an oppressive king, but several factors contributed to the onset of the Revolutionary War, including events, processes, and ideas. For example, the ideas of 17th-century philosopher John Locke strongly influenced the nation's founding fathers.

Locke's theory of the "social contract," which implies the right of people to overthrow an oppressive government, and his commitment to religious tolerance form the basis of modern democracy. The idea of a *representative democracy* (a process for electing representatives) like that in the United States was first practiced in ancient Greece. And numerous events occurred prior to the war to encourage France to form an alliance with the colonists against Britain.

You're likely to encounter at least one question on the GED Social Studies test that requires you to read a passage and answer questions about how particular events, processes, and ideas influence a certain event or outcome. For example, most students learn that the assassination of Archduke Franz Ferdinand, heir to the Austrian-Hungarian Imperial Throne, and his wife, led to World War I. Ferdinand's empire consisted of many nationalities and religions — Austrians, Serbs, Hungarians, Christians, Jews, and Muslims — and many of the minorities, especially the Serbians, wanted independence from Austro-Hungary. The investigation into the assassination appeared to show that the Serbian governments, or some members of the government, were involved. However, the question remains whether the assassination of Franz Ferdinand and his wife was the actual cause of the war or only the trigger.

The following passage analyzes interactions among events, processes, and ideas to shed light on possible causes of World War I that go beyond the assassination of the archduke and his wife. Following the passage are questions similar to those you're likely to encounter on the test.

One must differentiate between triggers and causes. Though the assassinations of Archduke Franz Ferdinand and his wife may have triggered WWI, they were far from the cause.

Austro-Hungary was facing a crisis. An arms race between Great Britain, Germany, and the other European countries was ongoing. With the development of new styles of battleships, especially the dreadnaughts, Austro-Hungary knew it would be unable to keep up. Yet it faced many enemies in the Balkans, beginning with Serbia and Russia, as well as internal dissension. For many among the leadership, Austro-Hungary would only become weaker over time, so if a war with Serbia to stabilize the eastern frontier was imminent, the sooner the better.

There was a general increase in militarism. France also expanded its military, still angry about its defeat by Prussia in the 1860s. It feared the rapid growth of German land forces while yearning for revenge. Competition for colonies had forced Great Britain to increase its navy in order to protect those colonies. Germany saw the British navy and colonies as tools for power and wanted to emulate that. In the years between 1900 and 1914, Germany built a large number of new warships, copying the design of the HMS Dreadnaught, a revolutionary British design that made all other warships obsolete. That allowed the kaiser's new navy to keep up with Britain's latest and best. The arms race was putting Britain's economy under severe strains, trying to stay ahead of the German naval buildup, and some feared it might fall behind.

Because of the fear of other nations, many countries banded together in alliances. They signed mutual defense agreements, promising to declare war on any country that attacked their allies. What should just have been a Balkan war between Austro-Hungary and Serbia spread as one nation after the other was pulled into the war by alliances.

Economic rivalries also played a role. German and British businesses were competing around the world, especially in South America, where the Germans were making great inroads at the expense of the British. German factories were more modern, and German scientists were often leaders in their fields. The competition for colonies and the heavy-handed German interference in international politics added to the rising tensions in Europe.

Here are a few practice questions related to the passage you just read:

1. Which of the following is not mentioned as a contributing factor of World War I?

   (A) growing nationalism in Germany and Britain

   (B) arms race between Germany and Britain

   (C) conflict between Austro-Hungary and Serbia

   (D) competition for colonies

2. According to this passage, which of the following emotional factors contributed most to causing World War I?

   (A) greed

   (B) anger

   (C) fear

   (D) hatred

3. Which of the following historical events mentioned in the passage contributed most significantly to the onset of World War I?

   (A) the Austro-Hungary Serbia War

   (B) the Franco-Prussian War

   (C) the Balkan War

   (D) the Franco-German War

Here are the answers.

1. Although growing *nationalism* (country-related pride) was certainly a contributing factor, it's not mentioned in the passage. The other three factors are, so Choice (A) is the correct answer.

2. The passage touches on both greed and anger, but it mentions fear, Choice (C), three times. (Though the passage doesn't deal directly with hatred, Choice (D), you can certainly infer its influence from the evidence.)

3. Choice (B) is the correct answer because the passage notes that France was still angry over its defeat by Prussia. Although it mentions conflict between Austro-Hungary and Serbia, it doesn't specifically describe that conflict as a war. The other wars in Choices (C) and (D) don't appear in the passage.

Scrutinizing Cause-and-Effect Relationships

Many events are related. Earlier events often cause, or at least influence the direction of, later ones. Analyzing these cause-and-effect relationships allows historians, economists, and geographers to study how modern events are shaped by what went before. Sometimes a direct causal relationship exists; other times, not so much.

The relationship among the rise of Hitler, the terms of the Treaty of Versailles (and how Germans perceived them), the Great Depression, and the outbreak of World War II is a good example of how events shape the future. Check out the following passage.

Hitler used the terms of the Treaty of Versailles to play on German anger at the wasted sacrifice in World War I. He railed against the limitations placed on the German military and the repeal of the peace settlement with Russia that ended WWI on the eastern front with a German victory. All the gains made there, as well as all German colonies and even part of the homeland, were lost in the treaty. Hitler directed that anger at the Allied powers and at the new German democracy, the Weimar republic.

Germany was forced to agree to huge reparation payments. At the time, economist John Maynard Keynes wrote that these reparations were far too harsh. He argued it would only make postwar recovery of the German economy impossible, damaging both the German economy and the other world economies as well. The amount was set at about $450 billion in modern dollars, but when Germany's economy collapsed and payments stopped, the debt grew to be in excess of $2.3 trillion. Consider that the entire national debt of the United States in 2014 was $18 trillion. This reparation amount was in addition to all the other national debts Germany owed.

The War Guilt clause infuriated Hitler. Germany had to accept complete guilt for the war, but Germans argued that the true war trigger was the assassination of Franz Ferdinand by a Bosnian-Serb terrorist and that Austro-Hungary's attack on Serbia was what began the fighting. Germany only entered the war when Russia refused to stop mobilizing its military, a direct threat to Austro-Hungary and Germany.

The other industrial economies had recovered quickly after the war, and the Roaring Twenties were just that. Economies boomed. Unemployment was low, and living and working conditions were improving rapidly. Germany's economy recovered much later and much more slowly. It was heavily dependent on trade and foreign loans. When the Great Depression hit in the fall of 1929, both foreign trade and loans evaporated. Germany's economy collapsed again, this time much faster than that of the United States or Great Britain. Unemployment rose higher, and the outlook was bleaker. Worse, Germany was financially ruined when foreign banks demanded it repay all debts in 90 days, and none would lend more funds.

The Weimar government applied traditional conservative measures to the crisis: It cut spending. With no help for the several million unemployed, people had no food and no money for clothing or to heat their homes. Many were starving in the streets. Hitler and the Nazi party had stirred up emotions against the Weimar government for accepting the Treaty of Versailles. Now Hitler could blame them for not dealing with the Great Depression. In 1928, the last election before the Great Depression, the Nazis held only 12 seats of 491 in the German parliament. In the 1930 election, the first after the Depression started, they won 107. That number climbed to 230 in the July 1932. That government failed, and a second election in November cost the Nazis seats, but Hitler outmaneuvered the other parties and was selected as chancellor. He used that position to become dictator two months later.

Even after the *Machtergreifung,* the seizure of absolute power, Hitler continued to rail against the Treaty of Versailles. When possible, he undermined the terms, refusing to make reparation payments. He ordered the secret rebuilding of the military, including new battleships, sent troops to reoccupy the Rhineland, built a new air force, and started a new submarine fleet.

Key terms of the Treaty of Versailles

In case you're wondering what the Treaty of Versailles was all about and how it likely contributed to World War II, here are the terms of the treaty in a nutshell:

Loss of territory:

- Surrender of all German colonies

- Alsace-Lorraine returned to France

- Eastern sections of Germany turned over to create an independent Poland

- Other eastern sections of Germany given to newly independent Lithuania and Czechoslovakia

- Danzig severed from Germany and turned into an independent state

- German territories of the Saar ceded to French control

- The Rhineland occupied for 15 years, and Germany forbidden to station troops there

Severe restrictions on Germany's military:

- Germany's military limited to 100,000, with no tanks, air force, or heavy weapons

- Germany's navy limited to a few old warships and small vessels; new ships restricted to under 100,000 tons, and submarines forbidden

Other conditions:

- Germany to pay reparations of roughly U.S. $450 billion in today's money

- Germany accepts sole guilt for the war

Here are a few practice questions related to the passage in this section:

1. Many historians suggest Hitler's constant speeches against the Treaty of Versailles helped bring him to power. Based on this passage, what led to his election to power?

   (A) the loss of German colonies and homeland territories

   (B) the limits on German military power

   (C) the War Guilt clause of the Treaty of Versailles

   (D) the government's inability to cope with the Great Depression

2. Why might the Germans have been particularly upset by the repeal of the 1917 peace treaty with Russia?

   (A) They lost all the gains made at great military sacrifice.

   (B) The treaty undid a major victory.

   (C) The victory over Russia was the only positive outcome of the war for Germany.

   (D) All of the above.

3. Why was the War Guilt clause a major issue for the Germans?

   (A) They argued Austro-Hungary had started the war.

   (B) They blamed the war on a Serbian terrorist.

   (C) They were unwilling to accept the blame.

   (D) They felt there was blame on all sides in causing the war.

Now check your answers.

1. The text states that Hitler and the Nazi party didn't make electoral gains until the Great Depression. With all the antitreaty rhetoric, Hitler and the party remained minor players until the economy collapsed. All the other choices may have lent Hitler public support, but they're not the best answers. Hitler's stance on Versailles didn't result in electoral seats. It was the Weimar government's failure to provide relief to Germans during the Great Depression, Choice (D), that made the electorate turn to his party.

2. The text discusses that the Germans saw their victory over Russia wiped out at the stroke of a pen by the Treaty of Versailles. That victory had been hard won. All the other points are part of that reasoning, but none is the complete answer, making Choice (D) the best option.

3. The text states that the Germans remembered that the assassination of the archduke and Austro-Hungary's attack on Serbia are what triggered and started the war, respectively. Though the Germans may have felt there was blame enough to go around (Choice (D)), the key statement is that Austro-Hungary launched the attack that started the war, Choice (A).

Cause and effect in a sequence is sometimes obvious and sometimes not. Work with the information presented. In this passage, the cause is twofold: Hitler's rhetoric against the Treaty of Versailles and the impact of the Great Depression. The anger over the treaty was one factor that led to the war. Hitler's agitation against the treaty's terms lent him a certain credibility, while the Weimar government's inability to help the people through the depression triggered his rise to power.

Sniffing Out Bias and Propaganda

All writers know the phrase "massaging the message." It refers to authors' ability to present information in whatever light they want. The media make their living by the art of persuasion, whether to sell people goods or services they didn't know they needed or to present a situation in the best or worst possible light. Presenting information subjectively rather than objectively is generally referred to as *bias*. When politicians do it, it's referred to as *spin*. When it's used to control the thinking and behavior of a group of people, it's called *propaganda*.

Some communications experts argue that all writing is biased because all truth is filtered through human perception, which is subjective. They may have a point, but everyone agrees that some writings are more biased than others. When asked to analyze passages that present an argument, examine the following areas for bias:

✔ **What's included and what's omitted:** Whether writing a newspaper story or history book, authors select the facts to present and omit others. When history books present the Cuban Missile Crisis resolution, they often overlook the fact that the United States also had missiles on the USSR's borders. The crisis was resolved only when the United States agreed to remove its missiles just as the USSR agreed to do in Cuba. Presenting only the fact that the USSR backed down when confronted in Cuba paints a different picture than stating that both sides had missiles on the other's borders and both sides agreed to remove them. This particular type of bias is difficult to detect because you're looking for something that's not there. However, if only one side of a complex issue is presented, then you can be fairly certain that the presentation is biased.

✔ **Language:** The words used to describe people or events can influence perceptions. For example, militants fighting against established governments often refer to themselves as "freedom fighters," whereas the established governments they're fighting against consider them "terrorists." These words are more than just descriptive; they carry an emotional overtone. When analyzing a passage, examine word choice carefully.

✔ **Sources:** Media content, from articles and video clips to research studies, is sometimes sponsored by people or corporations. Media outlets can be for or against political parties and views; corporations, such as tobacco or oil companies, may sponsor research into climate change or the health effects of smoking. Consider such sources when evaluating the credibility of any source.

✔ **Statistics:** Writers use statistics to support their arguments. These statistics may be selective, incomplete, or show only part of the picture. Even how a graph is designed can influence perceptions. Showing only part of the data can change how readers interpret the graph. Read statistics carefully and remember that unless you can verify the data in other ways, it may not be reliable.

Exploring History's Influence on an Author's Point of View

Politicians and historians often look to the past for an understanding of how events unfolded and to learn valuable lessons and glean guidance for their thoughts and decisions. In short, history often strongly influences a writer's point of view, as in the following extract from "Thoughts on Government" by John Adams.

All sober inquirers after truth, ancient and modern, pagan and Christian, have declared that the happiness of man, as well as his dignity, consists in virtue. Confucius, Zoroaster, Socrates, Mahomet, not to mention authorities really sacred, have agreed in this.

If there is a form of government, then, whose principle and foundation is virtue, will not every sober man acknowledge it better calculated to promote the general happiness than any other form?

Fear is the foundation of most governments; but it is so sordid and brutal a passion, and renders men in whose breasts it predominates so stupid and miserable, that Americans will not be likely to approve of any political institution which is founded on it.

Honor is truly sacred, but holds a lower rank in the scale of moral excellence than virtue. Indeed, the former is but a part of the latter, and consequently has not equal pretensions to support a frame of government productive of human happiness.

The foundation of every government is some principle or passion in the minds of the people. The noblest principles and most generous affections in our nature, then, have the fairest chance to support the noblest and most generous models of government.

A man must be indifferent to the sneers of modern English men, to mention in their company the names of Sidney, Harrington, Locke, Milton, Nedham, Neville, Burnet, and Hoadly. No small fortitude is necessary to confess that one has read them. The wretched condition of this country, however, for ten or fifteen years past, has frequently reminded me of their principles and reasoning. They will convince any candid mind, that there is no good government but what is republican. That the only valuable part of the British constitution is so; because the very definition of a republic is "an empire of laws, and not of men." That, as a republic is the best of governments, so that particular arrangement of the powers of society, or, in other words, that form of government which is best contrived to secure an impartial and exact execution of the laws, is the best of republics.

Questions on the Social Studies test may ask you to identify how history has influenced an author's point of view as conveyed in a written passage, as in these two sample questions.

1. What has Adams learned from Confucius, Zoroaster, Socrates, Mahomet, and other thinkers who came before him?

   (A) Fear is the foundation of most governments.

   (B) Honor holds a higher rank in the scale of moral excellence than virtue.

   (C) Virtue is the trait responsible for human dignity and happiness.

   (D) There is no good government but what is republican.

2. Modern thinkers have convinced Adams that

   (A) The best republics execute laws exactly and impartially.

   (B) A man must be indifferent to the sneers of modern English men.

   (C) No good government is republican.

   (D) Democracy is the best form of government.

What? You want to know the answers? Well, if you insist.

1. The answer is in the first paragraph, where Adams states that happiness and dignity are rooted in virtue. That matches Choice (C).

2. In the last paragraph, Adams describes the highest purpose of a republic: to enforce laws exactly and impartially, Choice (A).

Gauging an Author's Credibility

Evaluating whether an author is believable based on the information provided in a written passage and the citation isn't always easy, but you may be able to pick up clues by carefully examining the following areas:

- **Author's credentials:** Does the author have any special credentials relevant to the topic? Check the byline that accompanies the passage to determine whether the author has any special training that qualifies her as an expert in the field.

- **Citations:** Authors of nonfiction materials cite other sources to provide supporting evidence for their claims. Look at the sources they use. A large number of citations shows that the author has done her research. Check the citations themselves. Are the sources reliable? Do they show biases? For example, if a company sponsors a study, the researchers may be reluctant to release any results that reflect poorly on the company or its products.

- **Tone:** Objective passages present the facts in a matter-of-fact way, without a lot of emotion. A strident tone may indicate that the author is biased and isn't as objective as she's trying to present herself. Flip to the earlier section "Sniffing Out Bias and Propaganda" for details.

- **Balanced view:** Credible authors recognize and acknowledge different sides of an issue and address common or obvious objections to whatever claims they're making. An author loses credibility by not acknowledging other viewpoints or by presenting those other viewpoints as preposterous without providing evidence to prove it.

Compare the following two excerpts and determine which is more credible.

Passage One

From Bureau of Democracy, Human Rights and Labor, International Religious Freedom Report for 2013 (`www.state.gov/j/drl/rls/irf/religiousfreedom/index.htm#wrapper`)

In Syria, as in much of the Middle East, the Christian presence is becoming a shadow of its former self. After three years of civil war, hundreds of thousands fled the country desperate to escape the ongoing violence perpetrated by the government and extremist groups alike. In the city of Homs the number of Christians dwindled to as few as 1,000 from approximately 160,000 prior to the conflict. Elsewhere, in the Central African Republic, widespread lawlessness and an upsurge in sectarian violence between Christians and Muslims reportedly resulted in at least 700 deaths in Bangui in December alone and the displacement of more than one million people throughout the country during the year.

Passage Two

Letter to the editor

The problem with the Affordable Care Act purely from an economics perspective is that it increases demand for healthcare while doing absolutely nothing to increase the supply. The end result will be ever increasing prices for consumers in the form of both higher health insurance premiums and increases in out-of-pocket costs. My insurance company, for example, recently canceled the high-deductible policy I was paying $247 a month for because it did not comply with Affordable Care Act requirements. The "low cost" replacement plan the company recommended would cost me $448 a month. This is just one example of how the Affordable Care Act increases the cost of healthcare.

If you chose the first passage as the more credible, you answered correctly. The first passage contains plenty of facts presented objectively. The second begins by saying that the Affordable Care Act did "absolutely nothing" to increase the supply, which seems to be an exaggeration. In addition, the only evidence given to support the claim that the Affordable Care Act increases healthcare costs is a personal account of an increase in an insurance premium, which only proves that the author of the letter has reason to be biased against the Affordable Care Act.

Chapter 7

Applying Mathematical Reasoning to Social Studies

Although the questions on the Social Studies test focus on civics, government, U.S. history, economics, and geography, several questions test your ability to make sense of data that's presented visually (in maps, images, charts, and tables) and perform basic math — addition, subtraction, multiplication, and division and perhaps calculating an average or two.

In this chapter, we bring you up to speed on the skills required to apply mathematical reasoning to social studies questions, and we provide plenty of practice questions so you know what to expect when test day arrives.

Analyzing Maps and Images

Many questions on the Social Studies test are based on charts (graphs), maps, cartoons, photographs, and other visual materials. All these visual media provide ways to convey information visually. Some questions may combine text and a visual.

To do well on the Social Studies test, you need to be able to look at data or messages presented visually and extract or interpret the meaning from them to answer the questions that accompany the visuals. In this section, we start with maps and images.

Making sense of data in maps

Maps do more than show you where places are or give the names of streets and lakes. They also provide information, and knowing how to decode that information is essential. Maps are particularly effective at revealing patterns of distribution and changes in patterns in geographical areas. They may show you land use; climate patterns; resource locations; and distribution of crops, people, and resources and indicate how those have changed over time.

Start analyzing maps by examining the print information on the map: the title and *legend* (explanation of symbols or colors used on the map). Read the "fine print," as you'd do when reading a contract, because that's often where useful information is hidden that helps you decode the contents of the map. Then look at what the question requires you to find. You can then find that information quickly by relating the answer choices to what the map shows.

For example, in the map shown in Figure 7-1, the title tells you that the map shows the change in the total population of each state and Puerto Rico between April 1, 2010, and July 1, 2012. The color scheme indicates the change in population by state.

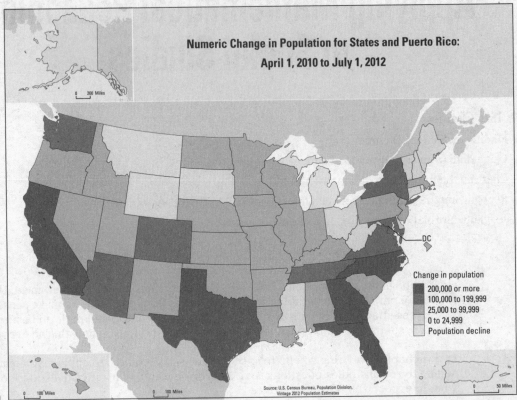

Numeric Change in Population for States and Puerto Rico:

April 1, 2010 to July 1, 2012

Change in population

- 200,000 or more
- 100,000 to 199,999
- 25,000 to 99,999
- 0 to 24,999
- Population decline

Source: U.S. Census Bureau, Population Division, Vintage 2012 Population Estimates

Source: U.S. Census Bureau, Population Division, Vintage 2012 Population Estimates

Figure 7-1:
Sample
map.

1. What two states or territories show a decline in population?

   (A) Michigan and Puerto Rico

   (B) Puerto Rico and Alabama

   (C) Florida and Texas

   (D) Maine and Connecticut

2. Which state had the largest population in 2012?

   (A) Michigan

   (B) Florida

   (C) Texas

   (D) cannot be determined

Here are the answers.

1. The only areas to show a decline are Michigan and Puerto Rico. The correct answer is Choice (A). You can figure that out by looking at the legend and seeing that white shading — shown only in Michigan and Puerto Rico — indicates a declining population.

2. This map doesn't show total population, only changes in population, so the correct answer is Choice (D).

Interpreting images

Pictures, cartoons, and posters all convey information, from geographical or historical information to economics and propaganda. Figure 7-2 is a typical example of a World War II propaganda poster John Philip Falter created for the U.S. government in 1942. The U.S. government used such posters to stir up patriotism and prepare people for the sacrifices the war required. This type of visual uses several techniques, including symbolism, to convey a message.

Figure 7-2: Symbolic World War II poster.

Library of Congress (http://www.loc.gov/pictures/item/91784720/)

Analyze cartoons and posters by identifying the images that make them up. Then look for the key elements in the message these images create. Examine the text for information and identify any symbolic representations. In the poster shown in Figure 7-2, for example, a family is cowering against a brick wall, indicating that there is no escape.

Here are a couple of questions about the image in Figure 7-2 that are similar to questions you may encounter on the Social Studies test.

1. Who is threatening to enslave half the world, according to this poster?

(A) the Japanese

(B) the Germans

(C) some military force, presumably German and/or Japanese

(D) impossible to tell from this image

2. What part of the image reinforces the idea of enslavement?

    (A) the whip

    (B) the cowering people

    (C) what appears to be a person in military uniform

    (D) all of the above

Check your answers.

1. The oppressor is a shadowy figure with a peaked military cap, which may represent either the Japanese or the Germans, considering the enemies of the time. Therefore, Choice (C) is the best answer.

2. The whip has been a symbol of slavery and oppression for centuries, so the correct answer is Choice (A). Choice (B) is partially correct, but people cower out of all kinds of fear, not necessarily just the fear of being enslaved. Choice (C) is wrong because the military doesn't necessarily enslave people.

Photos can also be used to convey information. Analyze the photo shown in Figure 7-3 from the FDR Presidential Library.

Figure 7-3:
Sample
photo.

Source: FDR Presidential Library, Public Domain http://docs.fdrlibrary.
marist.edu/gdphotos.html

Which of the following periods does this photo most likely depict?

    (A) The Roaring Twenties

    (B) The Great Depression

    (C) The cold war

    (D) The civil rights era

The correct answer is Choice (B). The lease signs indicate that the business is closed, and the man leaning against the wall looks destitute, which are both signs of a poor economy. In addition, you can tell that the photo is from quite a long time ago because MUSH & MILK is selling for five cents. You can eliminate Choice (A) because the Roaring Twenties were a time of economic boom. Eliminate Choice (C) because the cold war didn't start until 1947 or so and didn't end until 1991. You can also eliminate Choice (D) because nothing in the image suggests the civil rights movement, when African Americans protested for equality.

Extracting Data from Charts (Graphs) and Tables

In addition to presenting information in the form of text, maps, and images, the Social Studies test uses charts and tables and asks questions that challenge your ability to make sense of the data presented. (In this section, we use the terms *graph* and *chart* interchangeably.) For example, government statistical data is often presented in the form of charts and tables. In this section, we present several different types of charts and one table that you're likely to encounter on the Social Studies test and provide sample questions that test your ability to extract data from charts and tables.

Grappling with charts

Every time you turn around, someone in the media is trying to make a point with a chart. The reason people use charts to explain themselves is because charts clearly show trends and relationships between different sets of information. For example, the bar charts shown in Figure 7-4 are ideal for comparing unemployment and weekly earnings by educational attainment. The charts show clear relationships among the three factors.

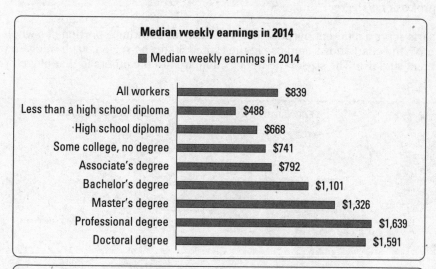

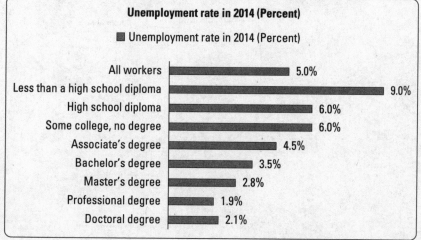

Figure 7-4: Bar charts comparing earnings.

John Wiley & Sons, Inc. (Source of info used in image: Current Population Survey, U.S. Bureau of Labor Statistics, U.S. Department of Labor)

1. What is the correlation between education and income?

   (A) Higher education results in higher income.

   (B) Higher education almost always results in higher income.

   (C) Lower education has no effect on income.

   (D) cannot be determined from these charts

2. Which of these groups is least likely to be unemployed?

   (A) people with a high school diploma

   (B) people with a bachelor's degree

   (C) people with a professional degree

   (D) people with a doctoral degree

Here are the answers.

   1. The correct answer is Choice (B). Higher education almost always means higher income. The weekly earnings chart shows a slight drop for the highest level of education, the doctoral level, so higher education doesn't always result in higher income, but it usually does.

   2. The unemployment rate chart shows the lowest unemployment is among people with a professional degree, Choice (C).

Pie charts serve a different purpose. They're ideal for showing a portion of a whole. In Figure 7-5, the chart shows land use in the United States by region. Each wedge represents a different land use. The size of the wedge compared to the others in that pie tell you the

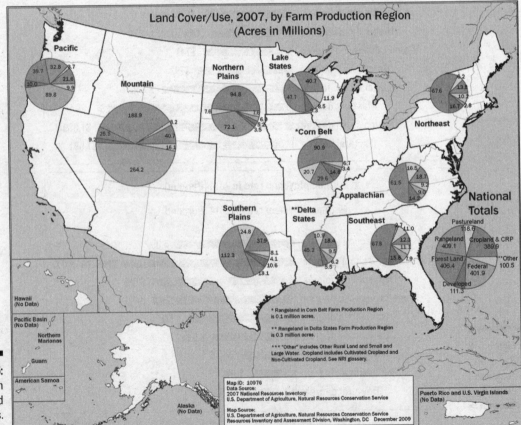

Figure 7-5: Map with embedded pie charts.

Source: U.S. Department of Agriculture, Natural Resources Conservation Service Resources Inventory and Assessment Division, Washington, DC

relative share of the total land use each represents. However, when comparing regions, the overall size of the pie is also proportional to the total available area, which is a unique use of pie charts.

Approximately how many millions of acres of rangeland are in the region with the greatest number of total acres?

(A) 264.2

(B) 188.9

(C) 112.3

(D) 72.1

The correct answer is Choice (B). The mountain region has the biggest pie, so it has the greatest number of total acres, 188.9 of which are represented as rangeland.

Line charts, such as the one shown in Figure 7-6, are good for illustrating trends over time.

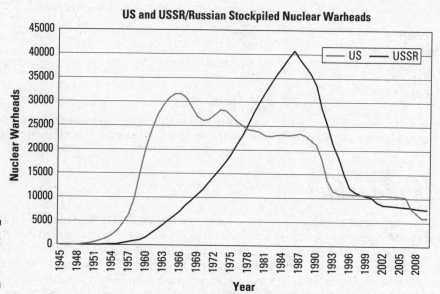

US and USSR/Russian Stockpiled Nuclear Warheads

Figure 7-6:
Sample line chart.

Illustration by John Wiley & Sons, Inc. (Source info from National Resources Defense Council)

Approximately how many years after the United States started reducing its stockpile of nuclear warheads did the USSR/Russia begin reducing its stockpile?

(A) 30 years

(B) 25 years

(C) 20 years

(D) 15 years

Choice (C) is the best answer. The United States began reducing its stockpile of nuclear weapons in 1965. The USSR/Russia continued to build its stockpile until 1985, at which point it began to reduce it. That's a difference of 20 years.

Column charts are useful for comparing data side by side. The column chart in Figure 7-7, for example, compares average wages of union and nonunion workers, clearly showing that union workers earn significantly more in wages in every category.

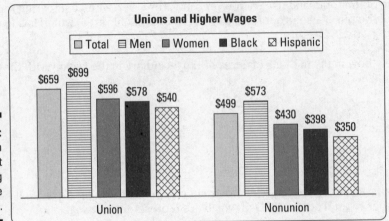

Unions and Higher Wages

☐ Total ☐ Men ■ Women ■ Black ☒ Hispanic

Figure 7-7:
Column
chart
illustrating
average
wages.

Illustration by John Wiley & Sons, Inc. (Source info from United States Department of Labor)

Male union workers earned how much more per week than nonunion women?

(A) $126

(B) $269

(C) $301

(D) $200

The correct answer is Choice (B). The chart shows that male union workers earned $699 per week, whereas female nonunion workers earned $430 per week, a difference of $269.

Tackling tables

Tables arrange data in columns (vertical) and rows (horizontal). You need to be able to extract and interpret information from any table even if the info isn't stated directly. From nutrition labels on food products to specifications for a new car, you have to be able to read a table. For practice, study any table you can find, whether in a newspaper or on the back of a can of cat food. The table in Figure 7-8 is an example of the kinds of tabled data you may see on the test. This table breaks down the population into ethnicities and places of birth.

Place of Birth in the United States
Hawaii
  Powered by The American Community Survey

	Total*:	One Race						Two or More Races	Hispanic or Latino (any race)
		White	Black or African American	American Indian and Alaska Native	Asian	Native Hawaiian and Other Pacific Islander	Some Other Race		
Total:	1,376,298	344,488	24,532	3,050	526,743	134,733	15,418	327,334	128,171
Born in state of residence	750,445	69,567	2,308	763	305,289	98,484	4,322	269,712	80,482
Born in other state in the United States	339,766	243,585	19,690	2,106	20,048	6,801	6,220	41,316	32,130
Native; born outside the United States	39,352	7,478	836	22	13,168	8,752	825	8,271	3,829
Foreign born	246,735	23,858	1,698	159	188,238	20,696	4,051	8,035	11,730

Source: U.S. Census Bureau, 2009-2013 American Community Survey 5-Year Estimates.
Except where noted, 'race' refers to people reporting only one race. 'Hispanic' refers to an ethnic category; Hispanics may be of any race.
An entry of '+/-0' in the margin of error column indicates that the estimate is controlled. A statistical test for sampling variability is not appropriate.
A 'Z' entry in the estimate or margin of error column indicates that the estimate or margin of error is not applicable or not available.
* Margins of Error are not provided for Totals but may be found for those estimates where available in American FactFinder or our FTP server. See Appendix 3 of 'What General Users Need to Know'
for instructions on calculating an approximate MOE for any totals not already provided within the ACS data tables.

Figure 7-8:
Sample
table.

Illustration by John Wiley & Sons, Inc. (Source info from U.S. Census Bureau, 2009–2013 American Community Survey 5-Year Estimates)

What percentage of Hawaii's population was not born in Hawaii? Round your answer to the nearest tenth of a percentage point: ☐ %.

You can't tell just by looking at the table. You need to do the math. The total number of people born in Hawaii is 750,445. Divide that by the total population of 1,376,298, and you get 0.54526345, which rounds to 0.545, which equals 54.5 percent. That's the percentage of the population born in Hawaii. Subtract that from 100 percent to get the answer: 45.5 percent of the population was *not* born in Hawaii.

Predicting Trends with Charts and Tables

One special feature of charts is that they allow you to make predictions based on the trends they show. The slopes of the lines can tell you what may happen in the future simply by extending the lines. The chart in Figure 7-9 shows trends in educational enrollment.

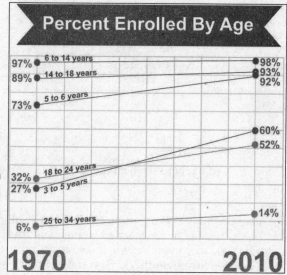

Figure 7-9
Chart showing trends in educational enrollment.

Illustration by Joe Kraynak (Source info from U.S. Census Bureau, 1970 Census of Population, American Community Survey 2010)

What will be the approximate percentage of people ages 25 to 34 enrolled in some form of education by 2050?

(A) 70%

(B) 30%

(C) 20%

(D) cannot be determined

The trend is upward, so you know it will increase. The percentage increase between 1970 and 2010 slightly more than doubled from 6 to 14 percent. In another 40 years, you can project that the percentage will slightly more than double again. Doubling 14 percent gives you 28 percent, so Choice (C) is definitely wrong. The answer you're looking for is slightly more than doubled, which describes 30 percent (Choice (B)) but isn't even close to 70 percent (Choice (A)). Choice (B) is the correct answer. However, this projection assumes the trend will continue at the same rate over 40 years, which is a *big* assumption. Making projections on so little data without the ability to verify is risky. However, in terms of the Social Studies test, it's acceptable.

You can also use numbers on tables to predict trends based on past experience. The table from the U.S. Census Bureau in Figure 7-10 is an example.

Historical Table 4f. Percent of Never-Married Women who are Mothers, by Selected Characteristics: Selected Years, 1990 to 2014
(Numbers in thousands.)

Characteristic	Women 15 to 44			Women 15 to 50[1]		
	Total number never married women	Number of never married mothers	Percent of never married women who are mothers	Total number never married women	Number of never married mothers	Percent of never married women who are mothers
TOTAL						
2014	31,886	7,567	23.7	33,506	8,314	24.8
2012	30,991	7,687	24.8	32,718	8,513	26.0
2010	29,648	6,884	23.2			
2008	28,426	6,491	22.8			
2006	27,730	6,481	23.4			
2004	26,385	5,679	21.5			
2002	25,782	5,878	22.8			
2000	25,095	5,844	23.3			
1998	24,185	5,451	22.5			
1995	22,846	4,778	20.9			
1990	20,739	3,756	18.1			

Figure 7-10: Chart showing year-to-year numbers of mothers who were never married.

Illustration by John Wiley & Sons, Inc. (Source info from U.S. Census Bureau, 1970 Census of Population, American Community Survey 2010)

What trend does this table show?

(A) Fewer women are getting married.

(B) More women are having children outside marriage.

(C) Women in the 45-to-50 age group are less likely to have children outside marriage.

(D) All of the above.

The correct answer is Choice (D), All of the above. The first three choices are obvious from the numbers. Between 1990 and 2014, the total of never-married women and the number of never-married mothers increased. However, when you include the 45-to-50 age group, you see a slight decline in the number of never-married mothers. That suggests that women in that age group are less likely to have children outside marriage.

This data is also suitable for other mathematical calculations. For example, you may want to know the average percentage of never-married mothers in the period between 2014 and 1990. Simply add up all the percentages in that column. You'd find that the average over that period is 22.45 percent. You may also want to compare the average for the 1990–2000 period to the 2002–2014 period to see whether the rate has changed. Calculate the total of the averages and divide by the number of entries. (Really, you're just averaging the averages.)

Analyzing the Relationship between Dependent and Independent Variables

Every chart has at least two axes, the vertical and horizontal, each of which represents a variable — a changing value such as year, population, income, expenses, or whatever. Data points are plotted on the chart to see how the *dependent variable* changes in response to changes in the *independent variable*. For example, data points may show how population increases or decreases over time. Time is the independent variable because it changes independent of population changes. Population is the dependent variable because its changes are dependent on the passing of time.

The chart in Figure 7-11 shows the declining population of WWII veterans living in the United States from the years 1950 to 2013. The two variables are the number of WWII vets (the dependent variable) and the year (the independent variable). In this case, the relationship between the dependent and independent variables is straightforward. As time goes on, the population of WWII veterans declines because they die and aren't replaced.

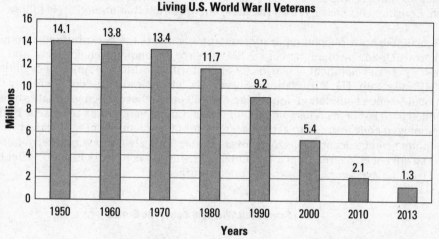

Living U.S. World War II Veterans

Figure 7-11: Chart tracking the declining population of WWII veterans.

John Wiley & Sons, Inc. (Source info from http://www.census.gov/content/dam/Census/newsroom/releases/2015/cb15-tps41_wwii_graphic.pdf)

Between 2004 and 2014, the federal debt held by the public increased by what percentage of the gross domestic product?

(A) 10%

(B) 20%

(C) 25%

(D) 35%

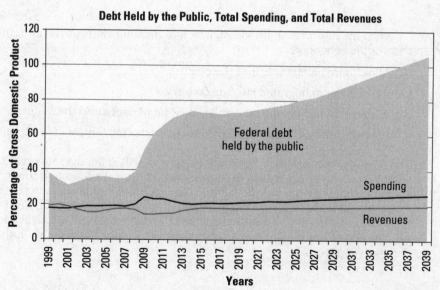

Debt Held by the Public, Total Spending, and Total Revenues

John Wiley & Sons, Inc. (Source info from http://www.cbo.gov/publication/45471)

From 2004 to 2014, the federal debt held by the public increased from just under 40 percent to between 70 and 80 percent, an increase of approximately 35 percent (Choice (D)).

Sorting Out Numerical, Technical, and Written Materials

Some questions include a short reading passage along with a chart or table. To answer the questions that accompany the materials provided, you typically must extract data from both. Consider this passage with the table and question that immediately follow:

An expanding body of contemporary research highlights the contributions to innovation and growth made by immigrants in STEM [science, technology, engineering, and math] fields, where development of world-class talent will be critical to America's continued global leadership. The 2010 National Survey of College Graduates, conducted by the National Science Foundation, found that over 60 percent of foreign graduate students were enrolled in STEM fields. The study found that although immigrants represent 14 percent of all employed college graduates, they account for 50 percent of PhDs working in math and computer science occupations. Moreover, studies indicate that every foreign-born student with an advanced degree from a U.S. university who stays to work in a STEM field is associated with, on average, 2.6 jobs for American workers.

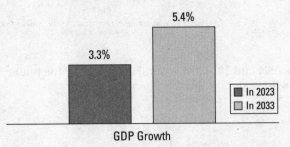

Senate Bill Will Spur Economic Growth

CBO estimate of percent increase in real GDP from enacting S. 744, Commonsense Immigration Reform

Illustration by John Wiley & Sons (Source info from https://www.whitehouse. gov/sites/default/files/docs/report.pdf)

Based on the information provided, which of the following conclusions about immigration is best for the economy?

(A) Allow more immigrants into the country.

(B) Allow fewer immigrants into the country.

(C) Allow more highly-educated and skilled immigrants into the country.

(D) Prevent uneducated and unskilled immigrants from entering the country.

The passage indicates that highly educated and skilled immigrants create jobs for American workers, so Choice (C) is the correct answer. The chart shows that immigration reform will spur economic growth, so you can rule out Choice (B). Although the chart without the passage may imply that allowing more immigrants into the country (Choice (A)) would be beneficial, the passage singles out the benefits of highly educated and skilled immigrants, so you can eliminate Choice (A). You can also eliminate Choice (D) because nothing in the chart or passage supports it.

Part III
Nurturing Your Knowledge: History, Civics, Economics, and Geography

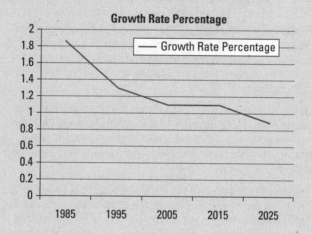

In this part . . .

✔ Find out more about the U.S. government and your rights and responsibilities as a citizen by brushing up on the purpose and goals of various governing bodies and branches, investigating how state governing bodies operate, and exploring politics and public policy.

✔ Get up to speed on U.S. history by glancing at historical documents, considering causes of the Revolutionary and Civil Wars, exploring the civil rights movement, finding out more about native populations and European immigrants, and investigating U.S. foreign policy.

✔ Tell the difference between capitalism, socialism, and communism; find out why FDR's New Deal was such a big deal; distinguish between micro- and macroeconomics; get schooled in how economics drives exploration and war; and explore how industrial and technology revolutions change the world.

✔ Go back in time to explore the ancient cultures of Athens and Rome and their influence on modern life; consider how population, environment, and development interact; examine borders and the conflicts they often trigger; and take a look at how human populations move and change around the world.

✔ Sharpen your Extended Response writing skills by finding out what the evaluators are looking for; how to decipher the reading passages and essay prompt; what ways you can structure your essay and support your claims; how to size up your audience, purpose, and message; and how to smooth out the rough spots.

Chapter 8

Brushing Up on Civics and Government

The GED Social Studies test isn't a citizenship test. You don't need to know the number of amendments to the Constitution (27), what the Bill of Rights is (the first ten amendments), who becomes president if the president and vice president die (the Speaker of the House), or the name of the person who said "Give me liberty, or give me death" (Patrick Henry). However, you do need to be able to read passages about government and specifically about the U.S. federal and state governments and answer questions about those passages. Having a familiarity with these topics beforehand improves your ability to understand the passages and the accompanying questions.

In this chapter, we cover some broad themes from *civics* (the study of the rights and duties of citizenship) and *governance* (the action and manner of managing a country and its people) so you have a firm foundation in those two concepts and the vocabulary necessary to understand them. We also provide plenty of questions along the way to let you practice with these topics and skills.

Perusing the Principles and Philosophy of Governance

George Washington once stated that "Government is not reason and it is not eloquence. It is force! Like fire it is a dangerous servant and a fearful master. Never for a moment should it be left to irresponsible action." Philosophers, historians, and politicians have many different views regarding the purpose and process of good governance, but government is essentially a way that all members of society agree to be governed and the rules by which they agree to live together. A more cynical definition is that government is all about who does what to whom, and how.

The form a government takes often arises out of how the most influential or powerful thinkers and leaders at the time view human nature. When they see human nature as evil, self-seeking, and power hungry, people gravitate toward forming harsh regimes capable of keeping the masses under control for everybody's benefit. When they view human nature in a positive light and see people as being kind and cooperative, milder forms of government such as democracy tend to take hold, with justice systems in place to keep the criminal element in check.

More than 2,000 years ago, writers and philosophers like Plato and Aristotle outlined what an ideal government should be and how it should work. Plato's (428–348 BCE) views were formed by living in a society where the wealthy and the poor were often in conflict with each other. A civil war in Athens and constant political turmoil had produced governments from absolute kings to participatory democracy. Plato thought that the ideal ruler was a philosopher king who ruled with grace and reason. Democracy, according to Plato, was flawed, a rule where men pursued their own desires with little care for others or society.

Thomas Hobbes (1588–1679) was an English philosopher who argued that nature is in a constant state of war and that people live in a constant fear of violence, chaos, and death. You may say he had a pessimistic view of human nature — that it led people to seek domination for personal gain, regardless of the needs of others. Because people were governed by their own appetites and lacked moral judgment, he concluded that the best form of government is an absolute monarchy. Only that form of power could keep society under some control. He agreed that people had the right to protest against unjust monarchs, but he also argued that people had no right to do away with a monarch after they had agreed to that rule. Tyrannical rulers can be opposed but not overthrown. He proposed a form of social contract by which people gave up some of their rights in return for security for all, enforced by an absolute monarch. Here's how Hobbes described it in his 1660 work *The Leviathan:*

> . . .they that are subjects to a monarch cannot without his leave cast off monarchy and return to the confusion of a disunited multitude; nor transfer their person from him that beareth it to another man, other assembly of men: for they are bound, every man to every man, to own and be reputed author of all that already is their sovereign shall do and judge fit to be done; so that any one man dissenting, all the rest should break their covenant made to that man, which is injustice: and they have also every man given the sovereignty to him that beareth their person; and therefore if they depose him, they take from him that which is his own, and so again it is injustice. . . .

Why may people not overthrow a monarch, regardless of the reasons, according to Hobbes?

(A) It would be an injustice.

(B) It would lead to chaos.

(C) It would break a covenant.

(D) cannot be determined from this passage

The best answer is Choice (A), It would be an injustice. Hobbes saw the relationship between the ruler and the ruled as a *covenant,* a contract, that neither could break. Twice he mentions that breaking that covenant would be an injustice. Although Choices (B) and (C) are partial answers, they're not the best choices.

The philosopher who arguably had the greatest influence on American political thought and the American Revolution was John Locke (1632–1704). He too saw governance as an agreement (a compact) between the ruler and the ruled. However, his views were opposed to those of Hobbes; he argued that all men were created equal by the Creator and that they did indeed have the right to resist unjust rulers.

Monarchs in Locke's time could seize the property of their subjects without compensation. Locke's key contributions to political discourse are two main concepts, private property and consent to be ruled. He maintained that because property was the result of personal labor, no one had the right to take it away. He also argued that government legitimacy depended on the consent of the governed. Like Hobbes, he argued that to have order, individuals surrender some of their individual authority to a ruler, who acts as a mediator, an arbitrator, of disputes. However, he also felt that when government abuses its power, the governed have the right to withdraw their consent and change government, views he outlined in his 1689 *Second Treatise on Government:*

Sect. 119. *Every man* being, as has been shewed, *naturally free,* and nothing being able to put him into subjection to any earthly power, but only his own *consent;* . . . I say, that every man, that hath any possessions, or enjoyment, of any part of the dominions of any government, doth thereby give his *tacit consent,* and is as far forth obliged to obedience to the laws of that government, during such enjoyment, as any one under it; whether this his possession be of land, to him and his heirs for ever, or a lodging only for a week; or whether it be barely travelling freely on the highway; and in effect, it reaches as far as the very being of any one within the territories of that government.

Sect. 122. . . . whenever the *legislators endeavor to take away, and destroy the property of the people,* or to reduce them to slavery under arbitrary power, they put themselves into a state of war with the people, who are thereupon absolved from any farther obedience. . . . Whensoever therefore the *legislative* shall transgress this fundamental rule of society . . . by this breach of trust they *forfeit the power* the people had put into their hands for quite contrary ends, and it devolves to the people, who have a right to resume their original liberty. . . .

How do Locke's views support the later events of the American Revolution?

(A) Rulers govern only with the consent of the ruled.

(B) Rulers who exert arbitrary power lose the right to govern.

(C) The people have the right to choose new rulers when government attacks personal or property right.

(D) All of the above.

The best answer is Choice (D), all of the above. All the answer options are correct. Locke's views became the philosophical underpinnings of the American Revolution. King George III issued edicts ignoring wishes of colonial legislatures, housed his soldiers in private homes without permission or compensation, directed courts in their decisions, and generally acted in an arbitrary manner. For the signers of the Declaration of Independence, these actions justified overthrowing a ruler they saw as tyrannical.

Surveying the Many Manifestations of Democracy

Democracy is practiced in many forms around the world. How these forms operate, the offices or individuals in which they are vested, and the relationships among them vary by type of government. The two major forms of democratic government in the world today are the parliamentary and the presidential (congressional) system. The Europeans and former British colonies have some form of parliamentary system, while the United States and much of South and Central America follow the American presidential or congressional system.

In this section, we examine the parliamentary and presidential forms of democracy and give you the opportunity to test your knowledge along the way.

The parliamentary system

The *parliamentary system* in Britain, Canada, and elsewhere separates the role of head of state and head of government. In many countries once part of the British Empire, Queen Elizabeth II is the head of state. She is queen of the United Kingdom, Australia, New Zealand, Canada, Jamaica, and several other Commonwealth realms. The British monarch, the head of state, has a purely ceremonial role with very few actual powers. The head of government, the real power, rests with the prime minister, who with the cabinet forms the executive branch. The judicial branch is the Supreme Court, which deals with constitutional issues.

The legislative branch of the British parliament consists of two houses, the elected House of Commons and the hereditary House of Lords. Most members of the House of Lords are aristocrats, who hold their position by right of birth, or bishops, who are members because of their positions. The House of Lords was once the most powerful part of parliament, existing to advise the monarch. Today the House of Lords has very limited powers. It may initiate legislation, which must then pass in the Commons, or it may delay (but not stop) legislation approved by the Commons. The same pattern exists in Canada, where the upper chamber, the Senate, has only very limited power to amend and delay legislation.

What is the difference between head of state and head of government in the British parliamentary system?

(A) The Head of State is the legal representative of the nation.

(B) The Head of Government is leader of the executive branch of government.

(C) The head of government may change, but the head of state is so for life.

(D) All of the above.

In Britain, the monarch is head of state for life, and the heirs to the throne become head of state upon the death or abdication (stepping down) of the present monarch. Queen Elizabeth II speaks for the country; she is the nation. The head of government is the elected prime minister, whose term in office is time limited. The individuals in that office change at the will of the electorate. Your best answer is Choice (D), All of the above.

Parliamentary elections

Elections in the parliamentary system are similar to those in most democracies. Candidates run in their electoral district, a *riding,* for a seat in the House of Commons. The candidate with the most votes in the riding is elected. Candidates may run for office as often as they want; they have no term limits. The political party that wins the most seats in the legislature forms the next government.

The voters don't elect the prime minister. He or she runs for a seat in parliament like any other candidate, as the representative for one riding. The leader of the winning party becomes prime minister, even if she doesn't win her personal election and has no seat in parliament. The leader of the party is chosen by a party convention, not by the public at large.

To form a government, a political party must have a majority of seats, or the ability to work together with a second or third party that will give it sufficient seats to provide majority in the House of Commons. The government has no fixed term; it stays in power for up to five years or until it loses a vote on a significant issue. If the governing party loses such a vote, it must resign and call an election. Otherwise, it may call an election any time before the end of the five-year limit.

How many times may a person serve as prime minister?

(A) for two terms

(B) for up to ten years

(C) The prime minister is elected for life.

(D) no limit

The prime minister in the parliamentary system is the leader of a political party and runs for a seat in parliament the same way any member runs for a seat. He's not elected to be prime minister, but only to be a member of parliament. As long as the individual is the leader of the winning party, that person is prime minister, even if he hasn't won a seat in parliament. The prime minister can remain in office as often as his party is reelected and he retains the party leadership. Canadian Prime Minister Mackenzie King served for more than 21 years, while Kim Campbell, Canada's first female prime minister, was in office for less than five months. The correct choice is Choice (D).

Parliamentary legislation

Legislation can be proposed by any member of parliament, but it usually comes from the prime minister or cabinet members. The governing party usually has an absolute majority in the House of Commons, the lower house, and can pass any legislation it wants. Opposition parties don't have a majority in the house and thus have little ability to block legislation. Deadlocks of the kind seen recently in the U.S. Congress simply don't happen unless there is a minority government. The upper chamber, the House of Lords, has only limited ability to block legislation. It may pass amendments or delay legislation but not stop it entirely. The final step is *royal assent,* meaning the monarch signs the legislation (or, in countries like Canada, the representative of the monarch, the governor-general, signs).

The monarch has few powers other than to advise, and even that is severely restricted. The remaining powers are the rights to dismiss parliament, call for elections, appoint the prime minister, and withhold royal assent to any legislation. In practice, the monarch always appoints the leader of the winning party prime minister, dismisses parliament only when asked by the prime minister, and never withholds assent to legislation.

The Supreme Court in countries with a parliamentary system has the same role as that of the U.S. Supreme Court. It deals with issues of law that have significance to the country as a whole, usually based on constitutional interpretation. The major difference is that judges of the Supreme Course in parliamentary governments are appointed for life by the monarch on advice of the prime minister.

Other countries also have adapted the parliamentary system. Germany, for example, uses a similar form, but the monarch is replaced as head of state by an elected president, also a largely ceremonial position.

What is the major difference between the U.S. Congress and the British Parliament?

(A) The governing party in Britain usually has an absolute majority and can pass any legislation it wants.

(B) Members of the U.S. Congress are solely responsible for proposing legislation.

(C) Supreme Court judges are appointed for life.

(D) None of the above.

In Britain, the ruling party has an absolute majority in the House of Commons, so it can pass any legislation it wants. In the United States, power is often distributed fairly equally between the two parties, significantly restricting the power of any one party to pass legislation. In the U.S. Congress, the House of Representatives may pass a bill only to have the Senate vote against it. And even if a bill passes both the House and Senate, the president can veto it, in which case a two-thirds vote in both the House and Senate is required to override the veto. Choice (A) is the correct answer.

The presidential system

The *presidential system* (also known as the *congressional system*) has been adopted in many parts of the world, especially in the United States and Central and South America. Like the parliamentary system, the presidential system comprises three branches of government:

- ✔ **Legislative:** The *legislative branch,* which is responsible for writing laws (legislation), consists of the House of Representatives and the Senate, collectively referred to as *Congress.* The legislative branch also confirms or rejects presidential appointments and has the power to declare war.

  The House of Representatives is intended to represent the popular views, while the Senate protects states' rights to balance individual and state rights. In fact, prior to the 17th Amendment, senators were elected by state legislatures, not directly by the people of the state as they are now.

- ✔ **Executive:** The president, vice president, and their cabinet form the *executive branch* of government, which is responsible for executing the laws passed by Congress. (The president combines the role of head of state and head of government.) The president also serves as commander-in-chief of the armed forces.

- ✔ **Judicial:** The *judicial branch,* consisting of the Supreme Court and lower federal courts, is responsible for reviewing laws and has the power to change laws through its review process, typically with the goal of making sure the laws comply with the Constitution. The justices of the Supreme Court are nominated by the president and approved by the Senate. They serve for life unless they resign or are impeached. Justices have their own political views, which can make the confirmation process difficult, especially when the president is of one party and the other party forms the Senate majority.

The powers of each branch are fixed by the Constitution.

What are the two branches of Congress?

(A) the Cabinet and the Supreme Court

(B) the Supreme Court and the Senate

(C) the Senate and the House of Representatives

(D) the House of Commons and the Senate

The correct answer is Choice (C), the Senate and the House of Representatives. The cabinet and the Supreme Court are other branches of government, and Choice (D) refers to the Canadian parliamentary system.

Elections in the presidential system

Members of the legislative and executive branch are elected. The president and vice president are elected for four-year terms; senators, for six-year terms; and representatives, for 2-year terms. The president may only serve two terms, but all other elected members of government may run for reelection as often as they want. Senators are elected directly in the state they represent — two senators per state regardless of size of the state. Terms of office of the Senate are staggered; one-third of the Senate is elected every two years, at the same time as the voting for the House of Representatives takes place. Representatives are elected directly in 435 electoral districts.

Although citizens cast ballots for president and vice president, their votes are assigned to *electors* in each state that collectively make up the *Electoral College.* Each state has a pre-determined number of electors in the college based on population. Originally, the electors were leaders of their communities, citizens of standing and repute who were entrusted with the right to choose the president and vice president. They could choose at will from among the candidates. However, today's electors are bound to the candidates of one party or the other based on the popular vote in the state. As a result, a presidential candidate can win with fewer popular votes if he wins a majority of electoral votes.

At first glance, this election process seems convoluted, but the founding fathers feared that an uneducated electorate could run wild and elect a popular but unsuitable president. They were also concerned that the entire legislature and executive could be voted out at the same time, virtually overthrowing the entire government. That's also why only one-third of the Senate is elected at any one time.

Separation of powers and the system of checks and balances

Significant features of the U.S. presidential system are the separation of powers and the system of checks and balances. The *separation of powers* keeps the three branches of government separate to prevent any one individual or group from dominating the government. The *system of checks and balances* subjects any branch of government to the scrutiny of the other branches so that all branches are held accountable for their actions and no one branch can run roughshod over the country. The idea is to force all branches of the government to work with each other cooperatively by reaching reasonable compromises among differing political positions. Here are a few examples of checks and balances:

- ✔ The president can veto a law passed by Congress.
- ✔ Congress can override a president's veto with a two-thirds vote.
- ✔ The Supreme Court can declare a law passed by Congress unconstitutional.
- ✔ The president nominates justices for the Supreme Court, but Congress must approve.
- ✔ Congress can impeach justices and remove them from the Supreme Court.
- ✔ Congress can impeach the president and remove him from office.
- ✔ The House and Senate can veto each other's bills.

1. What is the point of the checks and balances system in American government?

    (A) It allows for the impeachment of presidents.

    (B) It ensures that the legislative branch of government remains dominant.

    (C) It prevents the Supreme Court from being governed by any one political party.

    (D) It prevents any one branch of government from dominating all government.

2. What effect does the system of checks and balances have on the presidential veto of a bill?

    (A) It prevents a presidential veto.

    (B) It enables the legislature to override a president's veto.

    (C) It allows the legislation to be sent to the Supreme Court for reconsideration.

    (D) It has no effect on the presidential veto.

3. How can the legislative branch overrule a presidential veto?

    (A) It can simply vote on and pass the same legislation by a majority vote.

    (B) The legislative branch can't overrule a presidential veto.

    (C) The legislature can pass the same legislation with a two-thirds majority vote.

    (D) The legislative branch can appeal to the Supreme Court to overrule the president.

Here are the answers.

1. The system of checks and balances is just that: It allows for a balance of power among the three branches of government and provides checks so that one branch can prevent overreach by another. Choices (A) and (C) are correct as statements but aren't the best answers. The only complete answer is Choice (D).

2. The system of checks and balances enables the legislature (Congress) to override a president's veto, Choice (B).

3. Choice (A) is only partially correct, while Choices (B) and (D) are wrong. The only correct answer is Choice (C); Congress can vote on the same legislation and pass it with a two-thirds majority.

Checking Out the Structure and Design of U.S. State Governments

The state governments are a step down from the federal government. Under the U.S. Constitution, states have the right to organize their administrations any way they like, but most follow a very similar pattern. Each has an executive branch headed by a governor, a legislative branch typically made up of an upper and lower chamber, and the judicial branch consisting of a state supreme court. It also has a state constitution, which is considered supreme in that state as long as the terms don't conflict with the U.S. Constitution.

State governors are directly elected (usually every four years by popular vote), along with a lieutenant governor, attorney general, and other cabinet positions. Their powers are largely similar to that of the president: to make appointments, veto legislation, and implement laws passed by the legislature. However, at the state level the executive branch has somewhat greater powers, including the power to prepare the state budget.

State legislatures also follow the federal pattern. With the exception of Nebraska, they all have two houses with members elected by direct election. In most states, the upper house is referred to as the senate and the lower house as the assembly. In most states, the lower house has a two-year term, while the upper house generally has a four-year term. These houses also may have term limits. For example, in California, legislators may serve no more than 12 years combined in both houses, but Texas has no term limits on either house.

The state supreme court justices are generally elected with terms of office ranging from 6 to 12 years. In several states, justices are appointed. For example, in New Hampshire, the governor appoints supreme court justices for life. In some states, supreme court justices run for election with party affiliations, while in other states the elections are nonpartisan. The state supreme courts function as appellate courts, hearing cases when lower courts may have made serious errors.

State governments also have some form of checks and balances. Governors can veto legislation, and legislatures can overrule those vetoes, for example. Usually the state judiciary doesn't play a role in this process.

A distinct division of powers exists between the federal government and state governments. The U.S. Constitution assigns the federal government responsibilities for foreign relations, war and peace, interstate commerce, and other enumerated powers. The state governments have responsibilities for education, the establishment of local governments, and commerce within the state. Both levels of government levy taxes, build highways, borrow money, and maintain law and order.

The federal Constitution also states that any powers not specifically granted to the federal government are delegated to state governments. This principle goes back in part to the idea that the United States was in fact at one time a group of individual, sovereign colonies that joined together to form one nation. Disputes often arise between the federal and state governments over jurisdiction, especially in areas where new technology has changed lives. Many issues that the founding fathers had never considered are now part of everyday life, engendering debates about which level of government should be responsible. A case in point is the regulation of broadcast frequencies and cellular telephones. Because they're not mentioned in the Constitution, some argue that states should have jurisdiction over broadcast frequencies and cellphones; however, because this issue has national and international impact, the federal government became the authority.

Who is the head of state at the state level of government?

(A) the governor

(B) the president

(C) the mayor

(D) the attorney general

The correct choice is Choice (A), the governor. All states refer to their head of state as the governor, assisted by a lieutenant governor. There is only one president, the head of the federal government. Though the attorney general is the head lawyer in a state, that doesn't make her the highest official in the state.

Understanding the Legislative Process

The legislative process consists of the steps required to pass a bill into law. Any member of the Senate or the House of Representatives can propose a bill, but party leaders typically introduce the bill. Often both chambers of Congress introduce similar bills at the same time. After the initial reading, a bill is referred to a committee (and perhaps a subcommittee), which reviews the legislation, makes amendments, and may request input from government agencies and the public. Committees can kill legislation by simply refusing to consider it.

After the committee approves a bill, it returns to its chamber of origin, where the Speaker of the House or the Senate Majority Leader schedules a debate and vote. They, too, can kill a bill simply by not scheduling it. After debate and possible further amendment, members of the chamber vote on the bill. If it passes and no similar bill is in the other chamber, the bill is sent to the other chamber, where it undergoes the same cycle of committee consideration, debate, and vote. If the other chamber passes the bill, it proceeds to the president, who can then sign the bill into law or veto it. If both the chambers pass similar bills, the legislation is then referred to the conference committee made up of members of both chambers. If that committee can reach a compromise on the content of the bill, it sends a report to both chambers outlining the agreement. That report, if approved, then goes to the president for approval.

If the president signs the bill, it becomes law. The president can also veto it, which returns it to the congressional body that originated it for a possible override vote. If Congress is in session and the president does nothing with the bill, it automatically becomes law after ten days. However, if Congress adjourns before the ten days pass, the bill dies.

1. Who can introduce a bill?

   (A) only a senator

   (B) any member of Congress

   (C) only a member of the House of Representatives

   (D) only the president

2. After either chamber of Congress passes a bill, it is sent to

   (A) committee for further review

   (B) the president to sign into law

   (C) the conference committee

   (D) the other chamber of Congress

Now check your answers.

1. The correct answer is Choice (B). Any member of Congress — House of Representatives or Senate — can introduce a bill.

2. After passing one chamber of Congress, the bill goes to the other chamber for review, debate, and vote, so Choice (D) is the correct answer. A bill must pass both chambers before proceeding to the president.

Contemplating Citizen Rights and Responsibilities

The theme of individual rights and freedoms has been part of American life since the Declaration of Independence. Thomas Jefferson, one of the authors of the U.S. Constitution, wanted specific guarantees for the rights of the individual. The first 10 amendments to the Constitution are known as the Bill of Rights. Those amendments detail the basic rights of all American citizens. The interpretation of some of these rights has changed over the years as the Supreme Court has been asked to interpret their meanings to the Constitution. The Supreme Court is the ultimate arbiter of that Bill of Rights as well as the Constitution.

Along with those rights come responsibilities of citizenship. Table 8-1 provides a good overview of citizen rights and responsibilities as presented by the U.S. Citizenship and Immigration Services.

Table 8-1	U.S. Citizen Rights and Responsibilities
Rights	*Responsibilities*
Freedom to express yourself.	Support and defend the Constitution.
Freedom to worship as you choose.	Stay informed of the issues affecting your community.
Right to a prompt, fair trial by jury.	Participate in the democratic process.
Right to vote in elections for public officials.	Respect and obey federal, state, and local laws.
Right to apply for federal employment requiring U.S. citizenship.	Respect the rights, beliefs, and opinions of others.

Rights	Responsibilities
Right to run for elected office.	Participate in your local community.
Freedom to enjoy "life, liberty, and the pursuit of happiness."	Pay income and other taxes honestly and on time to federal, state, and local authorities.
	Serve on a jury when called on.
	Defend the country if the need arises.

Source: www.uscis.gov/citizenship/learners/citizenship-rights-and-responsibilities

Some amendments in the Bill of Rights have a more immediate impact on citizens than others. The first amendment guarantees freedom of religion, speech, and assembly. The fourth amendment guarantees individuals rights to the security of their person, houses, papers, and effects. Government agencies may not conduct searches or seizures without warrants issued for probable cause. The fifth and sixth amendments deal with criminal prosecution, guaranteeing the right to "a speedy and public trial" and the right to confront accusers and see all evidence. It also guarantees the individuals rights against self-incrimination, the right to call witnesses on their behalves, and to the assistance of a lawyer if desired.

The second amendment is perhaps the most contentious:

Amendment II

A well regulated Militia, being necessary to the security of a free State, the right of the people to keep and bear Arms, shall not be infringed.

This article has been subject to frequent reinterpretation by the Supreme Court. It was once interpreted to mean that individuals who were members of a militia regulated by government had the right to keep and bear arms. Subsequent interpretations emphasize the "well regulated" part, allowing government to put strict regulation on firearm ownership. The current interpretation is that any individual has the right to keep and bear arms. Though individual states have some regulation on ownership, in most instances all individuals have the right to bear arms.

Subsequent amendments abolished slavery (13th Amendment), guaranteed the rights of all citizens to vote regardless of race, color, or "previous condition of servitude" (15th Amendment), established the direct election of senators by popular vote (17th Amendment), granted women the right to vote (19th Amendment), prohibited the sale and distribution of alcoholic beverages (18th Amendment, known as Prohibition), and repealed Prohibition (21st Amendment).

1. An amendment is a

    (A) modification of the U.S. Constitution

    (B) correction of the U.S. Constitution

    (C) statement of a citizen's rights and responsibilities

    (D) freedom granted to religious organizations

2. Why is the phrase "previous condition of servitude" included in the 15th Amendment?

    (A) to allow all people of color to exercise their right to vote

    (B) to allow former slaves to exercise their right to vote

    (C) to stop slaves from voting

    (D) none of the above

You want answers? Here you go:

1. An *amendment* is a modification to the U.S. Constitution (not to correct the Constitution but typically to clarify an issue that it doesn't address). The correct answer is Choice (A).

2. The phrase "previous condition of servitude" refers specifically to slavery, regardless of race or nationality, so Choice (B) is the best answer.

Looking Into Public Policy and Politics: Case Studies

If you've ever said, "the government should do something about . . ." you've begun to discuss public policy. The decision about the level of government intervention in any given issue in part depends on individual political views. Some people feel that government shouldn't be involved in the lives of people on a day-to-day basis; rather, individuals should take responsibility for their own lives. Others believe that not all individuals can cope with the challenges facing them and need help from government agencies. The decisions that all levels of government make become public policy.

Significant issues impact the lives of individuals and the country as a whole. These issues include policies regarding the death penalty, drug policy, gun control, economic affairs, and even environmental controls. The debate on these issues is in part controlled by the two political parties. Broadly speaking, the Republican Party tends to champion individual liberties and responsibilities, while the Democratic Party is more open to government interaction. However, these tendencies vary depending on the issue, and disagreements aren't always along party lines.

In the following sections, we explain how citizens influence public policy decisions, and look at two case studies of public policy issues.

Chiming in on public policy issues

In a representative democracy like that in the United States, citizens can't simply vote for the public policies they want. They must convince their representatives to sponsor legislation for those policies. To do so, citizens, including you, have the following options:

✔ **Vote.** You may not be able to vote for a specific policy, but you can support politicians who support the policy and perhaps work toward removing politicians who oppose it from office.

✔ **Write letters.** You can write letters to your representatives and to the president expressing your views on a particular issue or requesting support for a specific policy. All members of Congress and the president have websites where you can send an email message.

✔ **Circulate petitions.** Have people with similar interests sign a petition and send it to representatives in Congress and perhaps to the president to show that numerous people support or oppose a particular policy.

✔ **Make phone calls.** You can phone your representative to discuss issues personally.

✔ **Join/form a special-interest group.** Joining a special-interest group adds your voice to others, giving the group of people with shared interests more influence. Special-interest groups may be formed by individuals, businesses, or organizations with shared interests.

✔ **Hire a lobbyist.** Unions, businesses, and special-interest groups often hire lobbyists to speak with representatives on their behalves. Lobbyists often educate representatives about specific issues the representatives are unfamiliar with and may influence their decisions in the process.

✔ **Protest.** You can organize a protest in the hopes of popularizing your cause with the help of local and national media.

✔ **File a lawsuit against the government.** Thanks to the system of checks and balances, you may be able to change policy by suing the government. If your case manages to reach the Supreme Court and you're able to convince the justices, they could change a law that affects public policy.

Remember: Of course, certain approaches for changing public policy are illegal. Trespassing, destroying property, harming others, and other unlawful acts aren't permitted and typically do more harm than good in furthering a cause.

1. Why are citizens in the United States not allowed to vote on public policy issues?

   (A) The U.S. government is a popular democracy.

   (B) Only the president can change laws.

   (C) Only the Supreme Court can change laws.

   (D) The U.S. government is a representative democracy.

2. What is a special-interest group?

   (A) groups of companies pressuring governments into a certain direction

   (B) individuals wanting to promote an issue

   (C) organizations wanting to influence government decisions

   (D) all of the above

See how you fared.

1. The U.S. government is a representative democracy, meaning that citizens vote for candidates who serve as their representatives in formulating public policy. Choice (D) is the correct answer. There is an exception: Governments sometimes hold plebiscites, sometimes called initiatives, asking all citizens in a particular jurisdiction to vote on a specific issue, such as increased funding for education, legalizing marijuana, or building new public facilities.

2. The best answer is Choice (D), all of the above. Interest groups all want to influence governments at all levels. They can be companies, large organizations, or simply private citizens banded together for an issue.

Warming up to climate change

Public debate has been raging over whether climate change is real and to what extent humans are responsible for it. Environmental groups have long argued that this change is both real and caused to a large extent by human actions. The National Association of Manufacturers and the coal and oil industry associations are opposed to legislation restricting the burning of fossil fuels (coal, oil, and gas). In a recent poll, almost all Republican members of the federal legislature had expressed doubt about the reality of climate change. Yet polls show that over 70 percent of U.S. citizens believe climate change is happening, and more than 60 percent believe human activities are part of the cause. Democrats have supported some action on climate change, and in 2015, President Obama announced new reduction targets of some 26 percent of greenhouse gas emissions in the United States.

The support for such actions is split along party lines. The Republican Party and its supporters are generally opposed to legislation. A PEW Research poll in 2014 showed only 37 percent of Republicans agreed that solid evidence supported the existence of climate change, and only 25 percent agreed it's a major threat to the United States. Of Democrats polled, 79 agreed that the evidence of climate change is solid, and 68 saw it as a threat. Because any legislative action must pass Congress, these disagreements present a major stumbling block for any legislation attempting to reduce carbon emissions.

Which of the following scenarios would make legislation to curb carbon emissions most likely?

(A) 75 percent of voters support the legislation.

(B) The president supports the legislation.

(C) Over two-thirds of members in the House and Senate support the legislation.

(D) More than 50 percent of the representatives in Congress support the legislation.

The scenario most likely to result in the passing of legislation to curb carbon emissions is Choice (C). Even if the president vetoed such legislation, if over two-thirds in the House and Senate supported the legislation, they'd have enough votes to override the veto.

Entering the universal healthcare debate

Health insurance is another divisive public policy issue, and again, support is divided sharply along party lines. Since 2011, Congress has voted at least 60 times on legislation to rescind or limit the Affordable Care Act (ACA, sometimes known as Obamacare), all put forward by Republicans. None has survived. The divisions go further because in many states, Republican administrations have refused to work with the ACA and even refused funding to expand Medicare and Medicaid.

Finding accurate data on support and opposition is difficult. Only a slim majority seems opposed, but when you exclude older voters who wouldn't be covered by the ACA anyway, the vote is split evenly. According to a Bloomberg poll, only 35 percent say that the Affordable Care Act should be repealed. Other polls suggest that a majority are opposed to the ACA but also state that a portion of that opposition is there because the ACA doesn't go far enough.

A presidential candidate promises voters that if he gets elected, he will repeal the Affordable Care Act. Can he make good on that statement? Yes or No: [   ]

The correct answer is no. The U.S. Constitution doesn't give the president power to repeal or overturn laws. Only Congress and the Supreme Court can do so.

Chapter 9

Looking Back at U.S. History

∙∙∙

In This Chapter

▶ Examining U.S. documents from the past

▶ Considering the roots of the Revolutionary and Civil Wars

▶ Getting up to speed on the civil rights movement

▶ Examining the effects of European immigration on Native American populations

▶ Grasping the basics of isolationism, U.S. involvement in the world wars and the cold war, and U.S. foreign policy

∙∙∙

ou can study history using several approaches. The most common is chronologically, using a cause-and-effect approach. Sequences of events lead toward particular outcomes. It's a comfortable approach, providing lists of events in sequence and then pointing to an outcome as the result. Historians use this approach because it works.

A different approach is to study history thematically to focus on topics or themes for interaction rather than on chronologies. One model for this approach is the SPIRE model, an acronym for the five themes used:

✔ Social

✔ Political

✔ Intellectual

✔ Religious

✔ Economic

Though the impact of these five themes on historical events varies by event, they all contribute to a certain outcome. In this chapter, we don't follow the SPIRE model to the letter, but we do help you understand United States (U.S.) history by looking at it through a thematic lens. Along the way, we provide sample questions to help you retain your knowledge and insight.

Surveying Key U.S. Historical Documents

When studying for the history portion of the GED Social Studies test, familiarity with some of the most important historic documents in U.S. history is an important asset. Which are the most important is always a matter of opinion, and the selection here is arbitrary. You find extracts from the Declaration of Independence and the Bill of Rights, which built a foundation for the United States. The Emancipation Proclamation and the Gettysburg Address follow. The Supreme Court ruling on the *Plessy v. Ferguson* case extended racial inequality into the middle of the 20th century. In modern times, Wilson's Fourteen Points and the Truman Doctrine, which formulated some basic principles of American foreign policy, and the Marshall Plan, which rebuilt Europe after WWII, are important documents, while Martin Luther King's "I have a dream" speech and Lyndon Johnson's speech on the voting rights bill are important as representatives of an enduring issue in American social history.

This chapter presents extracts from most of these documents, but some you need to read elsewhere. Using your favorite online search engine, search for the name of the document or speech you're interested in reading, and the search results will contain numerous links to the work, along with commentary. One useful site is www.ushistory.org.

Answering questions in the history portion of the Social Studies GED exam requires close reading, along with the ability to extract key information and draw conclusions from what you read. For most people, reading the questions first and then the passages, looking for key words or ideas, works well. Some familiarity with the topics before the exam will help you work quickly, an asset on a timed test.

Investigating the Causes of America's Revolutionary War

America's Revolutionary War (also referred to as the American War of Independence or the American Revolution) was the armed conflict between Britain and the original 13 British colonies. The causes of the revolution in the American colonies create a rather neat chronology. The Declaration of Independence sums up the anger that built over time, which eventually led to the revolution. In the view of some American colonists, the abuses of power exceeded levels they could tolerate, and appeals to the monarch, King George III, brought no relief. It was the colonists' belief that they had no other option than to replace his government with one of their own choosing and design, as this extract from the Declaration of Independence reveals:

> . . . when a long train of abuses and usurpations, pursuing invariably the same Object evinces a design to reduce them under absolute Despotism, it is their right, it is their duty, to throw off such Government, and to provide new Guards for their future security. . . .

The rest of the declaration is a checklist of abuses. The events that led to the revolution are a chronology of British actions and increasing anger on the part of the colonists. The British had just finished a victorious but very expensive nine-year war against the French and the Native Americans. Their victory added all the territory that is now Ohio, Ontario, and Quebec to the empire. The British needed to cut costs. They expected the colonies to pay at least one-third of the cost of their defense. The British colonial office also wanted to maintain peace with the Native Americans and French settlers to reduce colonial defense costs. One way was a government prohibition (the Proclamation of 1763) on settlement beyond the Appalachian Mountains to preserve peace with the Native Americans.

However, the British government also needed to raise additional funds to pay for the defense of the colonies. Taxes in Britain were already high, so the colonies had to step up. The British government passed several pieces of legislation to raise money. The Revenue Acts (1764) and the Stamp Act (1765) implemented taxes, some of which British citizens had paid for years, on American colonists. When these failed to raise sufficient revenues, parliament passed the Townshend Act (1767), which added taxes on selected consumer goods, including tea. American colonists resented paying new taxes, a familiar theme to this day. They also resented the lack of consultation and lack of representation of colonial leaders in British Parliament.

Why would the colonists regard these measures as "a long train of abuse and usurpations"?

(A) They felt the defeated French were treated better than the American colonists.

(B) The British government did not consult the colonists before implementing taxes.

(C) The government prevented the westward expansion of the colonies into Native American lands.

(D) All of the above.

The correct answer is Choice (D), All of the above. The British allowed the conquered French to retain their language and continue the fur trade through their traditional territories. These were lands American colonists had been looking to as areas of expansion. The British government decided to raise taxes to pay for the defense of the colonies and certainly didn't ask the colonial governments for their approval or opinion. Although at this moment the British hadn't imposed a rigid ban on the westward expansion of the American colonies, it was discouraged. That too created friction between the British government and the American colonists.

Tensions between the British government and the colonists grew increasingly tense. A quarrel between some Bostonian pub-crawlers and off-duty British soldiers escalated into a riot. It was quickly brought under control, but 11 people were either dead or wounded. The event was a gold mine for the anti-British colonial patriots, who promptly labeled the event "the Boston Massacre."

Taxation continued to aggravate relations, especially a tax on tea. The colonists circumvented it by snuggling tea into the country. In 1773, the British East India Company brought large shipments of tea to Boston. Colonists had often prevented British tea from being sold, and in 1773, they again attacked and looted three British cargo ships, dumping their cargoes of tea into the Boston Harbor in the infamous Boston Tea Party.

British reaction was as expected: a crackdown on those unruly colonists. Ignoring colonial legislatures, British parliament passed a series of measures that the colonists called the Intolerable Acts in 1774. They temporarily closed the Boston port, prohibited colonial courts from trying British officials, gave British officials control over all town meetings, and revoked colonial charters. The Quartering Act allowed the forcible *quartering* (housing) British soldiers in private colonial homes. The final straw was the Quebec Act of 1774, which defined the boundaries of the new province of Quebec and extended rights to the conquered French that were denied to the American colonists.

From that point, a revolution was almost inevitable, even though only about a third of the colonists actually supported independence. Another third considered themselves loyal to Britain. The remaining third just wanted to be left alone.

Based on the text, what was the most important reason for the American Revolution?

(A) subversion of the colonial justice system

(B) the Tea Tax

(C) the Proclamation Act

(D) all taxation without representation

The colonists who wanted independence were most upset about the imposition of taxes without consultation. The British parliament rejected requests by colonial leaders for representation in Parliament. Taxes were imposed without consultation of the colonial legislatures. Although Choice (B) the tea tax was a major irritant, as were the subversion of colonial courts (Choice (A)) and the Proclamation Act (Choice (C)), it was the total taxation issue, Choice (D), that underlay all the colonial anger.

Covering the Causes of the Civil War

No war — civil, revolutionary, or international — is ever based on a single reason. The Civil War the United States fought in the 1860s was never merely a war over slavery or the emancipation of slaves. Other issues contributed, including social, political, intellectual, religious, and political ones, which makes the SPIRE model a useful tool for studying the causes of the Civil War.

The key issue in the Civil War was the end of slavery, but slavery wasn't just a moral issue; it was also an economic and social one for some, and an intellectual and religious one for others, all of which combined into the political issues that led to the war.

Here, we use the SPIRE model to look at the various factors that contributed to causing the Civil War, but in a slightly different sequence starting with economics.

Economics

By the 1820s, the northern states were developing into an urban, industrial society. Factories produced an array of consumer and industrial goods and needed certain economic policies to sustain their growth. Northern industrialists were competing with imported goods for the domestic market. Their concern with protecting their markets from imports led for a push for import duties and restrictions on trade.

The southern states were a largely agrarian society, more and more focused on the production of cotton. That required large estates and cheap labor (slaves) and cheap imported goods. The southern states enjoyed great wealth from cotton exports. Maintaining open and free trade was a key economic concern. Slaves had become an increasingly valuable commodity, especially since Congress had banned the importation of slaves in 1808.

One measure of the difference in economic development was the railway system. The northern states had a unified system with some 22,000 miles of track, while the South had barely 9,000 miles, split even further by incompatible tracks and lack of investment in new equipment.

How would the rail systems make a statement about economic development?

(A) Businesspeople of the day preferred trains to stagecoaches.

(B) Railways were a status symbol of strong economies.

(C) The disparity in the rail systems reflected uneven economic development.

(D) The South could not afford railways.

The measurable difference in rail system development demonstrates the disparity in the level of industrial development between North and South, which reflects a potential point of contentions over economic strength. Although Choices (A), (B), and (D) are all partially true, Choice (C) is the most complete answer.

Social

The difference in the economic base also produced social differences. By the 1850s, the cost of a slave was so high that the slaves on most plantations were worth more than the entire estate. The South developed a wealthy elite, a plantation-owning aristocracy resting on a pinnacle of slave labor. This wealth produced a brilliant society and elegant cities. Beautiful Charleston is but one example. Southerners were also very aware of the fragility of their social pyramid, and the resulting political goals were all about preserving that society, which meant preserving slavery. At the same time, a new generation of leaders was coming up in the South, proud and increasingly southern nationalists. They were less willing to compromise and more ready to consider secession.

Religious and intellectual

Many religious leaders in northern states were *abolitionists* (those who supported ending slavery). Southern churches supported slavery and promoted the concept of white racial superiority, of which slavery was a natural outcome. Alexander Stephens, who became vice president of the Confederate States of America, stated the following:

> [Our] foundations are laid, its cornerstone rests, upon the great truth that the Negro is not equal to the white man; that slavery, subordination to the superior race is his natural and normal condition.

For many in northern states, ending slavery became a moral issue. Didn't the Constitution state that all men were created equal? Legislation to forcibly return escaped slaves caught in northern states (the Fugitive Slave Act of 1850) to their southern owners exacerbated problems. Books such as Harriet Beecher Stowe's *Uncle Tom's Cabin* and works by Frederick Douglass, an escaped slave, further fueled the moral anger against slavery.

Politics

The concerns we outline in the preceding sections demanded solutions, which moved the issue into the political sphere. Maintaining slavery was a political issue because Congress could vote to restrict or abolish slavery. The result was the formation of voting blocs: one of southern slave states and one of northern free states. Congress had a balance between senators from states supporting slavery and the southern cotton industry and senators from northern states that wanted higher tariffs and the abolition or limitation of slavery.

This balance itself became an issue because any change in voting power would affect the economy and slavery. A pattern was set in 1820 with the Missouri Compromise, when Missouri was admitted into the Union as a slave state. To balance voting power, Maine was admitted at the same time as a free state, and slavery was banned on western lands north of the northern borders of present-day Oklahoma, New Mexico, and Arizona, extending west. The issue arose again when the United States added new territories after a victory over Mexico in 1848. An agreement, the Compromise of 1850, tried to maintain a balance between the two competing interests. California was admitted as a free state but had to guarantee to support a stronger fugitive slave law.

When Congress passed the fugitive slave laws, requiring all free states to return escaped slaves to their owners, abolitionists were furious, and the antislavery campaign received tremendous new support. The Dredd Scott decision of 1857 added to that anger; the Supreme Court ruled that blacks could never be citizens. The court then went on to rule that the federal government had no authority to prohibit slavery in lands that hadn't yet become states or decide on the status of slavery on their lands.

Why would a rule requiring the returning of fugitive slaves to their owners be a huge political issue?

(A) Citizens who refused to assist in the recovery of fugitive slaves could be prosecuted.

(B) There were organizations dedicated to helping slaves escape, increasing potential for conflict.

(C) The struggle of escaped slaves became symbolic of the entire slavery issue.

(D) All of the above.

The best answer is Choice (D), All of the above, because all the other answer choices are correct. The Underground Railroad, books by escaped slaves, and opposition from abolitionists all focused attention on the efforts to recapture slaves and return them to their owners. For the South, the return of escaped slaves was also a huge issue because slaves were worth large sums of money. Twenty slaves were worth as much as an entire cotton plantation, and because of the ban on importing slaves from Africa, prices had continued to climb.

Either political issues are settled or they explode. This issue exploded. When the Kansas territories (which were north of the line set by the Missouri Compromise) were considered for admission, the 1854 Kansas-Nebraska Act left the slavery decision to the settlers. Settlers were allowed to bring their property with them, and many brought slaves. The settlers elected a proslavery territorial government, resulting in many pitched battles between supporters and opponents of slavery. Abolitionists including John Brown brought their private militias to confront proslavery groups. The violence continued right into the outbreak of the Civil War.

The entire issue then peaked with the elections of 1860. Abraham Lincoln headed the new Republican Party, solidly in favor of abolition. Lincoln won most northern and western states but not a single southern state. The southern states decided to *secede,* leaving the Union and, that same year, forming the Confederate States of America. An attack by Confederate forces on a Union fort, Fort Sumter, triggered the war.

One key document for this period is the Emancipation Proclamation, which Lincoln issued January 1, 1863. After designating the affected territories, the proclamation states the following:

> . . . I do order and declare that all persons held as slaves within said designated States, and parts of States, are, and henceforward shall be free; and that the Executive government of the United States, including the military and naval authorities thereof, will recognize and maintain the freedom of said persons.

> And I hereby enjoin upon the people so declared to be free to abstain from all violence, unless in necessary self-defence; and I recommend to them that, in all cases when allowed, they labor faithfully for reasonable wages.

> And I further declare and make known, that such persons of suitable condition, will be received into the armed service of the United States to garrison forts, positions, stations, and other places, and to man vessels of all sorts in said service. . . .

The Emancipation Proclamation freed slaves in designated territories, the Confederate states, but not the rest of the country. Why?

(A) The emancipation was intended to interfere with the southern war effort.

(B) Lincoln wanted continuing support from abolitionists who were pressuring him.

(C) Lincoln hoped freed slaves would join the Union army.

(D) All of the above.

The Emancipation Proclamation spelled out that only slaves in Confederate states were to be freed and that all suitable persons would be received in the armed services. Therefore, Choices (A) and (C) are correct. Even if you didn't know for sure, you could assume that Lincoln wanted to retain the support of the abolitionists, Choice (B). The best choice is Choice (D), All of the above.

Delving into Key Issues in the Civil Rights Movement

The end of the Civil War didn't grant equality to black Americans. When the state legislatures resumed their work, they introduced new legislation based on the old black codes, severely limiting black rights. Slaves had been freed, but they were no freer.

The immediate effect was to restrict blacks' voting rights. Poll taxes, literacy tests, and other measures made voting extremely difficult. Other restrictions created the segregationist South that survived until the 1960s. Legislation such as the Civil Rights Act of 1875 granted all people the right to "the full and equal enjoyment of any of the accommodations, advantages, facilities, and privileges of inns, public conveyances on land or water, theaters and other places of public amusement; subject only to the conditions and limitations established by law, and applicable alike to citizens of every race and color." Unfortunately, the law was rarely enforced and was often subverted. Schools and public facilities were divided into white and nonwhite, and private businesses simply refused to serve blacks. When segregation was appealed *(Plessy v. Ferguson),* the Supreme Court ruled in 1896 that segregation was legal as long as facilities for black and whites were equal (separate but equal). Of course, in practice, schools, hospitals, and other facilities for blacks were never equal to those for whites.

The ruling stated the following in part:

> Legislation is powerless to eradicate racial instincts, or to abolish distinctions based upon physical differences, and the attempt to do so can only result in accentuating the difficulties of the present situation. If the civil and political rights of both races be equal, one cannot be inferior to the other civilly or politically. If one race be inferior to the other socially, the constitution of the United States cannot put them upon the same plane.

It further ruled that segregation laws are state laws and don't fall under federal jurisdiction. That enabled the Jim Crow laws of the southern states to continue until the 1960s. Some laws even became more severe, such as a 1924 Virginia Racial Integrity Law that defined *nonwhite* as anyone with any nonwhite ancestors, no matter how far back, and made marriage between whites and nonwhites a criminal offence.

The issue of voting rights is a theme throughout the period of 1900 to today. The federal courts overruled state legislation restricting voting rights, and state legislatures implemented restrictions such as literacy tests and *gerrymandering* (manipulation of voting district boundaries to favor one party or class over another). The Civil Rights Act of 1964 finally ended segregation and state efforts to prevent blacks from voting. However, voting rights continued to be undermined. New legislation to strengthen voting rights followed. Initiated by John F. Kennedy and championed by Lyndon B. Johnson, the legislation finally became law when LBJ was president. Former President Johnson echoes Martin Luther King Jr., using the phrase "we shall overcome," in urging Congress to approve this legislation:

> Many of the issues of civil rights are very complex and most difficult. But about this there can and should be no argument. Every American citizen must have an equal right to vote. There is no reason which can excuse the denial of that right. There is no duty which weighs more heavily on us than the duty we have to ensure that right.

> Yet the harsh fact is that in many places in this country men and women are kept from voting simply because they are Negroes.

> Every device of which human ingenuity is capable has been used to deny this right. The Negro citizen may go to register only to be told that the day is wrong, or the hour is late, or the official in charge is absent. And if he persists, and if he manages to present himself to the registrar, he may be disqualified because he did not spell out his middle name or because he abbreviated a word on the application.

> And if he manages to fill out an application he is given a test. The registrar is the sole judge of whether he passes this test. He may be asked to recite the entire Constitution, or explain the most complex provisions of State law. And even a college degree cannot be used to prove that he can read and write.

> For the fact is that the only way to pass these barriers is to show a white skin.

> Experience has clearly shown that the existing process of law cannot overcome systematic and ingenious discrimination. No law that we now have on the books — and I have helped to put three of them there — can ensure the right to vote when local officials are determined to deny it.

> In such a case our duty must be clear to all of us. The Constitution says that no person shall be kept from voting because of his race or his color. We have all sworn an oath before God to support and to defend that Constitution. We must now act in obedience to that oath. . . .

> This great, rich, restless country can offer opportunity and education and hope to all — all black and white, all North and South, sharecropper and city dweller. These are the enemies — poverty, ignorance, disease — they are our enemies, not our fellow man, not our neighbor. And these enemies too — poverty, disease, and ignorance — we shall overcome.

The passage of the Voting Rights Act in 1965 worked: Black voter registration increased by over 50 percent. Today, civil rights issues revolve around institutional treatment of nonwhites. The focus is on police treatment of minorities and the institutional racism they represent. There are also attempts to remove protections from voting rights legislation (you can see President Obama's speech in Selma at www.c-span.org/video/?c4530514/president-obama-speech-selma-march-50th-anniversary).

If the Civil Rights Act of 1875 guaranteed all people full and equal rights to access public facilities, accommodations, and transportation, why did segregation happen and last until the 1960s?

(A) The legislation was ruled unconstitutional in 1887.

(B) Enforcement was left to the states.

(C) Racism continued, regardless of legislation.

(D) The Supreme Court argued segregation was acceptable if facilities offered were equal.

The legislation wasn't ruled unconstitutional, so Choice (A) is wrong. Choices (B) and (C) are correct but give only partial answers. The best choice is Choice (D). The Supreme Court ruled that it could not legislate equality and that as long as facilities were of equal quality and accessibility, they satisfied the Civil Rights Act.

Exploring European Settlement and the Native Population of the Americas

The European settlement of North America profoundly changed the lives of Native Americans. The French came in the 1500s, mainly to trade, and had relatively peaceful relations with the Algonquin tribes around the Great Lakes and lands stretching to Ohio, Wisconsin, and Illinois. The English came in the 1600s to settle. They settled in lands that became known as the 13 colonies, and over time the English displaced the natives as settlers took over the lands they wanted.

The European ability to push natives aside rested on two factors: disease and guns. Europeans brought with them smallpox, measles, cholera, diphtheria, and many other diseases. Natives had no previous exposure to these diseases, and so no immunity; their populations were decimated by repeated epidemics. The natives had no firearms, and bows and spears were no match for the flintlocks and other firearms the Europeans had. In battles where natives had no firearms, the Europeans generally won. However, that advantage was lost when natives acquired these goods through trade.

Initial contact with the English settlers and natives was also cordial. The settlers needed help. Most were the disenfranchised of England, poor rabble and refugees of persecution. They had little knowledge of farming or hunting and depended on the natives, who taught them the skills they needed to survive. Captain John Smith's Virginia colony survived only because the local tribe sent food. However, as the colonies expanded inland, contact became hostile, especially over the concept of land ownership. The natives considered all land communal property, and although they were willing to share, they could not accept the European idea of land ownership.

The Vikings tried to settle in North America well before the Spanish, French, or English. They too were met by the local natives. After only a few years, the Vikings abandoned their settlements in the face of native hostility. Why might the Vikings have fared worse than the later Europeans?

(A) The level of technology of the Vikings was not much higher than that of the Native Americans. They both fought mainly with spears and bows.

(B) The natives were resistant to diseases the Vikings carried.

(C) The local environment was not suitable for Viking settlement.

(D) The Vikings just decided to return home.

The correct answer is Choice (A). The first contact between Vikings and the local Native Americans very quickly turned hostile. Because the Vikings didn't have any great technological advantage and were far fewer in number, they could not resist the natives' attacks and decided to abandon their settlement.

Many Native American tribes allied with the French before the American Revolution. The French had generally left native lands alone because their primary focus was on the fur trade. After the defeat of the French and the coming of the American Revolution, many tribes, especially the Iroquois, sided with the British. They argued that the British had done much to keep settler spread into Native American lands to a minimum and hoped to preserve their lands against colonial expansion. For the same reasons, they supported the British again during the War of 1812, where the American military feared them more than they did the British or Canadian forces. The Iroquois, more than British soldiers, prevented Americans from conquering Canada.

As the settlers prospered, they needed more lands, and a cycle of conflict started. Successive wars with the Native Americans led to massacres, both of colonists and Native Americans. Natives made agreements with colonial governments to give up lands to the settlers in return of guarantees that their other territories would be left alone and settlers would not move into new territories. After a few years, when the settlers needed more lands, they again invaded Native American territories, and after a brief conflict, new treaties were signed and the process began over again. Native Americans also lost their reservations, pressured by state governments to leave, opening the land for settlement. Few reservations guaranteed by various treaties survived the original 13 colonies.

Understanding Isolationism and the U.S. Role in World Wars I and II

Americans have always been split between isolationism and interventionism. For many, the conflicts in other parts of the world mattered little. They overwhelmingly felt that those conflicts were of no concern to them and had no impact on life in America. In his 1796 Farewell Address, George Washington said, "The great rule for us in regard to foreign nations is . . . to have with them as little political connection as possible. . . . It is our true policy to steer clear of permanent alliances with any portion of the foreign world." That remained the basic view of most Americans. As World War I broke out in Europe, President Woodrow Wilson declared neutrality but allowed trade and commerce with both sides. Both Germany and Britain tried to change American opinion. The British made great propaganda out of the brutality of German soldiers invading Belgium and France, but despite the anti-German feelings, the U.S. remained neutral. In 1916, Wilson won reelection, running on the slogan "He Kept Us Out Of War."

Americans were allowed to trade with both sides of the conflict, which created the problems that ended American neutrality. Britain faced American anger in 1915 when it began seizing American ships and cargoes bound for Germany. Wilson's government protested but did little more. German actions provided more cause for anger. When the British blockaded German ports, the Germans retaliated by declaring the waters around Britain a war zone, where all merchant ships were subject to attack. Wilson's response was to declare that America would hold Germany strictly responsible for any American loss of life. German U-boats launched a major campaign against Allied shipping, hoping to stifle trade with Britain. The first major casualty was the sinking of the *Lusitania,* a British liner carrying American passengers bound for England, in 1915. Hit by German torpedoes, the ship sank in only 15 minutes, drowning hundreds of passengers, including 128 Americans. American pressure forced Germany to agree to end unrestricted submarine warfare but had little other effect. The German government justified the attack and pointed out how quickly the ship sank, arguing it proved the Lusitania was carrying war materials, which violated law.

How did the sinking of the *RMS Lusitania* affect American neutrality?

(A) It outraged Americans but made little difference.

(B) It directly led to the selling of war material to Britain.

(C) The U.S. agreed to take on an antisubmarine campaign on the Atlantic.

(D) Wilson asked Congress to declare war on Germany.

The only answer supported by the text is Choice (A). The loss of the *Lusitania* changed nothing with regard to the selling of war materials or active American participation in the war. Certainly, Wilson didn't ask Congress to declare war.

Why were the Germans unable to take advantage of the American willingness to sell to both sides in the conflict?

(A) They could not afford the prices American business was demanding.

(B) The German merchant fleet was not big enough.

(C) The Royal Navy managed to intercept most German vessels.

(D) The Germans did not need American supplies.

The Germans certainly needed and could afford American war materials, so Choices (A) and (D) are wrong. The German fleet may have been large enough, but that wasn't a primary concern, so Choice (B) is also incorrect. The best answer supported by the text is Choice (C). The Royal Navy managed to control all traffic flowing to German ports and capture or sink most German merchant vessels.

American neutrality ended because of two German actions. The first was the Zimmerman Telegram, intercepted by British intelligence. It proposed an alliance between Mexico, Japan, and Germany for the purpose of attacking the United States to (re)gain territory: Mexico, lost lands in the southern United States; Japan, the West Coast; and Germany, the Atlantic regions. When Germany restarted unrestricted submarine warfare, the American public was convinced that war was the only alternative. On April 2, 1917, Wilson appeared before Congress, which approved a declaration of war against Germany.

Few American troops saw combat in Europe in any real strength before 1918. The immediate flow of war materials was far more important. However, as a morale booster, their arrival was of major significance to the Europeans, and as American soldiers gained experience, their impact on the front increased. By September 1918, some 500,000 Americans were on the front lines, taking part in several major battles, including the second battle of the Marne, as the war came to an end.

The isolationist movement returned even more strongly after WWI, so strongly in fact that Wilson lost his efforts to have Congress ratify the Treaty of Versailles. America was the only major country that didn't sign the treaty. Isolationism was promoted by many organizations in the United States, such as the Women's International League. They had some major successes, including the Pact of Paris (the Kellogg-Briand Pact), in which Japan, Great Britain, and the United States agreed to reduce the size of their navies. Isolationist pressure also resulted in the passing of a series of Neutrality Acts designed to keep America out of any future wars. They aimed to counter business pressure to sell to any country, even countries at war. In their view, that trade was part of the reason America was pulled into the First World War. The new legislation prohibited such sales but, after 1939, also made helping Great Britain against Nazi Germany difficult.

President Franklin Delano Roosevelt (FDR) wasn't an isolationist. When Japan attacked China in 1937, he didn't proclaim the Neutrality Acts. China was able to continue obtaining war material from the United States. He also made the famous quarantine speech suggesting aggressor nations should be isolated, but he faced a strong backlash from isolationists.

That isolationist sentiment and the Neutrality Acts didn't unravel until November 1939, when Congress passed a further neutrality act that allowed sales of arms on a cash-and-carry basis. Because Germany was largely unable to safely transport goods across the Atlantic to Germany, this legislation was a large benefit to Britain. When Britain ran out of money to pay for supplies, FDR instituted the lend-lease program, trading military bases for supplies, or simply "renting" them to Britain. When German submarines again began taking a toll on shipping, he authorized the U.S. Navy to attack Axis warships without an actual declaration of war. FDR's State of the Union address in January 1941 stated:

> . . . by an impressive expression of the public will and without regard to partisanship, we are committed to full support of all those resolute peoples, everywhere, who are resisting aggression and are thereby keeping war away from our hemisphere. By this support, we express our determination that the democratic cause shall prevail; and we strengthen the defense and the security of our own nation.

America didn't enter the Second World War for more than two years, and then only after an attack by the Japanese on U.S. naval holdings at Pearl Harbor. America was largely preoccupied by the War in the Pacific, which turned into a battle between the American and Japanese navies fought with aircraft carrier and submarine attacks that finally turned into a savage ground war as marines and army personnel cleared one Japanese-occupied island after another. Often these battles were bloody, with horrendous casualties on all sides. Major victories such as those at the Battle of Midway and in Guadalcanal turned the tide against Japan, but the casualties convinced President Harry Truman (FDR's successor) and the Pentagon to use the atomic bomb on Japan rather than risk an invasion of the main Japanese islands.

What was the main reason for the use of the atomic bomb on Japan?

(A) The U.S. government feared heavy casualties in invading the Japanese mainland.

(B) The U.S. government wanted proof the bombs worked.

(C) The Pentagon wanted a quick end to the war.

(D) The military thought it was just a big bomb; no one knew about radiation hazards.

Choices (B) and (D) are possible answers, but the text doesn't support them. Choice (C) is certainly true but isn't the best answer. Choice (A) is your best answer based on the discussion of heavy casualties in the Pacific war.

Tracing the Origins and Outcomes of the Cold War

As World War II was ending, the Allies worried about the USSR's intentions toward Eastern Europe. Harry Truman, the new president of the United States, took a personal dislike to Joseph Stalin, leader of the USSR. The Four Powers — the USSR, the United States, Great Britain, and France — met at the Potsdam conference in 1945 to work out the future of Europe and relations among the four countries. The western Allies were seriously worried about Russia's intentions in the occupied territories of Eastern Europe. At the conference, the USSR refused to guarantee free elections in the Eastern European countries they had occupied. Truman and British Prime Minister Winston Churchill were convinced the Soviets were preparing to overrun the rest of Europe. But there was plenty of suspicion to go around. The Soviets were worried about the Allies' objectives. Twice the Soviets had been invaded from western Europe, and they wanted to ensure that it couldn't happen again. They created puppet states in their occupied Eastern European countries and used them as buffer states against any possible invasion. They were also worried about the American atomic bomb and had started a massive program to develop their own. Any efforts at cooperation ceased, and what became known as the Iron Curtain (a name Churchill popularized) descended from the Baltic Sea to the Mediterranean Sea, separating Eastern Europe from the West. In 1947, Truman learned that the British could no longer afford to send aid to

Greece and Turkey, who were fighting a communist-backed insurrection. He recommended, with this speech to Congress, that the United States approve aid to those countries:

> . . . At the present moment in world history nearly every nation must choose between alternative ways of life. The choice is too often not a free one. One way of life is based upon the will of the majority, and is distinguished by free institutions, representative government, free elections, guarantees of individual liberty, freedom of speech and religion, and freedom from political oppression. The second way of life is based upon the will of a minority forcibly imposed upon the majority. It relies upon terror and oppression, a controlled press and radio, fixed elections, and the suppression of personal freedoms. I believe that it must be the policy of the United States to support free peoples who are resisting attempted subjugation by armed minorities or by outside pressures. I believe that we must assist free peoples to work out their own destinies in their own way. I believe that our help should be primarily through economic stability and orderly political process. . . .

The policy he proposed became known as the Truman Doctrine. It formed the basis of American foreign policy for the next three decades. Wherever countries needed help to oppose Soviet domination, Americans would be prepared to send aid, both financial and military.

Truman's Secretary of State, George C. Marshall, introduced an economic aid program to send billions of dollars to help the western European economies. That included aid to western-occupied Germany, which had been forcibly separated from the Soviet-occupied portion. That led to the first outright confrontation between the western Allies and the Soviets. On April 1, 1948, the Soviets blocked all ground access to West Berlin, hoping that the western Allies would abandon West Berlin and allow the Soviets to take over. The Allies responded with the Berlin Airlift, which for over a year flew in supplies for the entire population of West Berlin, including food, coal, and all the other necessities of life. On May 12, 1949, the Soviets reopened the roads. Shortly thereafter, West Berlin and Ally-occupied Western Germany were united to create the Federal Republic of West Germany.

Truman refers to the USSR in his speech without ever mentioning the country by name. What evidence from the passage supports this conclusion?

(A) his description of a minority imposing its will on the majority

(B) references to terror and suppression

(C) statements about fixed elections and subjugation by outside pressures

(D) all of the above

Each of the answer choices is correct regarding the regimes imposed by the Soviets on the countries they liberated from Nazi rule, so Choice (D) is the best answer. Making pointed comments about a specific individual or country without ever mentioning it by name is a common tactic in political diplomacy. By this time, the public certainly knew what methods the Soviets were using to impose their will on occupied territories.

Confrontation between the Soviets and the western Allies continued. The Soviets managed to develop their own atomic bomb, and Americans and Soviets built up vast arsenals of weapons, aircraft, and missiles. The European Allies, the United States, and Canada formed NATO, a military alliance, to contain the Soviet threat. The Soviets retaliated by creating the Warsaw Pact, an alliance of Eastern European nations and the USSR. Further confrontations followed. Some were wars that involved direct confrontations with Soviet or American forces, and others were *proxy wars,* where the two powers backed others in conflict on their behalf. Both the Soviets and the Americans aided revolutions in other countries to support or fight against communist rebels.

The war in Korea was a direct conflict, although the Soviets' actual participation was very limited. The Soviets had occupied the northern half of Korea after the surrender of Japan. They refused to allow democratic elections in the north and instead created their own North Korean Republic. The United States supported the government of South Korea, and the peninsula was divided. In 1950, North Korea invaded the south, and United Nations forces were sent to repel the invasion. Canada, the United States, Great Britain, and countries as far away as Australia, New Zealand, and Colombia all sent forces to fight the invasion. After several years of bloody fighting, an armistice was reached in July 1953. That armistice line continues to this day.

The war in Angola was a proxy war in which Soviets used Cuban forces to aid communist rebels and Americans provided funds and weapons to the other side.

EXAMPLE
EXAM

What is a *proxy war?*

(A) a war between two major powers

(B) a war between major powers fought in another country

(C) a colonial war

(D) a war in which major countries confront each other without taking part in the actual combat

A proxy war certainly involves two major powers and is usually fought in another country; it can be a colonial war but doesn't have to be. Therefore, Choices (A), (B), and (C) are all partially correct. However, the best answer is Choice (D), a war between major powers who use others to fight for them.

The most serious confrontation, one that almost led to a nuclear war, was the Cuban Missile Crisis of 1962. Fidel Castro, a young Cuban communist, had led a successful revolution against the corrupt leader of Cuba, establishing the first communist country in the Western Hemisphere. Concern about the close relationship between Cuba and the Soviets led the United States to break off relationships with Cuba and establish a total embargo. In October 1962, American spy planes photographed what appeared to be Soviet missile installations in Cuba and then discovered Soviet freighters on their way to Cuba with what appeared to be missiles as deck cargo. The missiles of the day didn't have intercontinental range yet, so placing missiles close to America was a significant new threat. Missiles launched from Cuba could reach most of the United States, Central America, and parts of Canada.

When the Soviets ignored initial demands that the missiles be removed, President John F. Kennedy was under extreme pressure from his military advisors and some cabinet members to launch an all-out missile attack on the Soviets. Kennedy ordered a naval blockade of Cuba, and the Soviet freighters responded by slowing their progress toward the island. Kennedy resisted calls to bomb the missile sites in Cuba and instead confronted Soviet leader Nikita Khrushchev directly. In a series of telegrams and telephone calls, Khrushchev first offered to remove the missiles in return for a promise that America would not invade Cuba. He then sent a second, tougher message, offering to remove the missiles only if the United States removed its missiles on the Soviet border with Turkey. Kennedy publicly accepted the first offer, and privately agreed to the second message as well. They avoided a nuclear war.

Other confrontations between America and the Soviet Union continued, culminating in the savage war in Vietnam. The Vietnam War was devastating for the United States, both in terms of casualties and economic burden. President Nixon finally withdrew U.S. forces from Vietnam, but America struggled with a massive debt and rampant inflation. However, the arms race was also taking its toll on the Soviet economy. Estimates suggest that the Soviets allocated almost half of their annual budget to defense and the arms race. They invaded

Afghanistan in 1979, and the Americans fought a proxy war there by supporting the Taliban. The Soviets eventually gave up in 1989 and withdrew. During the Reagan administration, the United States rapidly increased its military spending, forcing the Soviets to spend vast sums they didn't have to keep up. The economic burden was too great for the Soviets and ultimately resulted in the end of the cold war.

Soviet President Mikhail Gorbachev had to deal with the economic fallout. The average Soviet citizens were resentful of the sacrifices, especially when they could see that the other Eastern European countries were offering their citizens a better life. Gorbachev introduced some liberal reforms, but that merely increased unrest. The Eastern European countries also created difficulties, exerting their independence again. In 1989, Lithuania declared independence from the Soviet Union, and Poland had its first free elections. That summer, thousands of people began to flee from East Germany. Later that year, the East Germans had their first free elections since WWII, and in 1990, East and West Germany were reunited. On December 25, 1991, the USSR ceased to exist. Russia and the republics that made up the USSR became independent countries.

How did the arms race end the cold war?

(A) The technology became too dangerous.

(B) The United Nations enforced disarmament agreements.

(C) The high cost led to unrest that caused the Soviet Union to collapse.

(D) The U.S. and USSR agreed to end the arms race.

The technology war certainly dangerous — so dangerous that the acronym for the arms race became MAD (mutually assured destruction) because both sides had more than enough nuclear weapons to utterly destroy the other. The consequences of a war using atomic weapons were simply terrifying. There were disarmament agreements, but the UN had nothing to do with them; they were agreements between the USSR and the United States, but only to limit, not to end, the arms race. So Choices (A), (B), and (D) are all wrong. The only correct choice is Choice (C) because the high cost of the arms race led to unrest among Russians, leading to the collapse of the Soviet government and the dissolution of the USSR.

Probing Shifts in U.S. Foreign Policy Since 9/11

American foreign policy after WWII was largely dominated by the Truman Doctrine, supported by both Democrats and Republicans, which was focused on the containment of Soviet expansionism. President Reagan, a staunch conservative, even negotiated a nuclear disarmament treaty with the Soviets. However, that doctrine died along with the Soviet Union. New issues arose in the Middle East, especially involving Saddam Hussein in Iraq and the U.S.-backed Taliban who had defeated the Soviets in Afghanistan. A more conservative view of politics became dominant, one that argued the United States shouldn't compromise with its enemies. The first example of that policy in action was the first Gulf War, (1990–1991) when the United States and many other nations including Great Britain and France invaded Iraq. More significant changes came after September 11, 2001. Americans hadn't experienced attacks on their homeland since Pearl Harbor. The events of 9/11 were a major shock. President George W. Bush outlined what would become known as the Bush Doctrine, the new approach to American foreign relations.

On September 18, 2001, Congress passed a joint resolution granting the president the right to use force against other nations and groups without a declaration of war (from www.govtrack.us/congress/bills/107/sjres23/text):

> . . . That the President is authorized to use all necessary and appropriate force against those nations, organizations, or persons he determines planned, authorized, committed, or aided the terrorist attacks that occurred on September 11, 2001, or harbored such organizations or persons, in order to prevent any future acts of international terrorism against the United States by such nations, organizations or persons. . . .

Then, on September 20, 2001, President G.W. Bush addressed a joint session of Congress, explaining what he intended to do:

> . . . This war will not be like the war against Iraq a decade ago, with a decisive liberation of territory and a swift conclusion. It will not look like the air war above Kosovo two years ago, where no ground troops were used and not a single American was lost in combat.

> Our response involves far more than instant retaliation and isolated strikes. Americans should not expect one battle, but a lengthy campaign, unlike any other we have ever seen. It may include dramatic strikes, visible on TV, and covert operations, secret even in success. We will starve terrorists of funding, turn them one against another, drive them from place to place, until there is no refuge or no rest. And we will pursue nations that provide aid or safe haven to terrorism. Every nation, in every region, now has a decision to make. Either you are with us, or you are with the terrorists. From this day forward, any nation that continues to harbor or support terrorism will be regarded by the United States as a hostile regime. . . .

In his State of the Union Address in January 2002, Bush went even further, introducing the idea of an Axis of Evil that the United States and the world had to confront:

> North Korea is a regime arming with missiles and weapons of mass destruction, while starving its citizens. . . .

> Iran aggressively pursues these weapons and exports terror. . . .

> Iraq continues to flaunt its hostility toward America and to support terror. . . .

> States like these, and their terrorist allies, constitute an axis of evil, arming to threaten the peace of the world.

> We'll be deliberate, yet time is not on our side. I will not wait on events while dangers gather. I will not stand by as peril draws closer and closer. The United States of America will not permit the world's most dangerous regimes to threaten us with the world's most destructive weapons.

In various speeches, Bush also called for preemptive action against nations or groups of perceived enemies or their supporters.

What does Bush mean by "I will not wait on events while dangers gather. I will not stand by as peril draws closer and closer"?

(A) the use of preemptive strikes against perceived enemies

(B) immediate military preparation

(C) U.S. pressure on the United Nations and Western allies to attack nations sponsoring terrorism

(D) all of the above

The correct answer is Choice (A), the use of preemptive strikes against perceived enemies. Choices (B) and (C) may be partially true; the U.S. government was increasing military expenditure, and the UN was applying pressure to gather support to attack nations sponsoring terrorism. However, Choice (A) is the most complete answer.

The immediate result of the Bush Doctrine was the invasion of Afghanistan, ostensibly to capture Osama bin Laden and to topple the Taliban government, a supporter of terrorism around the world. U.S. forces, along with forces from Great Britain, Australia, and Canada established a new government in 2001, but the war continued as the Taliban resorted to guerilla warfare. That was followed by the 2003 invasion of Iraq, which successfully removed Saddam Hussein government. Unfortunately, neither invasion solved the problem of terrorism, nor brought stability to the Middle East. The rise of ISIS proves that.

A further result of the Bush Doctrine has been the president's ability to order attacks on terrorist targets around the world. Drone attacks have been used to attack homes of terrorists, convoys of Taliban fighters, and other targets, even in sovereign countries not involved in any war with the United States.

Chapter 10

Shaking the Money Tree: Economics

*E*conomics is the study of production, distribution, and consumption of goods and services and the transfer of wealth. You don't have to be an economist or have a Master of Business Administration (MBA) degree to pass the GED Social Studies test, but having a general idea of how various economic systems, including capitalism, communism, and socialism, function and of the various factors that drive the transfer of wealth can help you score higher on the test.

In this chapter, we bring you up to speed on the different economies along with factors that shape economies and how economic factors impact the world. Along the way, we introduce and define relevant terminology that may be unfamiliar to you so you won't be thrown off if you encounter these terms on the test. We also present several sample questions to warm you up for test day.

Sorting Out the Different Economic Models

The difference among economic models all comes down to how much control the central government has over the economy and people's lives. The four main economic models you're likely to encounter on the GED Social Studies test are these:

✔ **Capitalism:** The most famous is Adam Smith's classic *capitalism,* which he developed in his 1776 work *The Wealth of Nations.* It called for a marketplace that would regulate itself through supply and demand.

✔ **Socialism:** *Socialism* argues that the state should intervene to ensure economic opportunity for all, to avoid exploitation of the working class, and promote the good for all.

✔ **Communism:** Communism is an extreme form of socialism in which the state owns all methods of production, and all economic activities are regulated. Unlike the Marxist model, communist states are also a police state with limited individual rights.

✔ **Keynesian economics:** *Keynesian economics* is less concerned about the relationships between workers and employers or prices and the market place and more concerned with controlling the inevitable economic slumps and booms of capitalist society.

In the following sections, we explain these different economic models in greater detail.

Grasping the basics of capitalism

Under classic capitalism, government plays no role in the economy. Smith argues that "the invisible hand" of the market place will regulate the economy. Ideally, capitalists produce goods to meet demand. If demand increases, increasing production to meet that demand is in the manufacturers' self-interest. Prices respond to the demand for goods. If demand is high, prices will rise, and manufacturers will increase production. As more manufacturers enter that particular market, more goods enter the market. As demand is satisfied and competition increases, prices will drop, and less-efficient manufacturers will leave the market. Having fewer producers will cause prices to rise again. Ideally, a balance will develop between prices and demand.

What does Adam Smith mean by "the invisible hand"?

(A) the hand of God

(B) government intervention

(C) the pressures of demand on prices and production

(D) economic regulations

Nothing in the text suggests a religious explanation, so Choice (A) is wrong. The text suggests that government plays no role in the economy, so Choices (B) and (D) are also wrong. The only answer the text supports is Choice (C), the pressures of demand on prices and production.

However, Smith wasn't blind to the rapacious effects of unbridled capitalism:

> In regards to the price of commodities, the rise of wages operates as simple interest does, the rise of profit operates like compound interest. . . . Our merchants and masters complain much of the bad effects of high wages in raising the price and lessening the sale of goods. They say nothing concerning the bad effects of high profits. They are silent with regard to the pernicious effects of their own gains. They complain only of those of other people.

What suggests that Smith left open the door to ideas of market regulations?

(A) Nothing in the text supports that statement.

(B) statements about merchants complaining about high wages

(C) statements about the bad effects of high profits

(D) complaints about government intervention

Choice (A) is wrong because Smith does in fact raise concerns. The text suggests Choice (B), but that choice doesn't answer the question. Choice (D) isn't supported by the text. Choice (C) is the correct answer; Smith states merchants never talk about the bad effects of high profits and are silent about the pernicious effects of their own gains.

Laissez-faire capitalism is an extreme version of capitalism whose proponents argue that the state should never interfere in any way with the economy. They want no government regulation of any kind, no minimum wages, no laws to prevent monopolies or price fixing, and no unions or any other restrictions. Although the United States and many other democracies operate with a version of capitalism, none have totally unfettered capitalism. Government regulations of various kinds, including safety and human rights laws, environmental, and anticollusion laws, govern business operations and transactions to varying degrees.

There are no truly laissez-faire economies to date, not even the United States. All capitalist countries, including the United States, regulate banking and business, set minimum wages, and provide state-backed insurance and pensions. At what point these regulations become socialism (discussed later in the chapter) is an open debate.

Coming to terms with communism

On the opposite end of the economic spectrum from laissez-faire capitalism is Soviet-style communism. The state owns all means of production and regulates inputs and outputs along with wages and prices. The state allocates resources and sets priorities, deciding how much of any item is produced and what it will cost. It sets quotas workers must meet. Because of state priorities, consumer goods are often in short supply, or of limited variety, and often of mediocre quality.

Karl Marx, a German philosopher and economist, popularized communism with the publication of his *Communist Manifesto*. The principle on which pure communism is based is "From each according to his ability, to each according to his need," a slogan that predated the *Communist Manifesto* but that was popularized by Marx.

In practice, communism has never achieved the ideal Marx had envisioned. Here's one example of how communism tends to fall short in terms of efficiency: After WWII, the East German government approved the production of private cars, including the Trabant. Because of steel shortages, the car body was made of a cotton and plastic resin body, and the car was equipped with a two-stroke engine. Consumers had to pay the full price in advance, the equivalent of several years' wages for the average worker, and then wait, sometimes several years, for delivery. When the Trabant's designers wanted to introduce a new and better model, the state regulators denied permission. That was a common theme throughout the communist states. The Soviet workers' car, the Lada, was a reproduction of a Fiat. It continued in production virtually unchanged for 30 years.

In what way can Soviet communism be viewed as a form of capitalism?

(A) It can't.

(B) The state, rather than private individuals, owns all the businesses in the country.

(C) The state is the only employer in the country.

(D) The government controls all sales.

In Soviet communism, the state owned all businesses just as individuals own businesses in a capitalist system. The correct answer is Choice (B). Choice (A) is wrong because, in a way, Soviet communism is capitalistic; the only difference is that the state, rather than individuals, owns and profits from the businesses. Choices (C) and (D) are partially correct if you view the state as a private business owner, but in capitalism, the state isn't the only employer in the country, nor does it control all sales.

Another problem with communism is that in the USSR and other communist states, consumer goods were not a priority. That was often given to industrial expansion to earn foreign currency to support the regime and for increasing production of military goods to expand borders and put down revolts, so shortages of consumer goods are common. However, communism does deliver some benefits to the people. In most communist countries, for example, healthcare and education are available at no cost.

Some experts are careful to point out that communism is an economic system and not a political system. As an economic system, it calls only for a reasonable approach to the division of labor and goods. However, the political system that often develops around communism is usually more dictatorial than democratic, giving rise to power and corruption that directs the flow of wealth to the country's leaders at the expense of the people.

Exploring the middle ground with socialism

Socialism falls between the two extremes of laissez-faire capitalism and communism, and it's practiced in several different forms. Some countries, including Sweden and Norway, combine private ownership of commercial enterprises with publicly owned corporations. Some socialist states have a highly regulated economy combined with high income taxes. Others, including Canada and Italy, may not consider themselves as socialist; they have less emphasis on public ownership but still provide many government services, ranging from free healthcare to free education and subsidized housing, paid for by taxes. However, socialist countries offer all the democratic benefits of free speech, free association, and other freedoms to all their citizens. The confusion between socialism and communism comes from the fact that many communist countries refer to themselves as socialist republics. In fact, communist countries are generally police states with few democratic rights.

Norway combines state and private enterprise with free education through graduate school and a free public healthcare system, all supported by high taxes. The wealthiest pay an income tax of 50 percent in addition to a wealth tax on all their assets. To avoid tax cheating, the government posts all tax returns on a publicly accessible website. As a result, the richest 20 percent in Norway own only 3.9 times the assets of the bottom 20 percent. (By comparison, that figure is 8.5 times for the wealthiest 20 percent in the United States.)

Canada's economic model is closer to that of the United States. Taxes are relatively low, but the government provides social services including subsidized housing and free medical care for all. Regulations are similar to those of the United States, from health and safety laws to environmental protection, while other areas such as banking are more heavily regulated. The federal government and provinces also own state enterprises known as *Crown corporations*. (In theory, they're owned by the Crown in the name of the people.) Air Canada started as a Crown corporation when a passenger airline was needed and no private enterprise was forthcoming. The Canadian Broadcasting Corporation (CBC) is still government owned, providing radio and television services across the country right up to the arctic. The provinces also own and operate electrical power corporations, and in one province, public automobile insurance. Provincially, alcohol sales are a government monopoly; all sales are through provincial Crown corporations. In Ontario, that Crown corporation earns the provincial treasury over a billion dollars a year.

Could the United States be considered a socialist country?

(A) yes

(B) no

(C) to a limited extent

(D) not enough information in the passage

Based on the text, the best answer is Choice (A). Though the United States government doesn't generally own and operate businesses that compete with the private sector, it does own many corporations that benefit the public. These include various credit and banking companies, the Corporation for Public Broadcasting, and the Tennessee Valley Authority. The government does, however, regulate commerce and trade, set minimum wages, and provide various social services. That exceeds the idea of "limited extent" in Choice (C).

Getting to know Keynesian economics

Keynesian economics is a special case. John Maynard Keynes developed his famous theory in England during the Great Depression. He was trying to understand why the Depression happened and how to solve the problem. He could see that classic economics didn't work to solve the crisis. In recession or depression, demand drops. People are reluctant to buy, fearing unemployment and the resulting lack of income. As demand continues to drop, companies lay off workers. However, prices are *sticky,* meaning they don't drop as the classic economic model would predict. Wages are also sticky because most workers won't agree to wage cuts. When companies lay off workers, unemployment and fear of unemployment cause demand for goods to drop even farther. Production continues to drop, unemployment continues to rise, and recovery from that cycle is much more difficult. In effect, recession and depression form a downward spiral in which reduced demand leads to unemployment, which leads to further reduction in demand, and so on.

Keynes argued that the traditional conservative way of cutting costs and instituting *austerity* (cost-cutting) programs isn't the way to get the economy running again. Austerity programs generally result in more layoffs. He argued that governments should encourage spending, increase hiring, and even use deficit financing to spur the economy.

After the recession of 2008, the U.S. federal government used that approach. The administration supported the banking sector (avoiding a collapse), invested billions in public-works programs, and even bailed out manufacturing companies including General Motors and Chrysler, saving tens of thousands of jobs. By 2015, unemployment in the United States was at 5.6 percent, a historic low; weekly earnings had started to climb again, corporate profits tripled, and the stock market recovered all the losses of 2008. However, the recovery was uneven. People at the lower end of the economic scale saw few benefits, even as more than 6 million jobs were created.

The major criticism of Keynesian economics is that it provides little guidance on how to end government spending when the recession or depression ends. Large government stimulus spending increases the risk of inflation. The question, then, is when and how to cut back on that spending and recover the money spent stimulating the economy. Governments are reluctant to raise taxes, and the economy may not yet be able to accept cutbacks to balance the books.

What do economists mean when they refer to sticky prices?

(A) prices that have too many agencies involved in their management

(B) prices that tend to remain low even when they should be rising

(C) the tendency for prices to change much more slowly than demand would suggest

(D) prices that "stick" to changes in the value of currency

The term *sticky prices* refers to the stability of prices despite changes in demand. Your best answer is Choice (C). Choice (B) is partially true but not the best answer. Nothing in the passage supports Choice (A) or Choice (D).

Finding Out What's New About the New Deal

When Franklin Delano Roosevelt (FDR) won the 1932 election, the Great Depression was in its second year. The previous Hoover administration had focused on providing indirect aid to banks and limited spending on public work projects, but refused to provide direct aid to citizens. FDR's first 100 days changed that. He began with legislation to bring stability to the banking system. Numerous banks had failed, and depositors lost millions. FDR brought in the Emergency Banking Relief Act and other banking reforms to protect people's savings if banks failed. Then his government created the Federal Deposit Insurance Corporation (FDIC) and implemented various regulations to limit speculation, one of the causes of the crash of 1929. The legislation prohibited banks from investing in the stock market, and the new Securities and Exchange Commission regulated stock market speculation.

The second stage was to deal with individuals and aid to the unemployed. The Civilian Conservation Corp, created in 1933, hired millions of unemployed young men to perform conservation work. In return for wages, food, and shelter, single young men worked outdoors to build and improve national parks and public roads. The Federal Emergency Relief Administration (FERA) and the Civilian Works Administration (CWA) provided financial relief to individual state and local governments and direct financial help to unemployed and destitute individuals.

The New Deal also boosted industry. The Tennessee Valley Authority (TVA) was created to build a huge hydroelectric project in the Tennessee River Valley. Construction of this project created thousands of jobs and provided training and housing for many people, and the resulting cheap electricity was a major benefit to the region. Despite criticism that the project represented socialism, the approach worked so well that the government built similar power projects, including the Hoover Dam, in other areas of the United States. The government also created other public works projects, building roads, public buildings, and other infrastructure, all to provide immediate employment.

By 1936, FDR faced growing opposition by the Republican Party in Congress. Resentment was building against higher taxes on corporations and wealthy individuals, and conservative judges in the Supreme Court overturned many of FDR's proposals on constitutional grounds. Roosevelt's campaign for the 1936 presidential elections proposed even more government interventions and social program changes. He won by a landslide.

The second New Deal emphasized social legislation. Just before the election, FDR introduced the Social Security and Wagner Acts, arguably the most important pieces of social legislation ever in the United States The Social Security Act provided state pensions and unemployment and disability insurance. The Wagner Act reinstated collective bargaining rights for unions.

The major opposition to the New Deal came from the conservative Supreme Court. It had overruled both a New York state law creating a minimum wage and New Deal legislation. The Court, supported by big business, threatened to do the same again. FDR proposed to reform the Supreme Court and appoint a large number of new justices who agreed with him. The Supreme Court didn't overrule the Social Security Act or the Wagner Act, both of which continue to this day.

Why was FDR's stabilization and regulation of the financial system in the first 100 days in 1932 significant?

(A) It stopped the runs on the bank that threatened to bankrupt thousands of private depositors.

(B) It prevented the kind of speculation by banks and stock market investors that had caused the crash of 1929.

(C) It restored confidence in the U.S. financial system.

(D) All of the above.

The correct choice is Choice (D), All of the above. FDR needed to provide financial stability before he could implement any of his other measures. Without that financial stability, neither individuals nor corporations would be willing to make the kinds of investments that would turn the Depression around.

How was the New Deal an example of Keynesian economics in action?

(A) It used deficit financing to create employment.

(B) It provided economic stimulus by significantly lowering income taxes.

(C) It reduced barriers to trade to stimulate exports.

(D) It created a minimum wage law to support workers.

The correct answer is Choice (A). Although Choices (B) and (C) may be true, nothing in the text supports those choices. The text also doesn't mention the creation of a minimum wage law (Choice (D)). You must select the best answer based on the information given, which means Choice (A) is your only choice. (If Keynesian economics sounds like Greek to you, flip to the earlier section "Getting to know Keynesian economics" for details.)

Wrapping Your Brain around Microeconomics and Macroeconomics

In *Economics For Dummies* (Wiley), Sean Flynn explains the difference between microeconomics and macroeconomics as follows:

- *Microeconomics* focuses on individual people and individual businesses. For individuals, it explains how they behave when faced with decisions about where to spend their money or how to invest their savings. For businesses, it explains how profit-maximizing firms behave individually and when competing against each other in markets.

- *Macroeconomics* looks at the economy as an organic whole, concentrating on factors such as interest rates, inflation, and unemployment. It also encompasses the study of economic growth and how governments try to moderate the harm caused by recessions.

In the following sections, we explain micro- and macroeconomics in greater detail.

Digging into microeconomics

On a microeconomic level, individuals make decisions about savings, spending, starting or closing businesses, and even investments. If enough people make decisions to buy a particular product, that may influence prices to rise or manufacturers to increase production of that product. Similarly, new products that don't find sufficient customers will quickly disappear in accordance with consumer choice theory. Adam Smith's "invisible hand" will determine success or failure. (Head to the earlier section "Grasping the basics of capitalism" for more on Smith's economic theory.) That "invisible hand" also influences the price of a product because a high demand coupled with a limited supply raises its price. As more manufacturers produce that product, increasing supply results in falling prices. Microeconomics also studies wages, employment, personal debt, and consumer choice.

Wages and employment

A number of forces influence both employment levels and employee income levels. Government can affect employment levels by imposing various taxes and by setting minimum wages. Unions can influence wage levels and job security through collective bargaining. An over- or under-supply of workers in a given economic sector has the same effect on wages as demand for goods has on prices. If unemployment is high and many workers are available, wages tend to remain low and stable. If unemployment is low, the reduced availability of workers applies an upward pressure on wages. Social action, such as the demand for a $15/hour minimum wage, can also create pressures to which employers respond, even without an accompanying shortage of labor.

A law that increases the minimum wage is most likely to

(A) increase job security

(B) lead to a recession

(C) discourage employers from hiring more workers

(D) encourage employers to hire more workers

A law that increases the minimum wage would probably cause employers to raise prices or lay off workers to mitigate the loss of profit from having to pay higher wages, so Choice (C) is the best answer.

Debt

Debt also affects the economy. Most people can't afford to pay cash for major purchases, so they borrow money to finance cars, homes, and even higher education. As long as debtors are able to repay their loans, the debt isn't a problem. The issue is *bad debts,* debts that can't be repaid or recovered. The crash in 2008 was caused in part because of a high volume of bad debts. Lenders had issued a large number of variable rate mortgages to individuals who couldn't afford their monthly payments when interest rates increased. In addition, lenders often approved loans in excess of the value of the homes used to secure those loans. When housing prices dropped, the value of many homes wasn't enough to cover the balance remaining on the loan. When homeowners couldn't make their monthly mortgage payments, they had to sell their homes, often for less than they had paid for them and less than they owed on their mortgages. Or they simply abandoned their homes, leaving the bank to deal with the financial shortfall. Banks foreclosing on these mortgages lost money — so much money that they faced serious financial problems.

Financial regulation can limit risks from certain types of loans and discourage speculation in the housing market by requiring minimum down payments, restricting the degree of debt leverage, or changing tax laws to discourage speculation and riskier loan types.

Consumer choice

Governments often use taxes to influence consumer behavior on a microeconomic scale. For example, the government charges a "sin" tax on tobacco and alcohol sales to discourage the use of these substances and collect money to help offset the medical and related costs (including lost tax revenue) associated with the consumption of these substances.

The government also uses a host of tax incentives to encourage certain behaviors, such as owning a home, investing in green energy products, making charitable contributions, obtaining health insurance, pursuing educational opportunities, and much more. These incentives come in the form of tax deductions and tax credits. A *tax deduction* is an amount you subtract from your income before calculating the taxes due on that income. A *tax credit* is an amount you subtract directly from the amount of taxes due.

A sin tax is designed to

(A) discourage certain consumer behaviors

(B) encourage certain consumer behaviors

(C) punish consumers

(D) reward consumers

A *sin tax* is designed to discourage certain consumer behaviors, such as the purchase of potentially harmful products, so Choice (A) is the correct answer.

Understanding macroeconomics fundamentals

Macroeconomics looks at the factors that affect the economy on a national and international level. It tries to explain the effect of government policies on the entire economy and what influences prices overall. Countries measure their economies by *gross domestic product* (GDP), and overall productivity by GDP per person. GDP represents the monetary value of all goods produced in a country over a given time, usually annually. The GDP per person divides that amount by the population of the country. It allows comparisons of year-to-year changes in one economy as well as comparisons of the economies worldwide. Two measures of how well the economy is doing are economic growth and inflation/deflation. *Growth* is monitored in terms of the annual increase or decrease in GDP, while *inflation* measures the rate at which prices are rising (or dropping, in the case of *deflation*).

Governments can influence macroeconomics in various ways, including the following:

- ✔ **Setting or removing tariffs:** They can charge fees on products coming into the country from foreign markets to prevent competition and lower prices that negatively affect domestic producers. Or they can remove tariffs to encourage the importation of goods, often resulting in lower prices for consumers. Tariffs tend to discourage trade for obvious reasons.

- ✔ **Increasing or decreasing government spending:** To create jobs and stimulate the economy, a government may increase spending. Of course, when the government has insufficient funds to cover its increased spending, they must resort to *deficit spending,* borrowing to spend, which increases the national debt and could result in problems down the road.

  National debt is the total amount the federal government owes. When you hear politicians discuss the *budget deficit,* they're talking about the annual shortfall, the difference between how much the government collects in revenue (mostly from taxes) and the amount it spends in any given year. With a *deficit reduction,* the national debt continues to grow. The government would need to have a *budget surplus* rather than a deficit for it to lower the national debt.

- ✔ **Increasing or decreasing interest rates:** In the United States, the Federal Reserve monitors economic conditions and either lowers or raises the interest rate on the money it lends to banks. The Federal Reserve attempts to maintain GDP growth at a rate of 2 to 3 percent annually. If the GDP grows slower than that, the Federal Reserve tends to lower interest rates to encourage consumer and business spending to stimulate the economy. When the GDP grows faster than that, the Federal Reserve tends to raise interest rates to keep inflation in check.

Why is GDP per person a more accurate measure of an economy than just the GDP?

(A) It shows individual incomes.

(B) It takes total population into account.

(C) It shows economies of small countries more accurately.

(D) All of the above.

GDP per person puts international comparisons on an equal footing. Economies like China may be producing far more than the economy of Great Britain or France, but taking China's huge population into account shows economic production more accurately. Your best option is Choice (B). Although Choices (A) and (C) are partially true, they're not the best choices.

Examining Income Inequality and Related Issues

In 2013, President Obama spoke out about income inequality, calling it the defining issue of our times:

> . . . Since 1979, when I graduated from high school, our productivity is up by more than 90 percent, but the income of the typical family has increased by less than 8 percent. Since 1979, our economy has more than doubled in size, but most of that growth has flowed to a fortunate few. . . .
>
> The top 10 percent no longer takes in one-third of our income — it now takes half. Whereas in the past, the average CEO made about 20 to 30 times the income of the average worker, today's CEO now makes 273 times more. And meanwhile, a family in the top 1 percent has a net worth 288 times higher than the typical family, which is a record for this country. . . .
>
> . . . This increasing inequality is most pronounced in our country, and it challenges the very essence of who we are as a people. Understand we've never begrudged success in America. We aspire to it. . . .
>
> The problem is that alongside increased inequality, we've seen diminished levels of upward mobility in recent years. A child born in the top 20 percent has about a 2-in-3 chance of staying at or near the top. A child born into the bottom 20 percent has a less than 1-in-20 shot at making it to the top. He's ten times likelier to stay where he is. In fact, statistics show not only that our levels of income inequality rank near countries like Jamaica and Argentina, but that it is harder today for a child born here in America to improve her station in life than it is for children in most of our wealthy allies — countries like Canada or Germany or France . . . the idea that a child may never be able to escape that poverty because she lacks a decent education or healthcare, or a community that views her future as their own, that should offend all of us and it should compel us to action. We are a better country than this.
>
> . . . These trends are bad for our economy. . . . When families have less to spend, that means businesses have fewer customers, and households rack up greater mortgage and credit card debt; meanwhile, concentrated wealth at the top is less likely to result in the kind of broadly based consumer spending that drives our economy, and together with lax regulation, may contribute to risky speculative bubbles.
>
> And rising inequality and declining mobility are also bad for our families and social cohesion — not just because we tend to trust our institutions less, but studies show we actually tend to trust each other less when there's greater inequality. And greater inequality is associated with less mobility between generations. That means it's not just temporary; the effects last. It creates a vicious cycle. . . .
>
> And finally, rising inequality and declining mobility are bad for our democracy. Ordinary folks can't write massive campaign checks or hire high-priced lobbyists and lawyers to secure policies that tilt the playing field in their favor at everyone else's expense. And so people get the bad taste that the system is rigged. . . .

Recent protests against the income inequality in the United States started with the Occupy Wall Street (OWS) movement in 2011. Though OWS has faded from the news, the frustrations continue, exemplified today by the $15/hour minimum wage movement. As fast food and retail giants are making major profits, workers are often left struggling with two or three jobs to make ends meet. This situation is exacerbated by the fact that many corporations won't offer minimum wage workers more than part-time work. That means many of these workers have no benefits, and their hours can be cut at will. Quite often minimum wage workers need government programs such as food stamps to survive. These programs have become a subsidy to employers because it enables them to continue to pay their workers such low wages.

Demonstrations in major cities across the United States reflect the anger of these workers, and the movement has met with some success. Governor Cuomo agreed to study creating a $15 minimum wage for New York State. Some cities such as Los Angeles and Seattle have set a $15 minimum wage, and San Francisco is raising minimum wages. New York Mayor Bill de Blasio in 2015 raised the minimum hourly wage for New Yorkers to $13.13

In his speech, President Obama also highlighted a different issue: massive student loan debt. That debt is estimated to be in excess of $1.2 trillion with 7 million debtors in default. Many students estimate they'll need decades to repay student loans. The problem is so significant because it limits educational opportunities for poor Americans. That debt load also affects the economy because failure to make payments on those loans reduces the amount of money available for other uses, limiting economic growth. The federal government has taken some steps recently to help alleviate the problem, including an option of tying repayment rates to income and family responsibilities.

Income disparity also has other serious effects. Studies have shown that life expectancy and health decrease as income decreases. A strong correlation between poverty and school dropout rates also exists. Dropout rates in poor U.S. states are significantly higher than in the wealthier ones. Many European countries have social programs specifically aimed at helping the poorest achieve better education. Some countries, like Germany, Norway, and Sweden, offer free university education to all. The income disparity is also reduced by higher taxes on the wealthy, and free healthcare.

Why would a poor child in countries like France or Germany (according to President Obama) have better chances for upward social mobility than a poor child in the United States?

(A) Those countries offer targeted social programs for the poor.

(B) France and Germany have higher taxes on the wealthy.

(C) France and Germany subsidize education for low-income earners.

(D) All of the above.

European countries have stronger socialist leanings, which means they offer many subsidies and other forms of help for the disadvantaged. This help is paid for by higher taxes on corporations and wealthy individuals. That means the best answer to this question is Choice (D).

Investigating Economic Causes and Fallout Related to War

Prior to the Industrial Revolution, wars were fought by largely mercenary armies out in a field somewhere to decide which king should sit on which throne. Dynastic succession triggered all the great wars of the 18th century.

Starting with the Industrial Revolution, economics became a much more significant factor. The American Civil War is a case in point. For the South, the survival of slavery was an economic issue, not a moral issue. Southern society couldn't survive as it was without the cotton trade, and the cotton trade depended on slavery.

World Wars I and II had similar economic components among the list of causes. World War I came about in part because of economic rivalries among Germany, Britain, and France. German industrialization since unification in 1871 had made it a modern industrial power-house. It outpaced Great Britain, where the Industrial Revolution had started. Germany's industries were more modern and its technology more up to date. Part of the hostility with France came from the Germans' seizure of Alsace and Lorraine, which also became an economic issue because it deprived France of much-needed coal.

Economics also contributed to the outbreak of World War II. Germany had a large popula-tion and a booming industrial economy but only limited raw materials and agricultural output. A common theme of Hitler's speeches was the requirement for more *Lebensraum* (living space) for the German people. Similarly, Japan risked war with the United States because it needed access to raw materials in China. The United States tried to force Japan to pull back from China and proposed an oil embargo as a pressure tactic. That oil embargo became a major trigger for the Japanese attack on Pearl Harbor.

Why would a possible oil embargo cause Japan to attack the United States?

(A) Japan wanted to seize U.S. oil fields.

(B) Japan's continuing military power depended on access to oil for its military.

(C) Japan needed to buy time to develop its own internal oil resources.

(D) All of the above.

The immediate cause was Japan's need for oil to maintain its military. Japan had no oil resources, and its leadership knew that an oil embargo would have a serious impact on its military combat readiness. The correct answer is Choice (B). Though Japan may have wanted to seize American oil fields (Choice (A)) or develop its own oil resources (Choice (C)), the text doesn't support these answers. (*Tip:* For more detail on the lead-up to major U.S. historical events, including the wars mentioned here, check out Chapter 9.)

The economic fallout of wars is obvious. According to a Congressional Budget Office (CBO) document from 2007, "total spending for U.S. operations in Iraq and Afghanistan and other activities related to the war on terrorism would amount to between $1.2 trillion and $1.7 trillion for fiscal years 2001 through 2017." Much of this cost is financed by borrowing because successive governments have reduced taxes and increased spending. That means the debt will be around for a long time. Table 10-1 compares U.S. war costs in dollars.

Table 10-1	Cost of U.S. Wars	
War or Conflict	*Year of Spending*	*Cost in Fiscal Year 2011 Dollars*
World War I	$20 billion	$334 billion
World War II	$296 billion	$4.1 trillion
Korea	$30 billion	$341 billion
Vietnam	$111 billion	$738 billion
Persian Gulf War	$61 billion	$102 billion
Iraq	$715 billion	$784 billion
Afghanistan	$297 billion	$321 billion

Source: Congressional Research Service, June 29, 2010 (cironline.org/sites/default/files/legacy/files/June2010CRScostofuswars.pdf)

The Vietnam War contributed to a unique economic problem: a combination of high inflation and a stagnant economy. Massive spending on the war put more money into circulation, increasing inflation. That increased interest rates, which impacted average Americans and the business community. Because much of the conflict was financed through debt, the government deficit increased significantly, with a major impact on the government's ability to provide other services.

What is the significance of presenting the costs of war in fiscal year 2011 dollars?

(A) It creates larger numbers.

(B) It makes the comparisons more accurate.

(C) It accounts for interest on the debt to 2011.

(D) All of the above.

Representing the cost of each war in 2011 dollar amounts provides a clearer comparison of the actual costs of the wars, Choice (B). For example, you may pay 65 cents for a candy bar now that would have cost a dime in 1970, but median household income was less than $10,000 in 1970 compared to over $50,000 in 2014. By translating the value of the dollar to a set time, you can compare expenditures over years on the same scale. Choice (A) is just silly. Choice (C) may be partially true, but accumulated interest charges are already calculated into the debt, so no extra calculations are required.

Looking into Economic Drivers of Exploration and Colonization

You can apply the SPIRE model we discuss in Chapter 9 to an analysis of exploration and colonization as well. Explorers from China traveled to Africa and India merely to explore. Europeans sailed around Africa and to the Americas primarily to find a faster sea route to India to cash in on the lucrative spice trade. Exploration of the Americas started for the same reason — expectation of future profits from trade with India. For the Spanish, Portuguese, and French explorers, a secondary motive was religion. After discovering native populations, the church wanted to bring religion to the people they mistakenly identified as "heathens."

Colonization had very strong economic motives. Europe was in the middle of the Industrial Revolution. Africa offered new resources, from minerals to rubber, palm oil, and lumber. The Europeans also realized the value of the slave trade, which became one of the more profitable sectors of the European economy.

The existence of 13 British colonies had a further impact. As wealth from the colonies became part of the English economy, the colonies needed to be defended. That required a stronger navy, which in turn spurred the iron and steel industry, the shipbuilding industry, and military expenditures. One result was that the Royal Navy became the largest, most powerful fleet in the world.

Weighing the Impact of the Agricultural, Industrial, and Technology Revolutions

The agricultural, industrial, and technology revolutions created profound changes in social organization, wealth, and social mobility. When nomadic herders learned how to grow crops, they created permanent settlements. While living as a nomadic tribe, individuals shared the wealth of the tribe. Because the animals in the tribe's herd were wealth, members of the tribe were equally wealthy. However, the creation of sedentary societies meant that land on which to grow crops equaled wealth. Individuals who were more successful in raising crops could buy more land on which to grow more crops and thus accumulate wealth, and less successful farmers became poor farmers. That's how society developed a class structure based on wealth. Sedentary agriculture also led to surplus food, which allowed some individuals other options for making a living. Now not everyone had to farm to survive, so some could specialize in pottery, weaving, or any other area dictated by their skills. That too allowed some to become wealthier than others.

The Industrial Revolution in the late 1700s had equally profound effects on society. Prior to that time, manufacturing was small scale on a family level. Guilds and an apprentice system trained individuals in the skills required. The guilds regulated the skills required and the number of individuals who could become masters. A master smith (such as a blacksmith) would run a family operation, usually in a facility attached to the home. He would train the oldest son to follow in the trade, while the wife and other children looked after the home and performed tasks required for the family's well-being. To be a master of the trade, the individual had to know all aspects of the trade and be able to manufacture an item from start to finish.

The Industrial Revolution changed that. The invention of the factory system of production meant that highly specialized tasks could be broken down into tiny pieces, each of which could be performed by individuals with minimal training. That also meant the individuals concerned could be paid far less for their skills, and the factory owners would make much higher profits. Machinery replaced skilled workers so that the number of people and the skill levels required to produce goods was reduced while the output of goods increased dramatically. That meant the cost of goods dropped significantly, too, and more members of society could afford to buy the products.

This shift created a vast dislocation within society. The wool and cotton industry in England is a good example. Traditionally, weavers controlled production and were able to set prices and earn a decent living. Beginning in the 1800s, factory owners replaced skilled weavers with automated looms. These machines worked around the clock without breaks and made no demands for salaries. The factory required only unskilled workers to feed the machines. Thousands of skilled weavers were displaced. Weavers were unemployed, and replacement factory workers earned starvation wages. Ned Ludd gave his name to the Luddite movement, which tried to stop the industrialization of the weaving trade. Luddites smashed weaving equipment whenever they could. They were so effective at slowing down the industrialization of their trade that the government was forced to offer a 200-pound reward for the capture of anyone guilty of such sabotage. The British government, under pressure from industrialists, made destroying machinery a hanging offense.

Who were the Luddites?

(A) unemployed weavers

(B) opponents of the mechanization of the weaving industry

(C) opponents of the factory system

(D) none of the above

The correct answer is Choice (B), opponents of the mechanization of the weaving industry. They may also have been unemployed workers (Choice (A)) or opponents of the factory system (Choice (C)), but those choices aren't the most precise answers.

Changes in technology had other effects. When Johannes Gutenberg created the printing press with movable type in 1440, he did more than print books; he made knowledge widely available. Before his printing press, books were handwritten, highly prized commodities that only the wealthy could afford. Because books were rare, few people needed to read. Gutenberg's printing press democratized knowledge and enabled the distribution of new ideas. It made books, and therefore knowledge, much more widely available. When Martin Luther nailed his famous Ninety-five Theses to the door of the church in Wittenberg, his message reached only those few who actually saw it. A friend copied the document and sent it to a printer. Within months, people throughout Europe had seen it. It became one of the instigating documents for the Protestant Reformation.

The impact of technology continues. The invention of transistors allowed the development of small portable radios. The integrated circuits that followed it allowed even greater minia-turization. The first computers occupied entire large rooms and required dust-free environ-ments and temperature controls but offered less computing power than today's hand-held calculators. The computer equipment onboard the space capsules that carried astronauts to the moon had less calculating power than a Commodore 64, and yet were a massive advance over previous technology.

The technology has also had social effects. In Gutenberg's days, sending the knowledge contained in a book from London to Berlin took weeks. Today that knowledge transfers around the whole world electronically in seconds. Thirty years ago, when workers left the office, they were done work for the day. Today cellphones and computers are an electronic leash requiring people to be available 24 hours a day. Technology has also created a new social dislocation as robotic assembly replaces skilled workers, leaving fewer well-paid jobs. At the same time, this displacement has created a new set of jobs requiring high skills to design, build, and maintain those robots.

Which of the following was a social effect of the introduction of the printing press in Europe?

(A) It led to the creation of public libraries.

(B) It made society more democratic.

(C) It allowed for a much wider distribution of knowledge.

(D) It led to a more standardized spelling.

Gutenberg's printing press had a profound social impact because it allowed for a much wider distribution of knowledge, Choice (C). The other choices are all true but not sup-ported by the text. You need to choose the best answer based on the material presented.

Chapter 11

Traveling through Time and Space with Social Studies Lessons

In This Chapter

▶ Digging up lessons from ancient Athens and Rome

▶ Considering interactions among population, environment, and development

▶ Looking into borders and border conflicts

▶ Tracing the movement of human populations

Although the GED Social Studies test involves a great deal of U.S. history, questions may also touch on ancient history (especially related to ancient Greece and Rome) along with topics related to population, environment, and development; borders and conflicts over borders; and the movement of populations as they seek resources and opportunities, or flee from areas that have become uninhabitable for a variety of reasons. Consider this chapter a mash-up of social studies topics not covered in the other chapters in this part. However, as we do in those other chapters, we provide sample questions in this chapter to help you retain the knowledge and warm up for the test.

As you read this chapter, you may wonder what it has to do with social studies, but keep in mind that social studies covers a lot of ground, including history, geography, and economics. In addition, it involves a variety of skills, including reading comprehension, analytical thinking, map-reading, data interpretation, and even a little math — skills covered in Part II of this book. If you have trouble answering any of the questions in this chapter, consider reading those earlier chapters.

Sizing Up Ancient Civilizations: Athens and Rome

Civilization today owes a huge debt to ancient civilizations in Athens (Greece) and Rome. Although ancient, these civilizations were ahead of their times and very modern by any standards. They served as the models of modern democracy and continue to influence nearly every academic discipline, including philosophy, science, medicine, mathematics, law, architecture, and art. In this section, we take you on a virtual tour of ancient Athens and Rome to help you appreciate their living legacies.

Turning back the clock to ancient Athens

Athens wasn't blessed with the natural resources typically required to become a center for culture and art. Greece is rocky with poor soil. The staple crop at the time was wheat, but growing conditions in Greece were far from ideal. Over time, grapes and olive trees replaced much of the wheat, which meant importing wheat and other goods not produced locally.

The rugged landscape made road building difficult, so travel by sea was simpler and faster. The Greeks focused on the sea, as fishermen and as traders. Wine and olive oil became important Greek exports for the entire Mediterranean. The Greek city states also created colonies in other parts of the Mediterranean where wheat could be grown successfully to ensure adequate supplies. They also had plenty of marble and clay to use for building materials along with copper and zinc and some gold and silver, which enabled them to fashion tools and weapons, construct buildings, and create beautiful sculptures. Trade and colonialism spread Athenian knowledge and ideals throughout the Mediterranean.

The Athenians developed democratic government. They had overthrown their kings early on, creating a government based on social class and property, where eventually even the smallest landowners had a say. The Athenian Assembly, open to all male citizens over 18 and land owners, met several times a month to discuss specific issues, from selecting political and military leaders to voting on laws and finances. The assembly had an additional, rather unique feature: Any citizen deemed to be too powerful or too much of a problem could be ostracized, expelled from Athens by an anonymous vote of the assembly. Judges and magistrates were chosen by lot and random selection from the upper classes, but at the end of their one-year term they had to justify their decisions to the assembly — an early form of checks and balances.

One Athenian leader, Pericles, summed it up this way:

> Athens' constitution is called a democracy because it respects the interests not of a minority but of the whole people. When it is a question of settling private disputes, everyone is equal before the law; when it is a question of putting one person before another in positions of public responsibility, what counts is not membership of a particular class but the actual ability which the man possesses. No one, so long as he has it in him to be of service to the state, is kept in political obscurity because of poverty.

Athenian democracy was far from perfect. Only about 20 percent of Athens's population had citizenship. Slaves composed a large part of the population, and women had no right to vote. Debtors and their families could be sold into slavery and lost all rights until the debt was repaid. Participants in the assembly could be paid expenses, but no salaries, limiting attendance to the wealthier class. Despite these limitations, it was a beginning.

Who was eligible vote in the Athenian assembly?

(A) everyone over the age of 18

(B) all males over the age of 18

(C) all male citizens over the age of 18 who were landowners

(D) all citizens over the age of 18 who owned land

The correct answer is Choice (C), all male citizens over 18 who were landowners. Women had no rights outside the home, and as in modern times, 18 was the age when youth were admitted to adult duties and rights. The minimum qualification for male citizens over 18 to vote was a requirement to own property.

What led the Greeks to become traders?

(A) poor conditions for most agriculture

(B) the need to buy food they could not produce easily

(C) concentration on large scale production of a few specialized crops

(D) all of the above

BC, AD, BCE, and CE

You may have noticed that we refer to certain eras by the acronyms BCE (before common era) and CE (common era), and you may wonder why we're not referring to these eras as BC (before Christ) and AD (*anno domini*, meaning "the year of our Lord" or "after Christ").

The reason we use BCE and CE is because these have become the universal standard due to the fact that not all people around the world are Christian. Although BCE is essentially the same as BC, and CE is essentially the same as AD, the new standard steers clear of any differences in religious beliefs that may offend. Think of it as the PC (politically correct) alternative.

The Greeks discovered that even with poor soils they could produce some crops very well, such as wine and olives. The only way to make that system pay off was to export these crops and use the revenue to pay for other goods they didn't or couldn't produce. Your best choice is Choice (D), all of the above.

Exploring the ancient Roman Empire

Roman civilization built on classical Greece and the Hellenic empire of Alexander the Great. Romans conquered an empire that lasted more than 500 years, longer than any other western European empire. Including the Eastern Roman Empire, the Roman Empire lasted an amazing 1,500 years. Although Greek civilization left behind theater, arts, democratic government, and philosophy, the Roman heritage is more practical. Roman roads crossed Europe, providing the first safe and rapid communications network from Britain to Greece and Rome to Spain. The Romans were great administrators, creating a legal code that is the foundation of modern law, and proved to be talented engineers and builders.

Ruling the day with Roman law

Roman law began with the Twelve Tablets, dating back to 449 BCE (see the nearby sidebar for more about BCE). These were written laws in the tradition of Greece and Babylon, defining legal rights and punishments, procedures, and duties. The laws were posted in the Roman forum for all to see.

The Romans believed in swift justice but also in terms people would consider strange today, as is demonstrated by the following example:

Tablet One 6-9:

When the litigants settle their case by compromise, let the magistrate announce it. If they do not compromise, let them state each his own side of the case, in the comitium of the forum before noon. Afterwards let them talk it out together, while both are present. After noon, in case either party has failed to appear, let the magistrate pronounce judgment in favor of the one who is present. If both are present the trial may last until sunset but no later.

Tablet Three:

1. One who has confessed a debt, or against whom judgment has been pronounced, shall have thirty days to pay it in. After that forcible seizure of his person is allowed. The creditor shall bring him before the magistrate. Unless he pays the amount of the judgment or someone in the presence of the magistrate interferes in his behalf as protector

the creditor so shall take him home and fasten him in stocks or fetters. He shall fasten him with not less than fifteen pounds of weight or, if he chooses, with more. If the prisoner chooses, he may furnish his own food. If he does not, the creditor must give him a pound of meal daily; if he chooses he may give him more.

2. On the third market day let them divide his body among them. If they cut more or less than each one's share it shall be no crime.

What was the Roman punishment for an unpaid debt?

(A) public humiliation in stocks

(B) a court order to pay

(C) a regulated repayment plan

(D) death

The debtor was certainly put in stocks, but not as a public humiliation, Choice (A). The Court did order repayment, but only allowed three days for payment to be made, Choice (B). There was no court-ordered regulated payment plan, Choice (C). If the debtor made no repayment within three days, the penalty was death, Choice (D); Tablet 3, paragraph 2 spells that out. The debt holders literally got their pound (or more) of flesh.

Roman law developed to include both fixed written laws and *common law,* which is based on precedent and tradition. That structure allowed laws to evolve as attitudes changed. Roman culture also showed the beginnings of a division of laws into criminal and commercial; in the case of Rome, laws were divided between those that involved the state and those for individuals, which included criminal, contract, and civil law. They also had laws limiting terms in office for elected officials, laws regulating inheritance and debt, and even procedures for the right of appeal of death sentences. These laws, and a later collection of them called the Justinian Code, became the foundation of the European legal code. Most significantly, as trade recovered after the collapse of the Roman Empire, merchants discovered that Roman contract law was a far better tool than the tribal traditions they had inherited.

Building up Roman construction

Roman building skills were based on two life-changing inventions: the arch and concrete. The Romans took the concept of the arch and applied it in new ways. They used it to span large spaces without the need for pillars. Because the arch could support more weight than a flat ceiling, the Romans were able to build much larger structures. Egyptian and Greek temples needed pillars every few feet, but Romans were able to create bridges with large spans and buildings with large, unobstructed interior spaces. When arches are combined, they create a barrel vault, like the tunnel entrance to a theater in Pompeii in Figure 11-1. Rotating the arch around a common center creates a dome, something totally impossible before this innovation.

Romans also improved on concrete, a vital building material. It was strong and lasted far better than modern concrete, as witnessed by the Roman structures still standing 2,000 years later. (Good luck saying that about your driveway in a few thousand years.) Combining arch technology and the ability to pour concrete into forms allowed Romans to build huge domed buildings like the Pantheon and the Coliseum.

What is the significance of the arch in Roman architecture?

(A) Romans created buildings with large open interior spaces.

(B) They explain how the pyramids were built.

(C) Arches were a fast way to build aqueducts and bridges.

(D) All of the above.

Figure 11-1:
Tunnel
entrance to
a theater in
Pompeii.

Photo courtesy of Achim Krull, 2012

Choice (A) is the best answer based on the text. Choice (B) is wrong because the text mentions nothing about pyramids, and arches didn't play a role in the architectural design or construction of the pyramids. Choice (C) may be partially correct but it's not the best answer.

Exploring Interactions among Population, Environment, and Development

The population of any species depends on the resource base available. In a well-established ecosystem, populations of all plants and animals remain relatively stable. Predators keep the populations of their prey in check, and food supplies and disease tend to prevent overpopulation of any one species. Human populations are subject to the same rules and regulations imposed by ecosystems, but humans have managed more effectively than most other beings to change their environments and to move when their environments become uninhabitable. The following sections introduce some ways of looking at population development.

Malthus: Regulating population growth to preserve the food supply

Thomas Malthus wrote in 1798 that population growth increased exponentially (2, 4, 8, 16, 32, and so on) while food availability increased only arithmetically (1, 2, 3, 4, 5, and so on). That meant humans would outgrow the food supply, and the world would ultimately descend into a struggle for survival over limited resources. He had no faith in human ability to regulate its own fertility and was opposed to birth control. He argued the only way to avoid such a fate was strict regulation on reproduction, including marrying later in life.

His ideas were justified at that time. Industrialization had allowed a population boom while reducing the number of people available to grow crops. With industrialization also came improvements to living conditions, especially sanitation. As a result, the infant mortality rate among the population dropped dramatically while the birthrate remained steady. The result was a population boom.

Rostow: All the development's a stage

One model of development, the *demographic transition model,* was proposed by American economist Walter Rostow. He divided societal and economic development into five stages:

- ✔ **Traditional (Stage One):** People are either nomadic herders or subsistence farmers, with limited urbanization and a cultural and societal development similar to that of medieval Europe. This stage is characterized by a high birthrate, high total fertility rate, high infant mortality rate, and a high death rate, with an overall relatively short life span.

- ✔ **Preconditions for takeoff (Stage Two):** In this stage, society has accumulated enough surplus wealth and scientific knowledge to enable development. Farming has improved, as has education. Birthrates and total fertility rates remain high, but a slight drop in death rates and infant mortality rates occurs, causing population growth. This stage would apply to much of Europe in the 1600s.

- ✔ **Takeoff (Stage Three):** This category is the beginning of an industrial revolution, similar to English society in the early 1800s. A few key industries lead to a rapid growth of production. Goods become cheaper and widely available. People migrate en masse from the countryside to the cities, and employment changes from largely agricultural or artisanal to mechanized agriculture and factory-based mass production. Society is disrupted as farmers and specialized craftspeople lose employment. At the same time, factory workers are poorly paid and live in appalling urban conditions. At this stage, birthrates and total fertility remain high, but death and infant mortality rates continue to drop, and life expectancy increases. The population boom continues.

- ✔ **Drive to maturity (Stage Four):** This stage is a long period of economic development. Mechanization and technology spread into all levels of society. The economy is based on the production and sales of large volumes of industrial goods. As production increases dramatically, the benefits begin to reach the lowest as well as the middle and upper classes. The need for workers brings universal education, and the literacy rate of the population increases. The greater wealth also brings improvements in sanitary conditions, one of the biggest factors in lowering infant and maternal mortality, as well as increasing longevity. At this point the birthrates and total fertility rates drop quickly; however, the infant mortality rates drop, so rapid population growth continues.

- ✔ **The age of high consumption (Stage Five):** During this period, industrial production shifts away from heavy manufacturing and extractive industries (such as mining) to service industries. Financial industries, mass media, and government activities increase dramatically. Socially and economically, this stage represents Europe and North America after World War II. Improvements to healthcare have caused maternal and infant mortality rates to bottom out, and the total fertility rate drops to replacement level (discussed in the following section). Longevity increases, and population growth slows. The material standard of living for all classes has improved substantially.

In which of Rostow's stages of development would the United States have been at the time of the Civil War?

(A) traditional

(B) preconditions for takeoff

(C) takeoff

(D) drive to maturity

The most applicable stage is Choice (C), takeoff. The country as a whole was past the first two stages of development; it had developed an industrial base, mining, and banking. Urbanization increased, and a massive influx of immigrants came to the northern cities. It wasn't quite at stage four, where even the lower classes were benefiting from increased production.

In which of Rostow's stages of development would the Plains Indians have been in the 1860s?

(A) traditional

(B) preconditions for takeoff

(C) takeoff

(D) drive to maturity

The Plains Indians were largely nomadic tribes that lived off the land. Though they had an extensive and developed culture and tradition, their economic development didn't include permanent settlements. That excludes them from the third and fourth stages of the Rostow model (takeoff and drive to maturity, Choices (C) and (D)). For stage two (preconditions for takeoff), the society would have to have a degree of scientific development and surplus wealth. Neither of these was part of the Plains Indians' society, so Choice (B) is incorrect. That means the correct answer is Choice (A).

All of these stages depend on the resources available to society and how that society uses those resources. In Great Britain, the precondition for takeoff included iron ore, a readily available supply of coal, and the knowledge to use coal to make steel. Virtually all developed societies went through a similar model as they became wealthier and experienced an intellectual boom. Research into technologies and medicine, especially those needed for colonialism and warfare, continued to improve the life of the domestic population. During the period of mass consumption, the 1950s to 1980s, access to goods and services for all classes improved dramatically. Education and healthcare were widely available, subject only to individual financial constraints. Socially, people began a debate about the role of government in looking after the interests of all levels of society. Various movements to protect the interests of the working class became more influential.

China: Bearing fertility and replacement rates in mind

Rostow's model didn't contemplate one further stage. He expected population growth rates to slow, and the birthrate to level off at replacement level. However, today in many developed countries, the *total fertility rate* (the number of children a woman is expected to have in a lifetime, or TFR) and birthrate are below the replacement level. To maintain a population, each man and woman must have a child to replace them when they die. The *replacement level* TFR is about 2.1. In many European countries, the United States, and Canada, the TFR has fallen below 2.0. In some cases, including Germany and Norway, the TFR has dropped below 1.7. Unless supplemented by immigration, those populations are destined to shrink.

In a world facing global warming, pollution, extinction of numerous species, and competition for resources that are being depleted (including nonrenewable resources such as oil and gas), you may think that the prospect of a smaller human population is a good thing. However, dwindling populations face serious problems, such as not having a sufficient number of younger workers to support an aging population or a bloated government. In many cases, countries must increase immigration to maintain a stable economy, but immigration poses challenges when cultures and religions clash over values.

The People's Republic of China (Communist China), went through all Rostow's stages of development (see the preceding section) and this additional one. Before the communist revolution, China remained largely at stage one of development, traditional. It was an *agrarian* (farming) society made up predominantly of peasant farmers and a few very wealthy individuals. Farming involved much manual labor and produced only limited surpluses. The birthrate was high, but so was the mortality rate, and population grew relatively slowly. After the communists took over, Mao Zedong worked aggressively to address the grievances of the peasants. Land was redistributed and corruption curtailed. Improvements to education and healthcare followed. The standard of living and health improved, but the high birthrate and population growth continued.

From 1959 through 1961, China experienced a massive famine. Estimates of deaths vary wildly, but the death toll is believed to be in the range of 30 million people. After the famine, Mao believed an increase in the population would help lead to industrialization. The birthrate increased, and so did the population. By 1970, the TFR for China had climbed to just under 6 and continued to rise. The government realized this growth would bring about a new famine because the available land wasn't enough to produce a sufficient amount of food. China introduced the one-child policy, limiting all families, with few exceptions, to only one child. By 1995, China's TFR had dropped below replacement levels. Industrialization, improved agriculture, and an emphasis on trade have put China in Rostow's fifth stage, drive to maturity. The rate of population growth has dropped from 2.8 percent in 1970 to 0.61 percent in 2015, with an estimated TFR of only 1.66 in 2018.

The one-child policy has been a success in that it reduced population growth faster than economic factors or social pressures alone. However, it's also an example of unintended consequences. The normal statistical division between males and females is a slight preponderance of males, usually 106 males to 100 females. In China, many couples practice gender selection, with a preference for male children. As a result, in 2004, the division in China was 121 boys for every 100 girls. Although more families have sons to take care of them, their sons have fewer women available as mates. In addition, few children in China have siblings, making for a very large number of single-child homes. Nobody really knows the implication that this trend will have on China in the long term.

This chart displays the proportion of males to females at different ages in the People's Republic of China (PRC) in 2015.

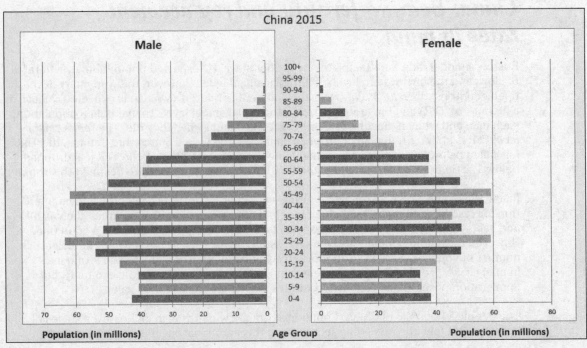

What is the proportion of males to females in the PRC in 2015 for people under 25, as compared to world averages?

(A) higher proportion of females

(B) higher proportion of males

(C) about world average

(D) cannot determine from the graph

The correct answer is Choice (B). China has significantly more males than females, especially in the younger age groups. Chinese tradition requires elderly parents to live with their oldest son. With only one child allowed, that's a problem.

Investigating Border Types and Conflicts

Borders cause no end of trouble. They seem like a good idea, indicating where one country's holdings end and another's begins, but problems arise when leaders disagree where exactly that line is. Natural borders are easy. They follow a river, a mountain range, a coastline, or some other physical feature that is easily identified. The people who live in states that border along the Mississippi know exactly when they enter or leave their state, at least on the river side. Natural borders have a further advantage: They are more easily defensible. Ancient Egypt was relatively safe from invasion, protected by desert on the west and south and the Red Sea to the east. Invading Italy required climbing over the Alps or sailing across the Mediterranean Sea first. Even lesser natural boundaries, such as the Rhine River, create defensible barriers.

Natural boundaries also divide cultures, which become nations. For example, people on the north side of the Alps spoke German, while those on the south side spoke Italian. The two cultures developed separately, intermingling when required but developing unique cultural identities and languages. The English Channel is a natural boundary between Britain and continental Europe, protecting the British Isles from invasion (with minor exceptions) and creating a culture and language different from those of the mainland.

Artificial borders can cause major geopolitical conflicts. Where you see a straight line on the map in Figure 11-2, you're looking at an artificial border. The settlers in the original 13 colonies landed on the coast and gradually moved inland. Because the colonies were started separately, they needed boundaries to keep themselves apart. In some cases, the boundaries followed a river or lake. The northern boundary of New York State follows parts of the Saint Lawrence River and Lakes Ontario and Erie. But the straight lines are where some negotiators decided to say, "Let's just call this the border." If both parties agree, as in the case of state or provincial borders in North America, there's no problem. Within the United States, the people on either side of the borders are the same, the culture is much the same, and so are the economies of adjacent states.

Elsewhere, such as on the African continent, artificial borders have become a major problem. They were drawn by the colonial powers of the day to delineate areas from which competing colonial powers could extract resources. The borders ignored local ethnic, cultural, tribal, or linguistic groups. When the colonial powers left, the newly independent countries faced the problem of integrating people who may have been traditional enemies. The tragic genocide in Rwanda was caused in part by such ethnic differences. Divisions of countries in the Middle East followed a similar pattern. Areas were severed and made into independent countries without regard for tribal or religious associations. One result is that in countries such as Iraq, people of different branches of Islam live within the same borders. Strong religious tensions among these branches have made the creation of a unified country very difficult. Rebellions and civil uprisings along ethnic lines are a common occurrence.

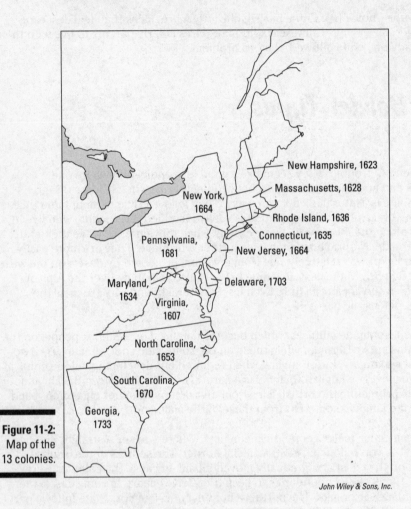

Figure 11-2:
Map of the
13 colonies.

John Wiley & Sons, Inc.

This map combines a satellite view with a standard map outline to show the state of New Hampshire.

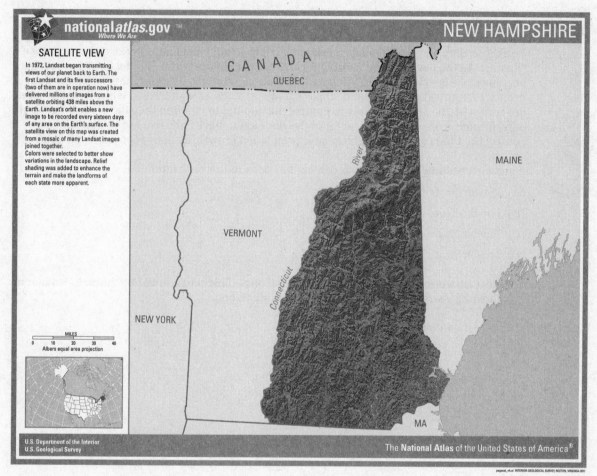

Judging by the image, which border is likely to be mostly a natural one?

(A) the border with Vermont

(B) the border with Maine

(C) the border with Maryland

(D) none of the above

The border between New Hampshire and Maine is almost completely straight for most of its length. That means it's probably an artificial border. The same can be said for the border with Maryland. That means Choices (B) and (C) are wrong. However, the border with Vermont is irregular, and a close look at the map tells you that the Connecticut River runs along that line. This boundary is a natural border following the Connecticut River. The correct answer is Choice (A).

Pondering the Population Puzzle

Several factors affect population growth, including migration and changes in the fertility rate. The following sections give you some insight into how these issues may crop up on the GED test.

Schooling yourself about education's impact on the TFR

The good news is that the growth rate of the world's population is slowing. The bad news is that it's still growing. The total fertility rate (which we discuss in the earlier section "China: Bearing fertility and replacement rates in mind") is steadily declining. In Rostow's model (see "Rostow: All the development's a stage" earlier in the chapter), the TFR declines as societies become more developed and switch to an industrial economy. Factors that encourage that drop are improved education and employment and a higher standard of living. When women are educated, they're more likely to control the number of children they have. In a wage economy, income is also a deciding factor in the decision to have children. Prohibition and state control like China's one-child policy slow population growth, as does economic well-being.

As women become better educated, what happens to the birthrate?

(A) The birthrate increases.

(B) The birthrate decreases.

(C) The birthrate stays the same.

(D) The birthrate fluctuates.

The best answer is Choice (B). Education is strongly linked to a lower birthrate in women of childbearing years. The other choices are simply wrong.

Consider the following charts.

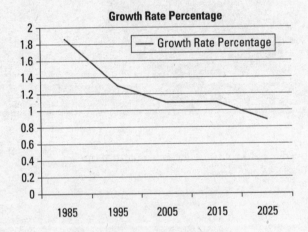

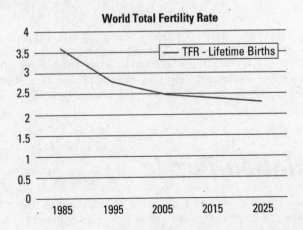

To maintain a population at its current level, the population's TFR must be 2.1. A mother and father must each be replaced, and a certain number of additional births must occur to make up the shortfalls due to infant mortality and other casualties. The first chart shows changes in growth rate to a certain population from 1985 to 2025. The second chart shows the world's total fertility rate. If the trend continues as shown, when is the total fertility rate likely to reach replacement level?

(A) 2015

(B) 2020

(C) 2025

(D) Sometime after 2040

You need to mentally project and extend the trend line. The line shows a decline, but that decline is slowing. Where the line ultimately ends is immaterial. You need to project when it would reach the 2.1 level. The line also shows the data for 2015, 2020, and 2025. For those dates the TFR hasn't yet reached replacement levels, so Choices (A), (B), and (C) are incorrect. Therefore, your best answer is Choice (D).

Making sense of migration

Whenever possible, people have tried to improve their living conditions. The Europeans who came to North America initially came here to explore and for adventure, seeking wealth. Those who followed came to make new lives for themselves. The French who settled in New France and Louisiana, the Spaniards in Mexico and California, and the English and Scots all along the Atlantic Coast all came to settle. When tens of thousands of Irish came here during the potato famine they were hoping for a better life in a new country. When Europeans left after World Wars I and II to come to North America they were looking for a better life.

When immigrants come to a new country, they bring with them their language, their customs, and many things about their culture. Whether through their music or their food, their skills or their attitudes, they affect the way of life in the country they come to.

The triggers of migration often are fear and desperation. When people flee from Central America to the United States or from North Africa and the Middle East to Europe, they're generally desperate. They sacrifice everything and put their lives at risk to escape. The illegal migration so common today is caused in part by immigration restrictions. The developed countries of the world are reluctant to accept immigrants from the less-developed regions. The fear is that immigrants will become a burden to society or, because they're so different, never become true members of the receiving society. People always fear "the other."

The vast numbers of refugees created by civil wars in rebellions in the Middle East and North Africa have indeed become an economic and political problem for Europe. Most of these refugees arrive with nothing, not even a local language, and do become at least temporarily a burden. A further question for the recipient countries is that the refugees often come with totally different cultural, ethical, and religious outlooks. Countries are often concerned over whether the immigrants will ever fit in.

America has long prided itself on being a melting pot, where migrants arrive and eventually blend in with the existing population. In the process, a little bit of "the other" rubs off on America, creating a vibrant society. The question that arises today is to what extent the melting pot is still working. Some ethnic communities in the United States (and in other countries) resist integration, remaining in distinct ethnic enclaves with their own cultures and languages rather than merging with the existing national culture.

France, Britain, Sweden, and Germany have all experienced difficulties with the assimilation of migrants. That struggle has created an inevitable backlash and social unrest as the migrants become the new have-nots in society. Integration is a growing issue.

Why do people emigrate?

(A) fleeing famine or war

(B) economic improvement

(C) fear of persecution

(D) all of the above

As the text shows, the best answer is Choice (D), all of the above. People leave their home countries for numerous reasons, all having to do with physical and economic survival. They want safer, better lives.

Chapter 12

Writing a First-Class Extended Response

· ·

In This Chapter

▶ Knowing what the evaluators are looking for

▶ Understanding the essay prompt and writing a clear, direct thesis statement

▶ Outlining your essay and finding evidence to support your claims

▶ Sizing up your audience, purpose, and message

▶ Smoothing out the rough spots

· ·

The Social Studies Extended Response item asks you to write an essay in 25 minutes on an *enduring issue,* one that "reflects the founding principles of the United States and is an important idea that people often grapple with as new situations arise." This part of the test assesses your literacy and understanding. You must demonstrate an ability to read and comprehend any source content provided (from a quotation and an excerpt from a reading passage), incorporate your own knowledge, present a coherent and well-organized written response, and follow the rules of Standard English grammar, usage, punctuation, and spelling.

Keep in mind that writing this essay isn't that different from writing a letter or a blog post — except that you must explain and clarify the subject for the reader without rambling on until you run out of space.

In this chapter, we explain the criteria used to score the Extended Response and walk you through the process to ensure that your essay meets the criteria. Although writing isn't necessarily a linear process, we present a sequential approach to writing your Extended Response. As you revise your essay, you may need or want to revisit earlier steps in the process.

Checking Out the Extended Response Guidelines

Whenever you write an essay, knowing how it's going to be scored helps to ensure that you meet the requirements of the assignment. In the case of the Social Studies Extended Response, the people reading your essay will be scoring it based on how well you do the following:

✔ **Stick to the topic.** Read the passage (usually a quote and a longer passage) and the prompt, which tells you what to write about, and carefully stick to the topic. The prompt tells you to consider the passage in terms of an enduring issue in U.S. history — an issue that reflects the founding principles of the United States and is still relevant today.

✔ **Present a well-thought-out argument in a well-organized manner.** Take and express a clear stand on the issue and present your case in a logical manner. Don't merely repeat what the passages already state. Your essay should follow a well-structured outline with your thesis supported by two or more claims, with each claim supported by evidence.

✔ **Support your claims.** Use multiple pieces from the passages as evidence to support your claims.

✔ **Incorporate your own knowledge.** Further support your claims with your own knowledge of history.

✔ **Transition smoothly from sentence to sentence and from one paragraph to the next.** Use transition words and other techniques to establish a smooth and logical flow.

✔ **Choose precise words and use them correctly.** Precise words express ideas clearly and efficiently, but don't use a word if you're unsure of its meaning.

✔ **Vary your sentence structure.** Compose sentences with different subjects, lengths, and types. Starting every sentence with "Roosevelt says" becomes repetitive. Likewise, using all short subject-verb sentences makes an essay monotonous.

✔ **Avoid errors in grammar, usage, punctuation, and spelling.** Use any remaining time at the end to proofread your essay and correct errors.

Sneaking a Peek at the Stimulus Material and the Essay Prompt

Within the 25 minutes that you have to write the Social Studies Extended Response essay, you have to read and analyze the *stimulus materials* (the quote and passage to which you're to respond) and the *prompt* (instructions that tell you what to write about). After that, you have to decide on your argument and rough out your answer. Finally, you must write your response in the form of a properly constructed essay.

Try to wrap it up in 20 minutes so you have 5 minutes at the end to review your work — to check for grammar and spelling errors and possibly consider areas of the paper that need rewriting. However, remember that the Extended Response doesn't need to be a polished, impeccably edited paper. Given the time constraints, the GED test evaluators expect the equivalent of a good first draft. Minor mechanical mistakes (punctuation errors and typos) are expected, but anything more than that will be penalized.

Checking out the stimulus material

The stimulus material consists of two passages: perhaps a short quote or an extract from a historical document and another passage. Here's an example:

Stimulus Material

Excerpt from the Constitution of the United States, Article I, Section 8

The Congress shall have Power . . . To make all Laws which shall be necessary and proper for carrying into Execution the foregoing Powers, and all other Powers vested by this Constitution in the Government of the United States, or in any Department or Officer thereof.

Press Release: House Speaker Boehner to President Obama: This Is Not How American Democracy Works

WASHINGTON, DC — House Speaker John Boehner (R-OH) released the following statement today regarding President Obama's unilateral action on immigration:

The American people want both parties to focus on solving problems together; they don't support unilateral action from a president who is more interested in partisan politics than working with the people's elected representatives. That is not how American democracy works. Not long ago, President Obama said the unilateral action he just announced was "not an option" and claimed he'd already "done everything that I can on my own." He said it would lead to a "surge in more illegal immigration." He said he was "not a king" and "not the emperor" and that he was "bound by the Constitution." He said an action like this would exceed his authority and be "difficult to justify legally." He may have changed his position, but that doesn't change the Constitution.

By ignoring the will of the American people, President Obama has cemented his legacy of lawlessness and squandered what little credibility he had left. His "my way or the highway" approach makes it harder to build the trust with the American people that is necessary to get things done on behalf of the country. Republicans are left with the serious responsibility of upholding our oath of office. We will not shrink from this duty, because our allegiance lies with the American people. We will listen to them, work with our members, and protect the Constitution.

NOTE: Before he changed his position, President Obama said at least 22 times that he could not make his own law without Congress, ignore current laws, or expand his 2012 executive action. He said doing so "would be both unwise and unfair" and "could lead to a surge in more illegal immigration." According to several surveys, a majority of Americans oppose his unilateral action. The administration has also gone to great lengths to hide the truth about its immigration policies from the American people.

In this example, both passages refer to the separation of powers as established in the Constitution of the United States, so that separation is obviously an enduring issue. If you know a little about the difference between democracy in the United States and in Britain, you could write a very compelling Extended Response about this enduring issue, explaining that in Britain, the prime minister holds power only so long as he or she commands a majority of votes in the House of Commons. So in Britain, if the prime minister's party wants immigration reform, it gets immigration reform; no unilateral action on the prime minister's part is necessary to override the opposition. Of course, you could respond in other clever ways as well.

Taking a look at the prompt

The prompt for the Extended Response always goes something like this:

In your response, develop an argument about how _____ reflects an enduring issue. Incorporate relevant and specific evidence from the stimulus material and your own knowledge of the enduring issue.

The GED testing service defines an enduring issue as an important topic or idea in American history, one that spans many eras and continues to shape policy. These are issues that have no simple solution and that American people continue to struggle to resolve.

The prompt is straightforward but can be quite a challenge because it requires that you read and understand the stimulus material and explain how the material represents an enduring issue in U.S. politics and policy.

Formulating a Clear, Direct Thesis Statement

A good essay must start with a clear thesis statement. That statement defines your argument, tells readers what to expect, and prepares them for the supporting evidence you present.

You can develop your thesis statement by following the terms of the prompt. The stimulus material presents a very specific event or topic. Your thesis indicates how the subject of the stimulus material qualifies as an enduring issue. For example, the passages may be about the utility of unions in the year 2015, but you should consider that the more general topic is labor relations and the struggles between employers and employees over economic issues. You can justify a thesis statement arguing that the enduring issue is the struggle between laborers' desire for acceptable working conditions and wages and employers' desire to keep their costs down.

Analyze the two passages, jotting down key statements. Ask yourself, what point are they making? Look at the specifics you've listed. What general point are they making? You can develop a stimulus passage about opposition to sending troops into combat somewhere into the enduring issue of American isolationism. Arguments about federal budgets or taxation may apply to the enduring issue of the distribution of wealth.

Place your thesis statement at the beginning of your paper. It should be the first sentence. Be blunt. Be precise. Say exactly what you mean to argue.

Avoid the pitfall of many high school essays. Think to yourself, "I intend to prove that," but don't actually write it. The readers know that's what you intend to do, so just do it.

Structuring Your Essay

An essay is like a house. To stand strong, your essay needs to be built on a firm foundation. Every premise must support the thesis and be supported by evidence.

In the following sections, we break down this approach by explaining the fundamentals of creating an outline for your Extended Response and demonstrating how premises and supporting evidence fit into the outline.

Treat each paragraph in the body of your essay as a mini-essay. The first sentence (the premise) serves as the thesis, and the remaining sentences support the premise.

Outlining your Extended Response

It's easy to drift off topic when writing an Extended Response. The prompt instructs you to write about the dancing hippos in a Disney movie, and suddenly you remember Dumbo, a cute, chubby little elephant. You decide to expand on the cute little elephant and suddenly find yourself writing about the zoo. Twenty-five minutes later, you realize that you haven't written anything about the dancing hippos.

Having an outline in place before you start writing serves two purposes: It keeps you from drifting off topic, and it enables you to determine whether your train of thought is really a train and not a train wreck before you invest a great deal of time developing a certain line of reasoning.

When outlining your Extended Response, you have two approaches that align with the two structures shown in Figure 12-1:

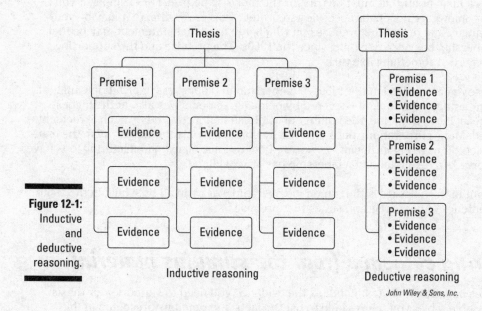

Figure 12-1:
Inductive
and
deductive
reasoning.

Inductive reasoning

Deductive reasoning

✔ **Inductive reasoning:** With inductive reasoning, your thesis statement is a conclusion drawn from the evidence you provide. For example, you may argue that a certain executive order from the president is constitutional (your thesis statement) based on two or three examples of executive orders issued by former presidents, each of which serves as a premise.

With inductive reasoning, each premise is independent, so you can arrange them however you want. We recommend starting with your weakest point and ending with your strongest for greater impact and to leave a strong impression at the end. However, you may also choose to lead with your strongest point or arrange them in the order that seems most logical.

✔ **Deductive reasoning:** With deductive reasoning, you draw conclusions with logical arguments. For example, you may argue that the Constitution states that only Congress can pass laws (premise 1), a certain executive order from the president constitutes a law (premise 2), and therefore the executive order is unconstitutional (thesis). Another option is to use cause-and-effect reasoning to explore the possible implications of a system in which executive orders are allowed to establish laws.

After outlining your argument, you still need an introductory paragraph at the beginning and a concluding paragraph at the end, but those are much easier to compose when you have a clear idea of what you want to say (your thesis) and how you're going to support it with evidence.

The GED test center provides you with three erasable tablets to help you organize your Extended Response. Write your thesis statement on one tablet and use each tablet to outline one premise or key point in your argument. Write the premise followed by a list of evidence from the stimulus material and your own knowledge. Glance at the tablets as you write your Extended Response to be sure you're sticking to the topic and not drifting off in some other direction.

Stating your premises (main points)

A *premise* is a main point that must be true for the thesis to be true. For example, if you're arguing that unions are no longer necessary to protect workers' rights, that may be your thesis statement, and one of the premises on which you base that statement may be that union membership has been declining since the 1960s. The premise and the supporting evidence may read something like this:

The labor movement peaked in the 1960s. Membership in unions was at an all-time high, and the number of establishments covered by union agreements was also at the highest level ever seen. Since that time, the number of establishments covered by such agreements has declined. Many corporations once covered by union agreements, especially in the manufacturing sector, have either declined or ceased operations. Many manufacturing jobs have gone offshore. As a result, union membership has also declined.

The key point in this passage is that union membership was at an all-time high in the 1960s. The first sentence of the paragraph states that premise.

Gathering evidence from the stimulus material

The stimulus material in the test contains the evidence you need to support your thesis. Use the erasable tablet you're provided to list the facts and opinions presented in the passages. Ask yourself how each point or opinion relates to the point of the entire passage. Add the useful points that support your thesis to the list. If part of the stimulus material is an original document or a speech, look for suitable phrases or short quotes to support your arguments.

The labor movement paragraph in the preceding section provides a number of facts to support the premise of the paragraph. On the test, you use your erasable tablet to briefly list those facts:

- Fewer establishments are covered by union agreements.
- Some union establishments have shrunk, employing fewer workers.
- Some union establishments have gone out of business.
- Some manufacturing has gone offshore reducing available union jobs.

You now have outlined the key points to support the premise about union membership being at its peak in the 1960s. Applying this approach to the stimulus passages on the Extended Response gives you both the key points to back your thesis and the evidence to back your key points.

Adding evidence from your own knowledge

When writing the Extended Response, draw from your own knowledge of history and current events to support your position and demonstrate to the evaluators that you know your stuff when it comes to social studies. We urge you to read, read, and read some more — history books, news stories, editorials, political commentaries, and other content related to social studies. Being familiar with the broad scope of American history, civics, and politics will help with the Extended Response. The evaluators are looking very specifically for evidence that you've done that.

If the labor movement paragraph in the earlier section "Stating your premises (main points)" was part of a stimulus for the Extended Response, you may include evidence from your own knowledge of changes to the employment scene or difficulties in negotiating union contracts. You could include information about the outsourcing of jobs to low-wage countries or even an example of management of the new Volkswagen plant in Chattanooga, stating that unions are actually a "good thing" for business.

You don't need to become a walking encyclopedia of American civics or history, but you should know the broad sweep and some current events and issues that you can incorporate into your Extended Response. Of course, you don't know what the Extended Response stimulus material and prompt will ask you to write about, so read broadly to get up to speed on a variety of enduring issues.

Mastering the formula essay

Even skilled and experienced writers struggle with outlines, feeling that they're too restrictive and that they essentially have to "write the essay" before they can write the outline. We think outlining is the best approach, however, because it prevents you from painting yourself into a corner — spending time writing only to reach a logical dead-end with no time to take a detour. If you still can't clear the outlining hurdle, think in terms of paragraphs and following a model.

Every writer has a favorite model. You've probably heard of the *hamburger, pyramid,* and *inverted pyramid* models. You can find plenty of information about those models online. We recommend a variation of another common model, the five-paragraph essay, which we call the *formula essay.* The Social Studies Extended Response can be shorter than the RLA essay (four or five paragraphs rather than five or six), so an introductory paragraph, a two-or-three paragraph middle section presenting supporting evidence, and a concluding paragraph restating your point and evidence should be enough. Here's the formula (outline), with each item in the list representing a paragraph:

1. **Introduction with thesis statement and, possibly, evidence preview.**

   This paragraph is where you state your position. You identify the issue introduced in the passages and explain why it's an enduring issue. Evaluators will look for a clear thesis statement and brief preview of the evidence — a summary of the arguments you intend to make to develop your thesis, to let the reader know what's coming next. Simply summarize the evidence without going into details.

2. **Premise 1 with supporting evidence.**

   State your first premise, your argument, and follow up with two or three sentences of supporting detail based primarily on the evidence presented in the two passages. Explain how this evidence supports your premise. Very brief quotes and references to the stimulus passages are fine, but make sure you link them to your thesis. Merely restating content from the stimulus material isn't sufficient.

3. **Premise 2 with supporting evidence.**

   State your second premise in the next paragraph, followed by two or three sentences of supporting detail based primarily on the evidence presented in the two passages. Use this section as an opportunity to work in your own knowledge because that's one of the traits that counts toward your score.

4. **(Optional) Premise 3 with supporting evidence.**

   State your third premise in the next paragraph, followed by two or three sentences of supporting detail based primarily on the evidence presented in the two passages.

5. **Conclusion with restatement of thesis and evidence recap.**

   Wrap it up. Restate your thesis clearly and briefly recap the key evidence you had in your introduction for your thesis. A strong closing leaves a positive and lasting impression.

Considering Purpose, Audience, and Message

Whenever you write anything — your GED Extended Response, a letter to the editor of your local paper, or a cover letter for your resume — you need to think about what you want the text to accomplish, the person(s) you're addressing, and the message you want to convey. You don't have to write all this information down or address it any formal way in your essay, but you do need to keep purpose, audience, and message in mind as you write your Extended Response. In the following sections, we describe each of these considerations in turn.

Purpose

You know why you're writing a Social Studies Extended Response. The purpose is to express your point of view and convince the reader that you're right. Of course, your underlying purpose is to score as high as possible on this portion of the test, but if you can convince the evaluators of your Extended Response argument, you'll achieve that goal, too.

Understanding purpose is important because it influences everything from organization to word choice. A letter to persuade your boss to give you a raise is quite different from instructions for connecting to a Wi-Fi hotspot.

Your purpose in an argumentative essay is to convince the reader. Don't get confused with purposes of other types of writing. Your purpose isn't to instruct, describe, or tell a story. Although you do need to inform the reader in terms of providing evidence to support your claims (thesis and premises), your primary objective isn't expository (to inform or explain). Your objective is to persuade.

Audience

Every essay focuses on a particular audience. A newspaper editorial is aimed at a particular readership. An Internet football fan blog focuses on a very specific and different readership. Before you put pen to paper, you need to think about who will be reading your essay. Your audience for every piece of writing will have a particular level of education and set of interests. Your audience may have specific political leanings, biases, and preconceptions. To persuade such an audience of your viewpoint, you need to write your essay in such a way that this audience will accept your points. Whether you're writing for preteens or adults, professors, or your neighbors, you must adjust the way you present the information.

Because readers have different levels of education, you tailor the vocabulary and level of information to that readership. The tone you adopt reflects the intended audience. In the case of the Social Studies Extended Response, your essay is aimed at the evaluators. Write your essay as if to convince your high school English teacher. The evaluators expect you to use Standard English and demonstrate a command of vocabulary, grammar, and mechanics (punctuation and spelling). More importantly, they want to see well-organized thinking and clear expression.

Message

The message is what you want the reader to understand and accept. Present that message clearly and in a way that your audience will accept it. After you've organized the key points you want to present in your essay, you need to review how well they prove your thesis. You also want to review how you present the information. You're dealing with a very specific topic on the Extended Response. Make sure you're presenting your premises and evidence factually; avoid wording that suggests bias. You want to be convincing without being harsh. The wording needs to be strong enough to make the message clear without becoming so aggressive that the audience rejects it.

Writing, Revising, and Editing Your Essay: Best Practices

Preparation is crucial in determining what to say, how to organize your thoughts, and how to present your message to a specific audience, but it's not going to write your essay for you. Preparation focuses on the big-picture component of good essay writing — content. Writing a top-notch essay also requires attention to detail — choosing precise words, expressing yourself efficiently, avoiding redundancy, transitioning smoothly from one thought to the next, varying your sentence structure, and avoiding errors in grammar, spelling, and punctuation.

In this section, we shift your focus to these and other details that help improve your writing overall.

Using precise language

Precise language is concise language — using a single word rather than two or three or five to express your intended meaning. When you're writing your Extended Response, you don't have a dictionary or thesaurus at your side, so you have to rely on only the words you know and can recall. Even so, you must try your best to use the most precise and accurate words you can think of to express your ideas. As you write, be especially carefully about the following:

- **Homonyms:** Words that sound the same but differ in meaning, such as *it's* (meaning "it is") and *its* (the possessive form of *it*) and *there* (meaning "not here") and *their* (meaning "belonging to them").

- **Frequently confused words:** Words such as *accept* and *except* and *principal* and *principle* that people commonly misuse.

- **Slang and other informal English:** Phrases such as *kind of* and *sort of* or, even worse, *kinda* and *sorta*.

- **Passive voice:** Sentences that start with anything other than the person or thing performing the action, such as "It was decided," which makes the reader wonder "Who decided?"

- **Negative phrases:** Phrases with "no" or "not" that can be rephrased into shorter, positive statements. You can reword "Nothing short of complete surrender was acceptable to General Patton" as "General Patton would accept only complete surrender."

- **Qualifiers:** Words such as *actually, really, basically, essential,* and *somewhat* are often unnecessary.

- **Redundancy:** Repetition of words, statements, details, or ideas, as in "The senator was only partially, not fully, committed to the legislation."

- **Nominalizations:** Verbs used as nouns, such as *indication* (indicate) and *stabilization* (stabilize).

- **Phrasal verbs:** Two or more words used together to express action, such as *decide on* (choose) and *hold up* (delay).

✔ **Unnecessary use of prepositions:** Prepositional phrases that can be reduced to one or two words, such as "view of the majority" (majority's view) or "on a regular basis" (regularly).

The English language has dozens of words meaning roughly the same thing. Synonyms have roughly the same meaning but their meanings have subtle differences. Choose the most precise word you can think of. Misusing vocabulary counts against you. However, don't get so obsessed with choosing the right word that you run out of time; express yourself as clearly as possible and then go back through if time remains and make adjustments.

Correct the following sentences.

1. Only after careful consideration did President Obama settle on a course of action.

    _____

2. The union movement was seen as incompatible with modern commerce.

    _____

3. The founding fathers established a set of principles to guide the formation of a representative democracy.

    _____

4. Protestors practiced resistance.

    _____

5. If a person is not at least 35 years old, she cannot be elected president of the United States.

    _____

Now compare your revised sentences to these:

1. After careful consideration, President Obama chose a course of action.

2. Opponents considered the union movement incompatible with modern commerce.

3. The founding fathers established a set of principles to form a representative democracy.

4. Protestors resisted.

5. To be elected president of the United States, a person must be at least 35 years old.

Being terse

Think of wordiness in terms of newspaper writing. A headline has to capture in a few words the entire point of the story. People use interjections in spoken language all the time. In writing, they use a lot of descriptive language to explain unclear points. They throw in extra adjectives and adverbs that simply repeat what the noun or verb already states. Some writers feel it sounds more academic or educated, but it merely confuses and irritates. *Terse* writing is to the point, uses direct statements, and avoids unnecessary embellishment.

Here's a wordy passage to practice on. Eliminate unnecessary words and phrases, and write your revision on a sheet of paper.

At any given moment, there are people who want to go for long drives and little automotive adventures on the weekend. It is obvious that this is something that car rental companies should exploit. We all know that rental companies can use all the extra revenues they can get, due to the fact that the economy has worsened, making renting a car a frivolous expense often cut.

When you're done, grade yourself. You can gauge your success by counting the number of words you eliminated or comparing your revision to the following version:

> Many people like long weekend drives. Because fewer people can afford to rent cars since the recession, car rental companies could target this market to improve revenues.

Evaluate your writing the same way. Does a particular word or phrase add anything to the text? Can it be replaced with simpler words or phrases?

Opting for active over passive voice

In a typical sentence, the actor enters first and then performs. You know from the beginning who's doing what. Passive voice flips the order:

Passive: The lesson was written on the blackboard by the teacher.

Active: The teacher wrote the lesson on the blackboard.

Passive: The cells were attacked by the virus.

Active: The virus attacked the cells.

As you can see, the passive voice is indirect, unclear, and wordy. However, passive voice comes in handy at times, such as when a politician wants to distance herself from an unpopular decision; she can simply say, for example, "The decision was made to increase taxes." It's also helpful in formal essays or scientific writing, when the writer must shift the focus from the observer to the observed.

Eliminating redundancy

Beware of phrases that state the same thing twice. Here are some common redundant phrases to avoid along with their succinct counterparts.

Redundant	Succinct
a total of a dozen eggs	a dozen eggs
briefly summarize	summarize
close proximity	close; nearby
cooperate together	cooperate
end result	result
exactly the same	identical; the same
period of two weeks	two weeks
revert back	revert

Transitioning smoothly from one point to the next

Your Extended Response is scored partially on how well you transition from one sentence to the next and from one paragraph to the next. Evaluators need to be able to follow your train of thought if you want to earn a high score. To build smooth transitions into your Extended Response, use the following techniques:

- ✔ **Stick to your outline.** A well-organized essay doesn't have to rely so much on heavy-duty transitional words and phrases, such as: *as a result, therefore,* and *consequently.*

- ✔ **Let the reader know what's coming.** You can look at writing as a process of making promises to the reader and delivering on those promises. For example, you may mention three reasons for taking a certain position. The reader then knows to expect three reasons, and your transitions become much easier to manage.

- ✔ **Repeat key words and phrases.** Frequently, you can subtly transition from sentence to sentence or paragraph to paragraph by repeating one or more key words from the previous sentence in the new sentence.

- ✔ **Use transitional phrases as needed.** Transitional phrases provide valuable information to readers regarding how two ideas are related, or they signal a shift or contrast between two ideas. Although you should use them sparingly, don't avoid using them altogether. Table 12-1 features a list of transition words that are likely to come in very handy as you compose your Extended Response.

Table 12-1	Transition Words
Purpose	*Transition words*
Addition	also, again, as well as, besides, furthermore, in addition
Consequence	accordingly, as a result, consequently, hence, otherwise, so then, subsequently, therefore, thus,
Comparison	but, by the same token, conversely, however, in contrast, instead, likewise, nevertheless, on one hand, on the contrary, on the other hand, rather, similarly, still, yet
Emphasis	above all, chiefly, especially, particularly, singularly, with attention to
Exception	aside from, barring, beside, except, excepting, excluding, exclusive of, other than, outside of
Example	chiefly, especially, for example, for instance, in particular, including, namely, particularly, primarily, specifically, such as
Generalization	as a rule, as usual, for the most part, generally, generally speaking, ordinarily, usually
Restatement	in brief, in essence, in other words, in short, namely, that is, that is to say
Sequence	afterward, at first, at the same time, earlier, first of all, for now, for the time being, in the first place, in the meantime, in time, in turn, later, later on, meanwhile, next, simultaneously, soon, the next step, then, to begin with, while
Summary	after all, all in all, all things considered, briefly, by and large, finally, in any case, in any event, in brief, in conclusion, in short, in summary, in the final analysis, on balance, on the whole, to sum up, to summarize

Here's a passage that shows transitional words (underlined) in action:

The technology boom and the move toward greater personalization have created a society that is much more fragmented. In the '70s and '80s, everyone watched the same movies and TV shows, listened to the same music, and grew up being involved in many of the same activities. <u>As a result</u>, people had closer personal bonds. <u>In contrast</u>, we now have hundreds of cable and network TV shows to choose from, a wide variety of music on radio and via the Internet, thousands of video games, and numerous social networks to choose from. <u>Consequently</u>, an individual's attention is drawn in numerous directions, and people don't have the shared knowledge and experience needed to form strong emotional attachments. <u>Therefore</u>, people would probably be better off with fewer choices.

Don't overuse transitional words or phrases, as we did in this sample passage. We used an abundance in this passage to illustrate their use. Moreover, be sure to use a variety of transitional words, and better yet, a variety of transitional techniques.

Avoiding overuse of the verb "to be" in all its forms

People who merely exist are boring, as is the verb *to be* in all of its forms: *be, being, been, is, am, are, was,* and *were.* Unless these are accompanied by an action verb, be on the lookout for a weak and/or wordy construction.

Rewrite the following sentences by replacing forms of the verb *to be* with more active, descriptive verbs.

1. There are many constituents who would disagree with the senator.

    _____

2. It is obvious that unenforced laws promote criminal activity.

    _____

3. The protesters were the people who looted the store.

    _____

4. Environmentalists were the major proponents of the new regulations.

    _____

Your revisions may vary. These are only examples:

1. Many constituents would disagree with the senator.
2. Obviously, unenforced laws promote crime.
3. The protesters looted the store.
4. Environmentalists promoted the new regulations.

Avoid starting a sentence with an "it + be" or "there + be" construction, such as "It is important that" and "There are people who." These are known as *expletives* and almost always produce weak, wordy sentences.

You can find entire websites devoted to concise writing, complete with plentiful examples, exercises, and even some sample questions. Search the web for "concise writing" or "eliminating wordiness."

Varying your sentence structure

Nothing is more boring than sentences that are all alike. That would be like a song consisting of only one note or the annoying drip, drip, drip of a leaky faucet. Vary your sentence structure by using the following techniques:

- **Combine short sentences.** If two short, adjacent sentences are related, consider combining them by joining them with a comma and a coordinate conjunction, such as *and, but, or, for, nor, so,* or *yet* to form a compound sentence. For example, if you have the sentences "In the 1960s, the union movement was strong." and "Corporations were growing quickly.", you can combine them to form this compound sentence:

  In the 1960s, the union movement was strong, and corporations were growing quickly.

  You can also combine two independent clauses (complete sentences) by joining them with a semicolon.

- **Divide long sentences.** If you run out of breath reading a sentence, consider breaking it into two or more sentences. Breaking long sentences into short sentences is often useful to stress an important point or achieve some other dramatic effect. For example, you can break this long sentence into shorter sentences: "If you are over the age of 18, we encourage you to become a registered voter and cast your ballot for your candidates at the next election because your vote counts and may put the country on a course that is more aligned with your vision for the world." Here's an example of this long sentence broken into shorter sentences for greater impact:

  Over 18? Register to vote. Cast your ballot. Help elect the candidate of your choice. Your vote counts. Make a difference. Change the course of history!

- **Use subordinate clauses to your advantage.** A *subordinate clause* isn't a complete sentence; it has a subject or a predicate but not both. You can add a subordinate clause to an independent clause or combine two independent clauses, making one of them subordinate to the other. For example, suppose you have the following two independent clauses: "Employment has risen." and "Corporations are outsourcing jobs." You can convert the first sentence into a subordinate clause and attach it to the second sentence to form this *complex sentence*:

  Even though unemployment has risen, corporations are still outsourcing jobs.

- **Rearrange words and phrases.** If you notice that all of your sentences start the same way, consider shuffling words and phrases. For example, you can reword the following sentence in numerous ways: "Ignoring colonial legislatures, British parliament passed a series of acts called the Intolerable Acts (1774) by the colonists." Here are a few versions:

  British parliament, ignoring colonial legislatures, passed a series of what the colonists referred to as the Intolerable Acts of 1774.

  British parliament ignored colonial legislatures and passed a series of acts called the Intolerable Acts (1774) by the colonists.

  Britain's passage of a series of acts despite protests by the colonial legislatures led the colonists to refer to them as the Intolerable Acts (1774).

Longer sentences are ideal for explaining, while short sentences are useful for emphasizing a point. Rearranging sections of a sentence can also add interest. Using two sentences in parallel structure can be useful to emphasize a particular point.

Avoiding the common pitfalls of writing with a computer

Writing with a computer rather than a pen presents unique challenges. Studies show people are more likely to skim and skip over text on screen than read thoroughly. Sometimes *subvocalizing*, reading "out loud" to yourself without actually speaking is a good technique to ensure more careful reading. The "to yourself" part is important because actually reading aloud can get you into trouble on test day.

As you read, remain especially sensitive to word choice, sentence patterns, and transitions, as we explained in the preceding sections. In addition, check the following:

- **Words or phrases that make you stumble:** If you have trouble reading something, your evaluators will have even more trouble. Rephrase to smooth out the bumps.

- **Meaningless phrases:** Sometimes a sentence or phrase seems important when you first write it. When you reread it, you find yourself asking, "What was I thinking?!" Get rid of these before the evaluator sees them.

- **Overly obvious phrases:** If a sentence or phrase tempts you to respond, "Yeah, duh!" it's probably too obvious to mention. Delete it.

- **Digressions:** Although the formula essay model is likely to keep you on track, one of the most common errors involves drifting off topic. If you start to rant, you're probably drifting off topic. Your Extended Response should follow a clear path from introduction to conclusion. One test to make sure that you stayed on topic: Read the introductory paragraph, the first and last sentence of each following paragraph, and the conclusion. They should all say pretty much the same thing. If your discussion of dancing hippos suddenly involves cute elephants, you need to revise.

Checking your grammar, spelling, and punctuation

Your Extended Response essay is complete. You've reread the essay for flow and transitions, and now you're going to check for mechanical errors. These points are important to your success on the Extended Response. Although you may not lose points for the occasional typo or grammatical error, serious or numerous errors that make reading the essay difficult can hurt your score.

If you have time after you complete your essay, read it closely to catch and eliminate grammar, usage, punctuation, and spelling errors. Ask yourself these questions:

- Is this a complete sentence? Does it have a subject (actor) and a verb (action)?

- Do the subject and verb agree in number? For example, if the subject is plural, is the verb form plural?

- Do pronouns and antecedents (the nouns they refer to) agree in person, gender, and number? For example, if a pronoun refers to one female, it should be *she, hers,* or *her,* not *they* or *their.*

- Are the modifiers (adjectives and adverbs) close to the words they modify?

- Have you kept the tenses the same throughout your essay?

- Have you used appropriate punctuation?

- Have you spelled everything correctly?

The word processor you use on the GED exam is very basic. It doesn't have a grammar- or spell-checker built into it. You're expected to be your own grammar- and spell-checker.

Part IV

Testing Your Social Studies Knowledge and Skills

Five Ways to Simulate the GED Social Studies Test Environment

- Find a quiet place to work where you won't be distracted or interrupted. Put away cellphones, music players, and all other electronic devices. They won't be permitted on test day.

- Set a timer to count down from the total time allocated for each section of the test.

- Don't go to the next section of the test until the time allotted for the current section is up. If you finish early, check your work for that section only.

- Don't take any breaks. You don't get a break between the question-and-answer portion of the test and the Extended Response.

- Type your Extended Response essay instead of using pen and paper. Use only a text editor, such as Windows Notepad or TextEdit on a Mac, and disable the spell- and grammar-checker on your word processor.

 Check out www.dummies.com/extras/gedsocialstudies for strategies to boost your GED Social Studies score on test day.

In this part . . .

✔ See how your stamina measures up by taking a full-length, 65-minute practice GED Social Studies test and then writing an Extended Response in 25 minutes or less, all without a break.

✔ Score your test quickly with the answer key.

✔ Discover how to improve your performance by reading through the answer explanations for all practice test questions and evaluating your Extended Response.

Chapter 13

Taking a Social Studies Practice Test

• •

This chapter gives you a chance to try your skills on a practice Social Studies test, including a sample Extended Response item. You can record your answers directly in this book or on a separate sheet of paper (if you're reading an e-book or think you'll want to revisit these practice questions at a later date). Mark only one answer for each item unless otherwise indicated. And be sure to have a couple of sheets of paper or your computer's text editor handy to practice preparing and writing an Extended Response.

The official Social Studies test consists mainly of multiple-choice items but also has some technology-enhanced question types that can't be replicated in print. Visit the official GED Testing Service website (www.gedtestingservice.com/ged-testing-service) to see what these look like. However, all questions end up working like standard multiple-choice items. Whether you select answers from a drop-down menu or drag-and-drop answer choices into empty boxes, you have four answers from which to choose.

The questions test social studies concepts. The items are based on a *stimulus,* the GED Testing Service's fancy way of saying you will be questioned on the content of materials that may include maps, graphs, charts, cartoons, text, or figures. Study the information provided and then answer the item(s) following it. Here are a few additional guidelines:

✔ Refer to the information as often as necessary in answering.

✔ Work carefully, but don't spend too much time on any one question. You can always skip it and come back if time remains at the end.

✔ Answer every question. If you know one choice is definitely wrong, you've improved your chance of guessing correctly by one-third. If you can eliminate two choices, you are now down to a 50/50 chance of guessing the correct answer. Wrong answers don't count against you, so you have nothing to lose and everything to gain from venturing a guess if you don't know the answer.

Chapter 14 provides detailed answer explanations. Take your time as you move through the explanations. They can help you understand why you missed the answers you did and confirm or clarify the thought process for the answers you got right.

The multiple-choice test and the essay are two separate, self-contained sections. You may not use any leftover time from the first portion to spend more time on the Extended Response or use extra time at the end of the essay to go back to the previous questions.

Answer Sheet for Social Studies Practice Test

1. (A) (B) (C) (D)	26. (A) (B) (C) (D)
2. (A) (B) (C) (D)	27. (A) (B) (C) (D)
3. (A) (B) (C) (D)	28. (A) (B) (C) (D)
4. (A) (B) (C) (D)	29. (A) (B) (C) (D)
5. (A) (B) (C) (D)	30. (A) (B) (C) (D)
6. (A) (B) (C) (D)	31. (A) (B) (C) (D)
7. (A) (B) (C) (D)	32. (A) (B) (C) (D)
8. (A) (B) (C) (D)	33. (A) (B) (C) (D)
9. (A) (B) (C) (D)	34. (A) (B) (C) (D)
10. (A) (B) (C) (D)	35. (A) (B) (C) (D)
11. (A) (B) (C) (D)	36. (A) (B) (C) (D)
12. (A) (B) (C) (D)	37. (A) (B) (C) (D)
13. (A) (B) (C) (D)	38. (A) (B) (C) (D)
14. (A) (B) (C) (D)	39. (A) (B) (C) (D)
15. (A) (B) (C) (D)	40. (A) (B) (C) (D)
16. (A) (B) (C) (D)	41. (A) (B) (C) (D)
17. (A) (B) (C) (D)	42. (A) (B) (C) (D)
18. (A) (B) (C) (D)	43. (A) (B) (C) (D)
19. (A) (B) (C) (D)	44. (A) (B) (C) (D)
20. (A) (B) (C) (D)	45. (A) (B) (C) (D)
21. (A) (B) (C) (D)	46. (A) (B) (C) (D)
22. (A) (B) (C) (D)	47. (A) (B) (C) (D)
23. (A) (B) (C) (D)	48. (A) (B) (C) (D)
24. (A) (B) (C) (D)	49. (A) (B) (C) (D)
25. (A) (B) (C) (D)	50. (A) (B) (C) (D)

Social Studies Test

Time: 65 minutes for 50 questions

Directions: Mark your answers on the answer sheet provided.

> *Question 1 is based on the following passage (*`www.senate.gov/civics/`
> `constitution_item/constitution.htm`*).*

The Constitution assigned to Congress responsibility for organizing the executive and judicial branches, raising revenue, declaring war, and making all laws necessary for executing these powers. The president is permitted to veto specific legislative acts, but Congress has the authority to override presidential vetoes by two-thirds majorities of both houses. The Constitution also provides that the Senate advise and consent on key executive and judicial appointments and on the ratification of treaties.

1. What is the purpose of the Constitution?

   (A) It permits a presidential veto over laws.

   (B) It selects the members of the executive branch of government.

   (C) It defines the responsibilities of the three branches of government.

   (D) It explains who may be a representative in government.

> *Questions 2–3 are based on Article I, Sections 1 and 2 of the Constitution (*`www.senate.`
> `gov/civics/constitution_item/constitution.htm`*).*

Section 1

All legislative Powers herein granted shall be vested in a Congress of the United States, which shall consist of a Senate and House of Representatives.

Section 2

The House of Representatives shall be composed of Members chosen every second Year by the People of the several States, and the Electors in each State shall have the Qualifications requisite for Electors of the most numerous Branch of the State Legislature.

No Person shall be a Representative who shall not have attained to the Age of twenty-five Years, and been seven Years a Citizen of the United States, and who shall not, when elected, be an Inhabitant of that State in which he shall be chosen.

Go on to next page

2. If the last federal election was in 2014, in what year will the next elections for members of the House of Representatives take place?

   (A) 2016

   (B) 2018

   (C) 2020

   (D) The date is yet to be determined.

3. George immigrated to the United States and became a citizen in January 2015. What is the first election year in which he will qualify to run for the House of Representatives?

   (A) 2018

   (B) 2020

   (C) 2022

   (D) Never. Only people born in the United States are eligible.

Questions 4–5 are based on Article VII, Section 1 of the Constitution of the United States (www.senate.gov/civics/constitution_item/constitution.htm).

Every Bill which shall have passed the House of Representatives and the Senate, shall, before it become a Law, be presented to the President of the United States; If he approve he shall sign it, but if not he shall return it, with his Objections to that House in which it shall have originated, who shall enter the Objections at large on their Journal, and proceed to reconsider it. If after such Reconsideration two thirds of that House shall agree to pass the Bill, it shall be sent, together with the Objections, to the other House, by which it shall likewise be reconsidered, and if approved by two thirds of that House, it shall become a Law. But in all such Cases the Votes of both Houses shall be determined by Yeas and Nays, and the Names of the Persons voting for and against the Bill shall be entered on the Journal of each House respectively, If any Bill shall not be returned by the President within ten Days (Sundays excepted) after it shall have been presented to him, the Same shall be a Law, in like Manner as if he had signed it, unless the Congress by their Adjournament prevent its Return, in which Case it shall not be a Law.

4. How can Congress force the implementation of a bill the president rejects and sends back to Congress?

   (A) It can't.

   (B) The presidential objection can be overturned if the bill in question is reapproved by a two-thirds vote in both houses of Congress.

   (C) Congress can lobby the president to change his mind.

   (D) Congress can appeal to the Supreme Court.

5. What happens to an unsigned bill if it spends more time than ten days in the president's possession?

   (A) It automatically becomes law.

   (B) It automatically dies.

   (C) It automatically becomes law if Congress is in session.

   (D) None of the above.

Questions 6–7 are based on the following passage from Article IV, Section 2 of the Constitution of the United States (www.senate.gov/civics/constitution_item/constitution.htm).

The Citizens of each State shall be entitled to all Privileges and Immunities of Citizens in the several States.

A Person charged in any State with Treason, Felony, or other Crime, who shall flee from Justice, and be found in another State, shall on Demand of the executive Authority of

Go on to next page

the State from which he fled, be delivered up, to be removed to the State having Jurisdiction of the Crime.

[No Person held to Service or Labour in one State, under the Laws thereof, escaping into another, shall, in Consequence of any Law or Regulation therein, be discharged from such Service or Labour, but shall be delivered up on Claim of the Party to whom such Service or Labour may be due.]

6. What does "The Citizens of each State shall be entitled to all Privileges and Immunities of Citizens in the several States" mean?

(A) The citizens of any state of the United States will have the same rights in all the states.

(B) Citizens granted immunity in one state will have the same immunity in every other state.

(C) A citizen's rights may apply only to several states.

(D) Immunities of citizens vary from state to state.

7. The police in New York State discover someone in their state has committed a crime in Texas. What happens when Texas demands that person's return?

(A) nothing

(B) Texas is offered the opportunity to try the person in New York State.

(C) New York State has to try that person.

(D) New York State must return the individual to Texas.

Question 8 is based on the following passage.

The people do not elect the president and vice president directly but rather vote for the members of an Electoral College. Each state has a predetermined number of electors in the College. The electors vote for the president and vice president. Originally, the electors were community leaders — citizens of standing and repute who were entrusted with the right to choose the president and vice president. They could choose at will from among the candidates. However, today's electors are bound to the candidates of one party or the other.

The founding fathers feared that an uneducated electorate could run wild and elect a popular but unsuitable president and/or vote out the legislature and executive, virtually overthrowing the entire government. That's why only one-third of the Senate is elected every two years and the president is elected by the Electoral College. Staggering elections and using an Electoral College as an intermediary are precautions intended to help maintain a stable governing body.

8. Why are American citizens not allowed to directly elect their president?

(A) The framers of the Constitution feared that an uneducated electorate might make bad choices.

(B) The framers of the Constitution believed the Electoral College would make a more educated choice.

(C) The Electoral College would be a moderating influence on popular passions in an election.

(D) All of the above.

Go on to next page

Questions 9–10 are based on the following graphic (www.census.gov/content/dam/ Census/newsroom/releases/2015/cb15-89_graphic.jpg).

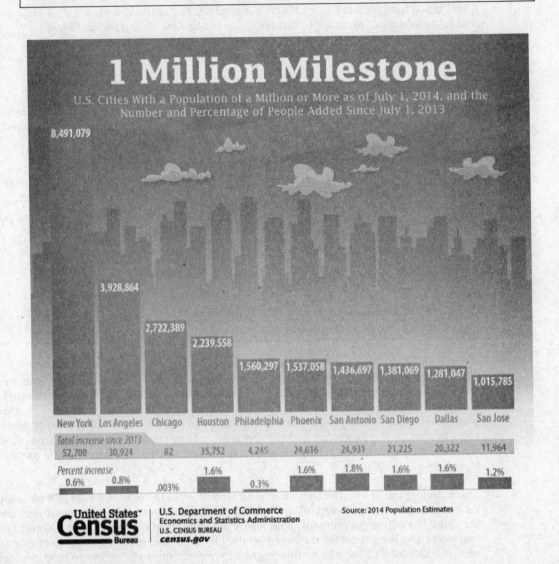

1 Million Milestone

U.S. Cities With a Population of a Million or More as of July 1, 2014, and the Number and Percentage of People Added Since July 1, 2013

	New York	Los Angeles	Chicago	Houston	Philadelphia	Phoenix	San Antonio	San Diego	Dallas	San Jose
Population	8,491,079	3,928,864	2,722,389	2,239,558	1,560,297	1,537,058	1,436,697	1,381,069	1,281,047	1,015,785
Total increase since 2013	52,700	30,924	82	35,752	4,245	24,616	24,931	21,225	20,322	11,964
Percent increase	0.6%	0.8%	.003%	1.6%	0.3%	1.6%	1.8%	1.6%	1.6%	1.2%

United States Census Bureau

U.S. Department of Commerce
Economics and Statistics Administration
U.S. CENSUS BUREAU
census.gov

Source: 2014 Population Estimates

9. Which city has shown the greatest percentage increase in this graph?

(A) New York

(B) Houston

(C) San Antonio

(D) Dallas

10. Over what period was the population increase measured?

(A) one year

(B) 10 years

(C) 15 years

(D) 20 years

Go on to next page

Questions 11–12 are based on the following graphic (www.census.gov/content/dam/ Census/newsroom/releases/2015/cb15-47_acsgraphic.pdf).

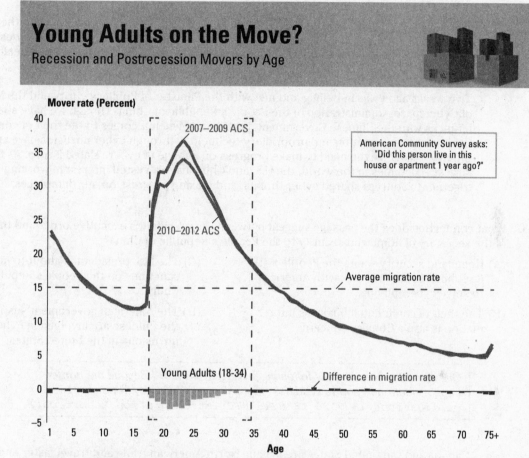

Young Adults on the Move?
Recession and Postrecession Movers by Age

Mover rate (Percent)

2007–2009 ACS

American Community Survey asks:
"Did this person live in this house or apartment 1 year ago?"

2010–2012 ACS

Average migration rate

Young Adults (18-34)

Difference in migration rate

Age

Note: Applies to movers age 1 and over.

United States
Census
Bureau

U.S. Department of Commerce
Economics and Statistics Administration
U.S. CENSUS BUREAU
census.gov

Sources: U.S. Census Bureau, 2007–2009 and 2010–2012
American Community Survey 3-Year Estimates.
For more information on the ACS, see
<http://www.census.gov/acs/www>

11. What generalization can you make based on this graph?

(A) The migration rate for seniors has decreased by about 10% since 2009.

(B) The migration rate for children has decreased from over 20% to about 10%.

(C) The migration rate of young adults has decreased since 2009.

(D) The migration rate has not changed.

12. What can you infer about the date of the recession mentioned in the subtitle of this graph?

(A) A recession occurred between 2007 and 2009.

(B) A recession occurred before 2007.

(C) A recession occurred after 2012.

(D) There was no recession.

Go on to next page

> *Question 13 is based on the following remarks by Secretary of Homeland Security Jeh Johnson at the RSA Conference 2015 (www.dhs.gov/news/2015/04/21/remarks-secretary-homeland-security-jeh-johnson-rsa-conference-2015).*

Just a few days ago President Obama signed an Executive Order which authorizes the Secretary of Treasury to impose financial sanctions on those who engage in malicious cyber-enabled activities that are a threat to national security, foreign policy, economic health, or the financial stability of our country.

Two weeks ago I was in Beijing and met with the Minister of Public Security and the Minister of Cyberspace Administration of the People's Republic of China. Though we have sharp differences with the Chinese Government, particularly when it comes to the theft of confidential business information and proprietary technology through cyber intrusions, we and the Chinese recognize the need to make progress on a range of cyber-related issues. As the two largest economies in the world, the U.S. and China have a vested interest in working together to address shared cyber threats, and making progress on our differences.

13. What connection does the passage suggest between the president's executive order and the visit of the secretary of homeland security to the People's Republic of China?

(A) Homeland security wants the People's Republic of China to work with America to solve cyberbullying.

(B) The theft of confidential business information is also a Chinese concern.

(C) The U.S. president is about to impose sanctions on the People's Republic of China.

(D) The American government suspects the Chinese are involved in cyber intrusions in the United States.

> *Question 14 is based on the following passage from "2014 Beyond the Border Implementation Report to Leaders" (www.dhs.gov/sites/default/files/publications/15_0320_15-0745_BTB_Implementation_Report.pdf).*

Canada and the United States are making North American trade and travel faster and more secure through enhanced information sharing, faster processing for business travelers, and an historic agreement on preclearance that provides a transformational framework for border management and facilitation of legitimate trade and travel in the land, rail, marine, and air modes. We have also moved towards a common approach to screening travelers through the ongoing implementation of automated sharing of biographic and biometric visa and immigration information; and, through the first two phases of an Entry/Exit initiative for all foreign nationals, with additional phases to come. Further, Canada is developing a pre-departure screening system for visa-exempt travelers flying to Canada from abroad, largely mirroring existing U.S. systems.

14. Why is it important that the United States and Canada use a common approach for screening travelers?

(A) Many travelers come from foreign countries through Canada to the United States.

(B) It makes exchanging information about travelers between Canada and the United States easier.

(C) Prescreening in Canada and the United States will make travel for regular visitors easier.

(D) All of the above.

Go on to next page

Questions 15–17 are based on the following passage from U.S. History For Dummies by Steve Wiegand (Wiley).

After going back to England and negotiating a charter to establish a colony, taking out a few loans, and forming a company, a group of 102 men, women, and children left England on September 16, 1620, on a ship called the *Mayflower.* (A second ship, the *Speedwell,* also started out but sprang a leak and had to turn back.) The *Mayflower* was usually used for shipping wine between France and England. Its cargo for this trip was decidedly more varied than usual. Although the Pilgrims didn't really pack any smarter than had the Jamestown colonists, they did show some imagination. Among the things they took to the wilderness of North America were musical instruments, all kinds of furniture, and even books on the history of Turkey (the country, not the bird). One guy even brought 139 pairs of shoes and boots.

Despite a rough crossing that took 65 days, only one passenger and four crewmen died, and one child was born. After some preliminary scouting, they dropped anchor in a broad, shallow bay now known as Plymouth. (No evidence exists to indicate they landed on any kind of rock.)

Two important things happened on the way over. One was that the Pilgrims missed their turnoff and failed to land within the borders laid out by their charter. That meant they were essentially squatters and didn't fall under the direct governance of anyone in England. Secondly, concerned by mutterings from some members of the group that they should go home, the colony's leaders drew up a *compact,* or set of rules, by which they all agreed to abide. This became known as the Mayflower Compact.

15. The passage refers to the Mayflower colonists as squatters. Why?

(A) They built their settlement outside the area they were granted in their charter.

(B) They simply took over Native American lands.

(C) They were homeless.

(D) None of the above.

16. How much smaller was the pilgrim party when it arrived in Plymouth compared to when it left England?

(A) six fewer people

(B) five fewer people

(C) four fewer people

(D) three fewer people

17. What is the best description of the Mayflower Compact?

(A) a tenancy agreement for the new colony

(B) a treaty with the local Native Americans

(C) a company charter granting them the right to colonize

(D) None of the above.

Questions 18–19 are based on the following passage from U.S. History For Dummies by Steve Wiegand (Wiley).

While enjoying the protections of the formidable British Empire's military, the average American colonist, if he paid any taxes at all, paid far less than his British cousin. The argument against British taxes, put forth by the eloquent Boston lawyer James Otis, that "taxation without representation is tyranny," was a bit hypocritical. After all, more than a few

Go on to next page

Americans had to pay taxes to American local governments and still couldn't vote or didn't have a representative in the colonial assemblies.

Moreover, for the most part, Britain didn't interfere in the colonies' internal affairs. Mostly, the mother country concerned itself with defense and trade issues, and many of the trade laws were mutually beneficial to both sides of the water (unless you happened to be a big-time smuggler like John Hancock, who later became the first to sign the Declaration of Independence and was Public Enemy Number One as far as the British were concerned). So, most Americans in the 1760s and early 1770s had no interest in independence from Britain. What they wanted was what they had: protection by the world's mightiest navy, generally cozy trade rules, and freedoms and rights unequalled in the rest of the world.

18. What does this passage suggest about the colonists' demands for independence from Britain?

    (A) Most American colonists were quite happy to be living in colonies of Britain.

    (B) The American colonists were absolutely right to demand their independence.

    (C) The British colonial government was indeed tyrannical.

    (D) The American colonists resented paying for British protections.

19. Who created the famous phrase "taxation without representation is tyranny"?

    (A) John Hancock

    (B) James Otis

    (C) Robert Lubinski

    (D) American colonists

> Questions 20–22 are based on the following passage from Economics For Dummies, *by Sean Flynn (Wiley).*

[Thomas Malthus] argued that living standards couldn't permanently rise because higher living standards would cause people to breed faster. He believed that population growth would outpace our ability to grow more food, so we would be doomed to return to subsistence levels of nutrition and living standards.

Even when Malthus first published this idea, lots of evidence indicated that it was bunk. For generations, living standards had been rising while birthrates had been falling. And because that trend has continued up to the present day, we're not going to breed our way to subsistence. Indeed, many nations now face an *under*population problem because birthrates have fallen below the replacement rate necessary to keep the population stable. The populations of Italy, Japan, and Russia, among others, have already begun to shrink.

A related problem is that rapidly falling birthrates are wreaking havoc on government-sponsored retirement systems because there aren't enough young workers to pay all the taxes needed to fund retirees' pensions.

20. Why does the passage suggest that underpopulation is a problem in the modern world?

    (A) Shrinking populations can't provide enough young workers.

    (B) Fewer young people means fewer taxpayers to fund government activities.

    (C) The population of some developed countries is already beginning to decline.

    (D) All of the above.

Go on to next page

21. What is the main argument in this passage?

    (A) Birthrates are continuing to fall.

    (B) Falling birthrates are a major problem.

    (C) We will not breed ourselves into subsistence.

    (D) Our population growth will outpace our ability to feed ourselves.

22. This passage has a relatively narrow focus. What is one key area it ignores?

    (A) the rapid population growth in the developing world

    (B) the limits to expanding food production

    (C) the fact that urbanization is freeing up more land for food production

    (D) None of the above.

Questions 23–24 are based on a press release from the USGS, May 28, 2015 (www.usgs.gov/newsroom/article.asp?ID=4239&from=rss_home#.VWzuhblViko).

Although record low precipitation has been the main driver of one of the worst droughts in California history, abnormally high temperatures have also played an important role in amplifying its adverse effects, according to a recent study by the U.S. Geological Survey and university partners.

Experiments with a hydrologic model for the period Oct. 2013–Sept. 2014 showed that if the air temperatures had been cooler, similar to the 1916–2012 average, there would have been an 86% chance that the winter snowpack would have been greater, the spring-summer runoff higher, and the spring-summer soil moisture deficits smaller. . . .

High heat has multiple damaging effects during drought, according to the study, increasing the vulnerability of California's water resources and agricultural industry. Not only does high heat intensify evaporative stress on soil, it has a powerful effect in reducing snowpack, a key to reliable water supply for the state. In addition to decreased snowpack, higher temperatures can cause the snowpack to melt earlier, dramatically decreasing the amount of water available for agriculture in summer when it is most needed.

23. How will climate change affect available water supplies?

    (A) It will bring dramatic increases.

    (B) It will increase the risk of drought.

    (C) It will have very little effect.

    (D) Worldwide cooler temperatures will reduce precipitation.

24. What effects have higher temperatures had on California?

    (A) They have increased tourism.

    (B) They have brought about a vast expansion of market farming.

    (C) They have reduced winter snowpack, decreasing spring-summer runoff.

    (D) They have caused the snowpack to melt much later, reducing available water.

Go on to next page

Questions 25–27 are based on the following maps from the Federal Election Commission (www.fec.gov/pubrec/fe2012/2012presmaps.pdf).

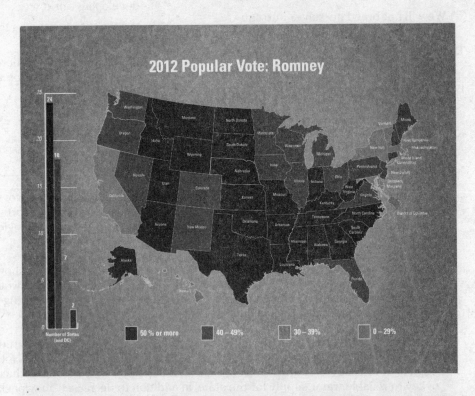

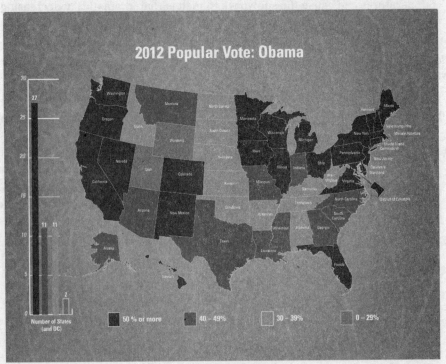

Go on to next page

25. How does the number of states in which each candidate won the popular vote compare?

    (A) Obama won the popular vote in more states than Romney.

    (B) Romney won the popular vote in more states than Obama.

    (C) Both candidates won about the same number of states by popular vote.

    (D) It's irrelevant. What matters is the size of the states they won.

26. According to the maps, which party do New England states most likely support?

    (A) Democrats

    (B) Republicans

    (C) It's probably a tie vote.

    (D) can't be determined from the maps

27. Which two states gave the lowest popular vote to Obama?

    (A) Texas and Florida

    (B) California and Vermont

    (C) Wyoming and Utah

    (D) New York and Kansas

> *Questions 28–30 are based on the following passage from the Economic Development Agency's website (www.eda.gov/news/blogs/2013/12/01/success-story.htm).*

. . . In April 2008, EDA awarded a $500,000 grant to support construction of interior road improvement and related utility upgrades on the Port's 8-acre industrial park [in Port of Hood River in Oregon's Hood River County]. . . .

Infrastructure expansion was needed to give the local economy a much needed boost. The area unemployment rate was 6%, and the average per capita income was $27,173, more than 20% below the U.S. average. However, any improvements would have to account for both the industrial and recreational uses of the Port. Further, local residents' concerns about increased business traffic had to be addressed. Planners had their work cut out for them.

. . . Changes were made both carefully and below original cost estimates, allowing for a finished project that has improved the local business climate, increased employment, and raised quality of life. . . . The area was particularly challenging because the industrial core borders active recreation sites. EDA's investment enabled the placement of necessary infrastructure at a critical time when local businesses were seeking to expand. The resulting private investment and job creation has provided an enormous benefit to our community. . . .

At the time of the grant, there were nine principal tenants on site, including the Full Sail Brewing Company, Boeing, and Turtle Island Foods that in aggregate occupied about 100,000 square feet of light industrial space. Seasonally adjusted employment on the site totaled just 24 persons.

Once construction was completed, several of the tenants were able to advance their expansion plans. The improvements also attracted additional tenants, including Hood River Juice Company, Pfriem Brewing, and DaKine. Today, 23 tenants occupy 233,000 square feet, total employment is 371 persons, and private sector investment has reached $33.85 million. . . . The Port anticipates future demand and is poised to accommodate up to an additional 40,000 square feet of light manufacturing space. Officials project that another 50 area jobs will be added as a result.

EDA sees the Port's success as an excellent example of how a small and targeted investment can quickly generate tangible and sustainable economic benefits for an entire community.

Go on to next page

28. What made the Port of Hood River a suitable area for an economic development grant?

   (A) The unemployment rate in the area was 6% above the national average.

   (B) The development plans could be completed below budget.

   (C) The area had economic difficulties and could not provide the seed money required to create improvements.

   (D) Local business was waiting for government to step in.

29. What was one complication making industrial development more difficult?

   (A) the high unemployment rate

   (B) the proximity of recreational land to the industrial areas

   (C) objections from existing port tenants

   (D) environmental assessment review programs

30. How has the grant changed availability of manufacturing space?

   (A) It brought in an additional 133,000 square feet of space.

   (B) It brought in an additional 233,000 square feet of space.

   (C) It brought in an additional 40,000 square feet of space.

   (D) It doubled the original amount.

Questions 31–32 are based on the following passage from the National Park Service (www.nps.gov/gett/learn/historyculture/civil-war-timeline.htm).

November 6, 1860: Abraham Lincoln is elected 16th president of the United States, the first Republican president in the nation who represents a party that opposes the spread of slavery in the territories of the United States.

December 17, 1860: The first Secession Convention meets in Columbia, South Carolina.

December 20, 1860: South Carolina secedes from the Union.

January 1861: Six additional southern states secede from the Union.

February 8–9, 1861: The southern states that seceded create a government at Montgomery, Alabama, and the Confederate States of America are formed.

February 18, 1861: Jefferson Davis is appointed the first President of the Confederate States of America at Montgomery, Alabama, a position he will hold until elections can be arranged.

March 4, 1861: Abraham Lincoln is inaugurated as the 16th president of the United States in Washington, D.C.

April 12, 1861: Southern forces fire upon Fort Sumter, South Carolina. The Civil War has formally begun.

April 15, 1861: President Lincoln issues a public declaration that an insurrection exists and calls for 75,000 militia to stop the rebellion. As a result of this call for volunteers, four additional southern states secede from the Union in the following weeks. Lincoln will respond on May 3 with an additional call for 43,000+ volunteers to serve for three years, expanding the size of the Regular Army.

Go on to next page

31. Who took office first, Abraham Lincoln or Jefferson Davis?

(A) Abraham Lincoln

(B) Jefferson Davis

(C) Both took office at the same time.

(D) can't be determined from the data

32. Which side fired the first shot in the Civil War?

(A) the South

(B) the North

(C) Both sides attacked at more or less the same time.

(D) can't be determined from the data

Questions 33–34 are based on the following passage from the Federal Court website, dealing with the establishment of Miranda rights (www.uscourts.gov/ educational-resources/educational-activities/facts-and- case-summary-miranda-v-arizona).

The following statement is the Supreme Court explanation for overturning the Miranda conviction. Miranda was arrested and interrogated in a room cut off from the outside for two hours and not given either warnings of his rights against self incrimination or legal advice. At the end of the two hours, Miranda signed a full confession.

The Court held that "there can be no doubt that the Fifth Amendment privilege is available outside of criminal court proceedings and serves to protect persons in all settings in which their freedom of action is curtailed in any significant way from being compelled to incriminate themselves." As such, "the prosecution may not use statements, whether exculpatory or inculpatory, stemming from custodial interrogation of the defendant unless it demonstrates the use of procedural safeguards effective to secure the privilege against self-incrimination. By custodial interrogation, we mean questioning initiated by law enforcement officers after a person has been taken into custody or otherwise deprived of his freedom of action in any significant way."

The Court further held that "without proper safeguards the process of in-custody interrogation of persons suspected or accused of crime contains inherently compelling pressures which work to undermine the individual's will to resist and to compel him to speak where he would otherwise do so freely." Therefore, a defendant "must be warned prior to any questioning that he has the right to remain silent, that anything he says can be used against him in a court of law, that he has the right to the presence of an attorney, and that if he cannot afford an attorney one will be appointed for him prior to any questioning if he so desires."

33. Which Constitutional amendment did the Court use to justify their decision?

(A) the First Amendment

(B) the Second Amendment

(C) the Fourth Amendment

(D) the Fifth Amendment

34. Why did the Court hold that in this particular case a signed confession was not acceptable as evidence in court?

(A) The prisoner was not advised of his right not to incriminate himself.

(B) The prisoner was not advised of his right to legal counsel during interrogation.

(C) The prisoner was not advised that anything he said could be used against him.

(D) All of the above.

Go on to next page

Question 35 is based on the following map from the U.S. Census Bureau (www.census.gov/population/apportionment/files/2010mapbw.pdf).

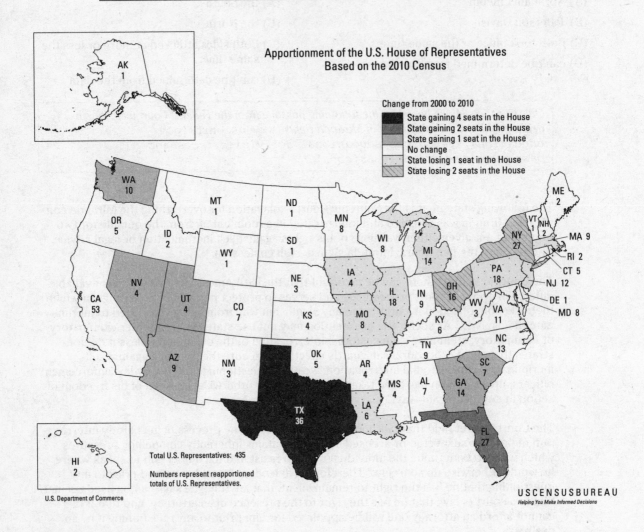

Apportionment of the U.S. House of Representatives
Based on the 2010 Census

35. Which state gained three seats in the House of Representatives?

(A) Texas

(B) Florida

(C) Arizona

(D) no state

Go on to next page

> *Question 36 is based on the following passage from the Department of Education* (`studentaid.ed.gov/sa/types`).

The U.S. Department of Education awards about $150 billion a year in grants, work-study funds, and low-interest loans to more than 15 million students. Federal student aid covers such expenses as tuition and fees, room and board, books and supplies, and transportation. Aid also can help pay for other related expenses, such as a computer and dependent care. Thousands of schools across the country participate in the federal student aid programs; ask the schools you're interested in whether they do!

Federal student aid includes

- Grants — financial aid that doesn't have to be repaid (unless, for example, you withdraw from school and owe a refund)

- Loans — borrowed money for college or career school; you must repay your loans, with interest

- Work-Study — a work program through which you earn money to help you pay for school

36. What is the difference between a loan and a grant in the Department of Education's award system?

(A) Grants are substantially larger.

(B) Loans can be forgiven.

(C) Grants have substantially lower interest rates.

(D) Grants do not have to be repaid under most circumstances.

> *Questions 37–38 are based on the following passage and graph from the Centers for Disease Control and Prevention* (`www.cdc.gov/measles/cases-outbreaks.html`).

Reasons for an increase in [measles] cases some years:

2015: The United States experienced a large, multi-state measles outbreak linked to an amusement park in California. The outbreak likely started from a traveler who became infected overseas with measles, then visited the amusement park while infectious; however, no source was identified. Analysis by CDC scientists showed that the measles virus type in this outbreak (B3) was identical to the virus type that caused the large measles outbreak in the Philippines in 2014.

2014: The U.S. experienced 23 measles outbreaks in 2014, including one large outbreak of 383 cases, occurring primarily among unvaccinated Amish communities in Ohio. Many of the cases in the U.S. in 2014 were associated with cases brought in from the Philippines, which experienced a large measles outbreak. . . .

2013: The U.S. experienced 11 outbreaks in 2013, three of which had more than 20 cases, including an outbreak with 58 cases. . . .

2011: In 2011, more than 30 countries in the WHO European Region reported an increase in measles, and France was experiencing a large outbreak. Most of the cases that were brought to the U.S. in 2011 came from France. . . .

2008: The increase in cases in 2008 was the result of spread in communities with groups of unvaccinated people. The U.S. experienced several outbreaks in 2008 including three large outbreaks. . . .

Go on to next page

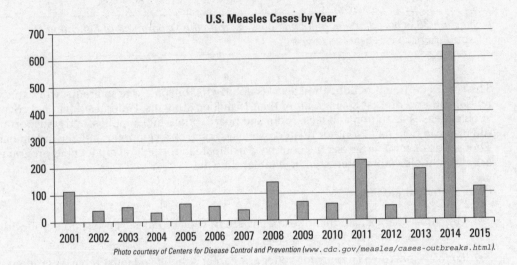

U.S. Measles Cases by Year

Photo courtesy of Centers for Disease Control and Prevention (www.cdc.gov/measles/cases-outbreaks.html).

37. Based on the graph, what is the general trend of the number of measles cases in the United States?

(A) increasing

(B) decreasing

(C) about the same

(D) can't be determined

38. What was the most likely source of the outbreak in the California amusement park in 2015?

(A) a traveler from France

(B) an unvaccinated traveler

(C) an unvaccinated traveler from the Philippines

(D) unvaccinated religious communities in the United States

Questions 39–41 are based on the following passage.

John Maynard Keynes developed his famous theory during the Great Depression in England. Keynes argued that the traditional conservative way of cutting costs and instituting austerity programs is not the way to fix a recession or depression. Austerity programs generally result in more layoffs. He argued that governments should encourage spending, increase hiring, and even use deficit financing to spur the economy.

When the World Financial Crisis of 2008 hit, Greece was carrying a debt load much higher than members in the European Union were allowed. Government revenues were not high enough to meet service requirements, salaries, and pensions, so Greece continued to borrow more money. A low tax regime and high tax avoidance exacerbated the problem. When Greece was unable to meet debt repayments, the European Central Bank and the World Bank gave Greece a bailout loan. In return, Greece had to introduce an austerity program aimed at balancing the budget.

The government cut the civil service, military spending, even civil-service pensions. Unfortunately, this coincided with an increasingly serious worldwide recession. Greek unemployment rose to over 20%, and youth unemployment to over 60% by 2013. That worsened the financial crisis; with fewer employed people, government revenues dropped sharply. Tens of thousands of people lost their homes. Despite the austerity measures and further loans, the government could not meet its debts and threatened again to default on the government debts. In 2015, a plebiscite rejected further austerity measures.

Go on to next page ⟶

39. What are austerity programs?

    (A) government restructuring whereby governments reduce the size of the civil service and cut spending on government programs

    (B) very lean social service programs

    (C) programs to privatize government services in an attempt to reduce costs

    (D) None of the above.

40. How would bailing out Greece help preserve the world economy in a recession?

    (A) It creates government jobs.

    (B) It forces lenders to write off their loans.

    (C) Lending money avoids a surge in Greek unemployment.

    (D) None of the above.

41. Would Keynes have considered the steps taken by Greece a successful application of his theory?

    (A) Yes

    (B) No

    (C) He would have argued the Greek government should have borrowed more money to finance greater government intervention in the economy.

    (D) He would have argued Greek austerity did not go far enough.

Questions 42–43 are based on the following speech by John F. Kennedy in Berlin on June 26, 1963 (www.jfklibrary.org/Asset-Viewer/oEX2uqSQGEGIdTYgd_JL_Q.aspx).

There are many people in the world who really don't understand, or say they don't, what is the great issue between the free world and the Communist world. Let them come to Berlin. There are some who say that communism is the wave of the future. Let them come to Berlin. And there are some who say in Europe and elsewhere we can work with the Communists. Let them come to Berlin. . . .

Freedom has many difficulties, and democracy is not perfect, but we have never had to put a wall up to keep our people in, to prevent them from leaving us. . . .

What is true of this city is true of Germany — real, lasting peace in Europe can never be assured as long as one German out of four is denied the elementary right of free men, and that is to make a free choice. . . .

Freedom is indivisible, and when one man is enslaved, all are not free. When all are free, then we can look forward to that day when this city will be joined as one and this country and this great continent of Europe in a peaceful and hopeful globe. When that day finally comes, as it will, the people of West Berlin can take sober satisfaction in the fact that they were in the front lines for almost two decades.

All free men, wherever they may live, are citizens of Berlin, and, therefore, as a free man, I take pride in the words "Ich bin ein Berliner."

42. Why does Kennedy suggest people should visit West Berlin?

    (A) He really enjoyed his own visit to West Berlin.

    (B) People could see the contrast between capitalism and communism just by looking at East and West Berlin.

    (C) The West Berlin economy needed the financial boost from tourism.

    (D) It would convince people that communism is the wave of the future.

Go on to next page

43. Why does Kennedy say he takes pride in the phrase "Ich bin ein Berliner" (I am a Berliner)?

    (A) West Berliners had become a strong symbol of free people's struggle against communism.

    (B) It made the Berliners feel better.

    (C) It created a dramatic ending for his speech.

    (D) He was promising American military support for West Berlin.

Questions 44–45 are based on the following graph (`www.census.gov/prod/2014pubs/p20-573.pdf`).

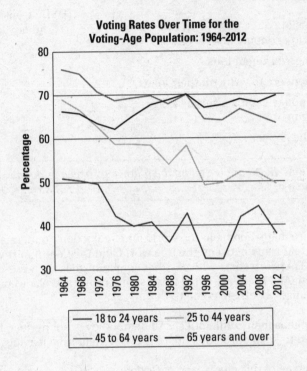

Voting Rates Over Time for the Voting-Age Population: 1964-2012

— 18 to 24 years   — 25 to 44 years
— 45 to 64 years   — 65 years and over

44. If an election campaign wanted to change possible election outcomes, which age group should it target?

    (A) 65 years and over

    (B) 45 to 64 years old

    (C) 25 to 44 years old

    (D) 18 to 24 years old

45. Bill Clinton's first presidential campaign was in 1992. How can you tell that Clinton had broad appeal during his first election campaign?

    (A) Voter participation in the 18-to-24-year-old group spiked.

    (B) Voter participation in the 25-to-44-year-old group spiked.

    (C) There's no such evidence. The general trend of voter participation continued to decline.

    (D) Voter participation of all age groups increased in 1992.

Go on to next page

*Question 46 is based on the following passage (*www.army.mil/asianpacificamericans*).*

"The principle on which this country was founded and by which it has always been governed is that Americanism is a matter of mind and heart; Americanism is not, and never was, a matter of race or ancestry."

—President Franklin Delano Roosevelt upon signing the executive order that created the 442nd Regimental Combat Team, the only entirely Japanese American unit during World War II, in February 1943

46. Why is this statement rather ironic?

   (A) The American army at this time was still segregated.

   (B) Japanese Americans had been incarcerated in internment camps.

   (C) both Choice (A) and Choice (B)

   (D) Nothing is ironic about this statement.

Question 47 is based on the following passage from U.S. History For Dummies *by Steve Wiegand (Wiley).*

One of the Progressives' ideas was that people who made more money could afford to pay more taxes. A federal income tax had been tried before — once during the Civil War and once during the hard economic times of 1894 — but neither attempt was successful. In fact, the U.S. Supreme Court, on a 5 to 4 vote, struck down the 1894 effort as unconstitutional. The 16th Amendment, which was pushed by Progressives, was proposed in 1909 and ratified in 1913. This amendment gave Congress the power to slap a federal tax on income, which it promptly did. Congress required a 1 percent tax on annual income above $4,000, and a 2 percent tax on income above $20,000. Of course, the rates have gone up since.

47. Why did the United States not have an income tax until after 1913?

   (A) There was popular opposition to the idea of income tax.

   (B) People remembered the slogan "taxation without representation is tyranny."

   (C) It failed to pass Congress.

   (D) Congress did not have the power to create a federal income tax until the passage of the 16th Amendment.

Question 48 is based on the following passage from U.S. History For Dummies *by Steve Wiegand (Wiley).*

On May 1, [2003,] [George W.] Bush landed on a U.S. aircraft carrier off the coast of San Diego and declared an end to major combat. Standing in front of a large banner proclaiming "Mission Accomplished," Bush told the crew that "because of you, the target has fallen, and Iraq is free. The war on terror is not over, yet it is not endless. We do not know the day of final victory, but we have seen the turning of the tide."

But if the tide had turned, it seemed to have turned the wrong way. The United States lacked a comprehensive postwar plan for rebuilding the country. Looting and riots dismantled much of Iraq's infrastructure and damaged public buildings. U.S. occupation leaders barred members of Saddam's Baath Party from serving in the provisional government and largely disbanded the Iraqi army. That resulted in a dearth of experienced political leaders and military officers to help with the country's reconstruction.

Go on to next page

In the aftermath, guerrilla warfare caused far more casualties than the brief war had, and fighting between militias of the rival Islamic Sunni and Shiite sects threatened to plunge the country into civil war. Worse for Bush, an intensive search failed to turn up any weapons of mass destruction, and it became clear that Saddam had almost no connection with al-Qaida.

48. Why do many critics today consider the invasion of Iraq during the George W. Bush administration a failure?

(A) There was no comprehensive plan to rebuild Iraq after the war.

(B) Members of the former Iraqi army became terrorists.

(C) A strong central Iraqi government refused to cooperate with American troops in Iraq.

(D) The Baath party continued to exert its influence on the provisional government.

Question 49 is based on the following from a State of the Union address by President Franklin Delano Roosevelt, January 6, 1941.

These are the simple, basic things that must never be lost sight of in the turmoil and unbelievable complexity of our modern world. The inner and abiding strength of our economic and political systems is dependent upon the degree to which they fulfill these expectations.

Many subjects connected with our social economy call for immediate improvement.

As examples:

- We should bring more citizens under the coverage of old-age pensions and unemployment insurance.

- We should widen the opportunities for adequate medical care.

- We should plan a better system by which persons deserving or needing gainful employment may obtain it.

I have called for personal sacrifice. I am assured of the willingness of almost all Americans to respond to that call.

49. What here indicates that some form of government medical care has been a long-term issue in American politics?

(A) FDR solved the issue of medical care for all in 1941.

(B) FDR argued it was needed to strengthen the American economy.

(C) FDR was talking about it in 1941, and it's still a major debate today.

(D) FDR was proposing to create a government healthcare plan.

Question 50 is based on the following passage from U.S. History For Dummies *by Steve Wiegand (Wiley).*

On the foreign front, Clinton was cautious. . . . But his biggest challenge came in what was the former country of Yugoslavia. It had split into smaller states after the collapse of Soviet dominance in Europe in the late 1980s. In Bosnia, which was one of those states, Serbian, Croatian, and Bosnian groups were fighting a civil war that threatened to spread. When diplomatic efforts failed, the United States and other nations sent in peacekeeping troops to

Go on to next page

enforce a fragile truce. Later in the decade, U.S. military forces and other countries also intervened (and eventually restored order) when the former Yugoslavian state of Serbia invaded and terrorized neighboring Kosovo.

Clinton was much less successful — and apparently less interested — in solving problems in Africa. He inherited a mess in Somalia, where U.S. troops had been sent in as part of a United Nations peacekeeping force. They failed to quiet things down. In October 1993, Americans were repulsed by video of the bodies of U.S. soldiers being dragged through the streets of Somalia's capital. U.S. troops were removed in 1994. Clinton also failed to intercede in the genocidal conflict in Rwanda, where millions were killed or forced to become refugees. A decade later, and presumably wiser, Clinton apologized for his "personal failure" to do more.

50. Which internal debate in the United States is reflected in this passage?

(A) interventionism versus isolationism

(B) American exceptionalism

(C) Pro- and anti-United Nations feelings in America

(D) globalization

The Extended Response

Time: 25 minutes for one essay.

Directions: Read this passage and write an essay in response to the prompt that follows it.

Passage

From "Remarks by the President on Economic Mobility," a speech by President Obama, December 4, 2013 (www.whitehouse.gov/the-press-office/2013/12/04/ remarks-president-economic-mobility).

Now, the premise that we're all created equal is the opening line in the American story. And while we don't promise equal outcomes, we have strived to deliver equal opportunity — the idea that success doesn't depend on being born into wealth or privilege, it depends on effort and merit. . . .

It was Abraham Lincoln, a self-described "poor man's son," who started a system of land grant colleges all over this country so that any poor man's son could go learn something new.

When farms gave way to factories, a rich man's son named Teddy Roosevelt fought for an eight-hour workday, protections for workers, and busted monopolies that kept prices high and wages low.

When millions lived in poverty, FDR fought for Social Security, and insurance for the unemployed, and a minimum wage.

When millions died without health insurance, LBJ fought for Medicare and Medicaid.

Together, we forged a New Deal, declared a War on Poverty in a great society. We built a ladder of opportunity to climb, and stretched out a safety net beneath so that if we fell, it wouldn't be too far, and we could bounce back. And as a result, America built the largest middle class the world has ever known. And for the three decades after World War II, it was the engine of our prosperity. . . .

. . . during the post-World War II years, the economic ground felt stable and secure for most Americans, and the future looked brighter than the past. . . .

But starting in the late '70s, this social compact began to unravel. . . . A more competitive world lets companies ship jobs anywhere. And as good manufacturing jobs automated or headed offshore, workers lost their leverage, jobs paid less and offered fewer benefits. . . .

And the result is an economy that's become profoundly unequal. . . . Since 1979, when I graduated from high school, our productivity is up by more than 90 percent, but the income of the typical family has increased by less than eight percent. Since 1979, our economy has more than doubled in size, but most of that growth has flowed to a fortunate few.

The top 10 percent no longer takes in one-third of our income — it now takes half. Whereas in the past, the average CEO made about 20 to 30 times the income of the average worker, today's CEO now makes 273 times more. And meanwhile, a family in the top 1 percent has a net worth 288 times higher than the typical family, which is a record for this country.

Go on to next page

So the basic bargain at the heart of our economy has frayed. . . .

. . . this increasing inequality is most pronounced in our country, and it challenges the very essence of who we are as a people. Understand we've never begrudged success in America. We aspire to it. We admire folks who start new businesses, create jobs, and invent the products that enrich our lives. . . . As Lincoln once said, "While we do not propose any war upon capital, we do wish to allow the humblest man an equal chance to get rich with everybody else."

The problem is that alongside increased inequality, we've seen diminished levels of upward mobility in recent years. A child born in the top 20 percent has about a 2-in-3 chance of staying at or near the top. A child born into the bottom 20 percent has a less than 1-in-20 shot at making it to the top. . . . In fact, statistics show . . . that it is harder today for a child born here in America to improve her station in life than it is for children in most of our wealthy allies — countries like Canada or Germany or France. They have greater mobility than we do, not less. . . .

. . . But here's an important point. The decades-long shifts in the economy have hurt all groups: poor and middle class; inner city and rural folks; men and women; and Americans of all races. . . .

This shouldn't be an ideological question. It was Adam Smith, the father of free-market economics, who once said, "They who feed, clothe, and lodge the whole body of the people should have such a share of the produce of their own labor as to be themselves tolerably well fed, clothed, and lodged." And for those of you who don't speak old English, let me translate. It means if you work hard, you should make a decent living. If you work hard, you should be able to support a family. . . .

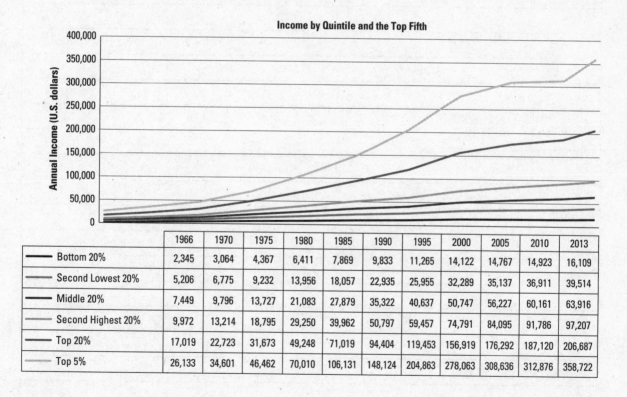

Income by Quintile and the Top Fifth

	1966	1970	1975	1980	1985	1990	1995	2000	2005	2010	2013
Bottom 20%	2,345	3,064	4,367	6,411	7,869	9,833	11,265	14,122	14,767	14,923	16,109
Second Lowest 20%	5,206	6,775	9,232	13,956	18,057	22,935	25,955	32,289	35,137	36,911	39,514
Middle 20%	7,449	9,796	13,727	21,083	27,879	35,322	40,637	50,747	56,227	60,161	63,916
Second Highest 20%	9,972	13,214	18,795	29,250	39,962	50,797	59,457	74,791	84,095	91,786	97,207
Top 20%	17,019	22,723	31,673	49,248	71,019	94,404	119,453	156,919	176,292	187,120	206,687
Top 5%	26,133	34,601	46,462	70,010	106,131	148,124	204,863	278,063	308,636	312,876	358,722

Go on to next page

Prompt

You have 25 minutes to write an essay based on the passage and graph. In your response, develop an argument about how income inequality reflects an enduring issue. Incorporate relevant and specific evidence from the stimulus material and your own knowledge of the enduring issue.

Go on to next page

Chapter 14

Answers and Explanations for the Social Studies Practice Test

*I*n this chapter, we provide the answers and explanations to every question in the Social Studies practice test in Chapter 13. If you just want a quick look at the answers, check out the abbreviated answer key at the end of this chapter. However, if you have the time, you're better off reading all the answer explanations carefully. Doing so helps you understand why some answers are correct and others aren't, especially when the choices are really close. It also points you to areas where you may need to do more review. Remember, you learn as much from your errors as from the correct answers.

Answers and Explanations

1. **C. It defines the responsibilities of the three branches of government.** Choices (A) and (D) are correct in that the Constitution allows for presidential veto and defines the selection of candidates for election to government, but they aren't the complete answer. Choice (B) is wrong because the Constitution doesn't select members of any branch of government. You must select the best answer from the options given, and here that's Choice (C).

2. **A. 2016.** Elections for members of the House of Representatives take place every two years.

3. **C. 2022.** George may run for election to the House of Representatives in the first election after seven years from the date of his citizenship. Elections for the House happen every two years, so the first year he would be eligible would be 2022. Candidates running for election to the House of Representatives don't have to have been born in the United States.

4. **B. The presidential objection can be overturned if the bill in question is reapproved by a two-thirds vote in both houses of Congress.** The president has the right to refuse to approve any bill passed by Congress. The president may refuse to sign the bill and return it to Congress, where legislators vote on it again. If a two-third's majority in both chambers approves the bill, it becomes law even without the president's support. Of the choices given, only Choice (B) is an actual governmental process.

5. **C. It automatically becomes law if Congress is in session.** If the president doesn't want to approve or directly veto a bill, he can also simply ignore it. However, if Congress is in session, the bill becomes law automatically after ten days.

6. **A. The citizens of any state of the United States will have the same rights in all the states.** This clause basically states that laws passed in any one state must be respected by the governments of all other states. Choice (B) is partially correct but not the complete answer. Choices (C) and (D) are wrong because they simply aren't true.

7. **D. New York State must return the individual to Texas.** The Constitution requires that any state return on demand a fugitive criminal to the state where he committed that crime. The process is called *extradition*.

8. **D. All of the above.** The framers of the Constitution wrote that document with two concerns in mind: a fear of the establishment of a tyrannical government and a fear that the uneducated masses would take over the government. The Electoral College was just one part of the division of power and the checks and balances built into the Constitution.

9. **C. San Antonio.** The upper graph shows the actual population numbers, and the lower graph shows percentage increase. You need to read the details on the graphs to make sure you're using the correct one.

10. **A. one year.** The information you need to find is the subtitle of the graph: "U.S. Cities with a Population of a Million or More as of July 1, 2014, and the Number and Percentage of People Added since July 1, 2013." Graphics show information in many areas, not just the charts themselves. You gotta read the famous "fine print."

11. **C. The migration rate of young adults has decreased since 2009.** Choices (A) and (B) are wrong because they confuse the general trend with the difference in the trend between 2007–2009 and 2010–2012. The general trend for both time periods is relatively the same. The two lines virtually overlap. However, the migration rate does change, so Choice (D) is wrong. You can verify a gap between the two time periods in the age group representing young adults by looking at the lower graph. The only significant change in migration that the graph shows is in the young adult age group. From the choices offered, Choice (C) is your best choice.

12. **A. A recession occurred between 2007 and 2009.** The correct answer is Choice (A) because of the two time periods selected. The two lines compare 2007–2009 to 2010–2012. The implication is the recession happened in the earlier period. Choices (B) and (C) make no sense based on the chart; the chart title clearly indicates a recession did take place, so Choice (D) is wrong.

13. **D. The American government suspects the Chinese are involved in cyber intrusions in the United States.** Several pieces of data in the passage allow the reader to connect the dots. The president signed an executive order to impose financial sanctions, the secretary of homeland security visited China, and the United States has "sharp differences with the Chinese Government, particularly when it comes to the theft of confidential business information and proprietary technology through cyber intrusions." The only valid conclusion you can draw from that information from among the choices offered is Choice (D). Though Choices (A) and (B) may be true, they're not the main point. Nothing in the text supports Choice (C).

14. **D. All of the above.** All three other options are valid choices, so the best answer is Choice (D).

15. **A. They built their settlement outside the area they were granted in their charter.** In modern terms, a *squatter* is someone who illegally occupies a property. The text states very specifically that the Pilgrims landed outside the borders of the territory laid out by their charter, so Choice (A) is the correct answer. Choices (B) and (C) are true statements, but they're not the best answers.

16. **C. four fewer people.** One passenger and four crew members died, but one child was born. The net decrease is four.

17. **D. None of the above.** The Mayflower Compact was a set of rules to live by, a simple constitution to which all the colonists agreed. It wasn't a tenancy agreement or a treaty with the local Native Americans, and it had nothing to do with the company charter.

18. **A. Most American colonists were quite happy to be living in colonies of Britain.** The passage suggests that most Americans were quite happy living in British colonies, which is reinforced by the fact that the only examples of people opposed to British rule are described as a "big-time smuggler" or "hypocritical." Nothing in the passage supports the other three options.

19. **B. James Otis.** You can find the answer in the first paragraph. The other names have no connection to that phrase.

20. **D. All of the above.** The passage lists all of these concerns as factors resulting from population decline.

21. **C. We will not breed ourselves into subsistence.** The author of the passage suggests that birthrates are indeed declining, contradicting Malthus's arguments that people will continue to breed faster than we can expand our food supply. Choices (A) and (B) are partially correct but not complete answers. Choice (D) is wrong based on the passage.

22. **A. the rapid population growth in the developing world.** The passage discusses living standards and birthrates in terms of developed countries only. Less-developed countries still have birthrates significantly above replacement level, and developed countries are balancing their lower birthrate with higher immigration. Choice (B) is partially correct, but the focus of the passage is on birthrates, not agriculture. Choice (C) may be partially true, but it doesn't answer the question.

23. **B. It will increase the risk of drought.** The passage states that if temperatures had been cooler, a larger snowpack would've been available for spring and summer runoff and therefore reduced the risk of drought. The other options are wrong based on the passage.

24. **C. It reduced winter snowpack, decreasing spring-summer runoff.** Higher temperatures cause the winter snowpack to melt earlier, making less water available during the summer. The passage also mentions that high heat increases evaporation of moisture from the soil, which in turn increases the need for water, which exacerbates the lack of available runoff water. Unstated is the fact that warmer temperatures also have a general effect of reducing precipitation. Though Choice (A) may be true, it has nothing to do with the theme of the passage, and the passage contradicts Choices (B) and (D).

25. **A. Obama won the popular vote in more states than Romney.** You have two ways of finding the answers for this question: You can count the actual number of states shown in the darkest color on each map for each candidate, or you can check the bar graph on the left side. According to the bar graphs, Obama won the popular vote in 27 states compared to Romney's win of 24 states. Choice (D) is a true statement — in the Electoral College system, a candidate can win the presidency by winning a smaller number of highly populated states but not the overall popular vote — but it doesn't answer the question asked. Choice (A) does.

26. **A. the Democrats.** Obama won all the New England states with 50 percent or more of the popular vote; in several states, he won by more than 60 percent. If those trends hold, then the most likely expectation would be support for the Democratic Party in future elections. Nothing in the maps indicates a possible tie vote.

27. **C. Wyoming and Utah.** Only two states are marked in that particular shade of gray

28. **C. The area had economic difficulties and could not provide the seed money required to create improvements.** Choice (A) is wrong; unemployment is 6 percent, not 6 percent above the national average. Choice (B) may be true, but that wasn't known at the time the economic development grant was made. Choice (D) may also be true, but nothing in the passage supports that choice. That means your best answer is Choice (C).

29. **B. the proximity of recreational land to the industrial areas.** Choices (A), (C), and (D) aren't supported in any way by the text. The passage makes no mention of an environmental assessment review or of objections from existing port tenants. The area may have high unemployment, but that's not a complication for economic development.

30. **A. It brought in an additional 133,000 square feet of space.** A quick math question: The passage states that the aggregate occupied space was about 100,000 square feet, and after construction, some 233,000 square feet were in use. The 40,000 figure comes from anticipated future demand.

31. **B. Jefferson Davis.** Abraham Lincoln was elected before Jefferson Davis took office, but Lincoln wasn't inaugurated until several weeks after Davis took office.

32. **A. the South.** According to the timeline, Confederate forces fired first, at Fort Sumter, South Carolina, on April 12, 1861. The other choices are wrong.

33. **D. the Fifth Amendment.** The Fifth Amendment states that no one shall be forced to give evidence against himself. The other amendments don't apply to this question.

34. **D. All of the above.** The court starts by suggesting that Fifth Amendment rights apply to all people, even those in custody. At the end of the statement, the court states very directly the advice that must be given before custodial interrogation to anyone under arrest. That advice includes all the answer options.

35. **D. no state.** This question is something of a trick question that requires a close interpretation of the legend and the math. The description of states gaining seats offers three increases: one seat, two seats, or four seats. No color is assigned for a three-seat gain. Therefore, no state could've increased its representation by three seats. The numbers on the map refer to the number of seats states have, not the changes in the number of seats.

36. **D. Grants do not have to be repaid under most circumstances.** Choices (A) and (B) may be correct but aren't supported by the passage. Choice (C) is true, but it's not the best answer. The key point is that, barring a drop-out, grants don't have to be repaid.

37. **A. increasing.** The graph shows more peaks toward more recent years, and 2014 was the highest of the displayed years.

38. **C. an unvaccinated traveler from the Philippines.** The text states that the outbreak was likely started by a traveler infected overseas, which means the person was unvaccinated. The text also indicates that the type of measles was identified as the same as one involved in an outbreak in the Philippines the previous year. You can reasonably connect the two for your answer. The link to France refers to measles outbreaks in 2011, and the unvaccinated religious community is linked to outbreaks in 2008 and 2014. The best answer choice is Choice (C).

39. **A. government restructuring whereby governments reduce the size of the civil service and cut spending on government programs.** Governments such as Greece that face financial crises often respond by drastically downsizing the civil service and government programs and cutting spending, all in an effort to balance the budget. Keynes's theory instead argued that the government indeed should be spending money, increasing services, and finding ways to create new employment. Although Choice (C) is partially true, none of the other choices is a complete answer.

40. **D. None of the above.** None of these answers applies. Bailing out Greece didn't create new government jobs. Choice (B) is wrong, since it did not force lenders to write off any or all of their loans. Choice (C) is just wrong, since austerity caused unemployment to surge.

41. **B. No.** Keynes's aim was to shorten the time it takes for an economy to recover from recession. The steps Greece took made the debt crisis and recession much worse. Based on that information, Choices (A), (C), and (D) don't fit the bill.

42. **B. People could see the contrast between capitalism and communism just by looking at East and West Berlin.** Though Kennedy may have enjoyed his own visit to West Berlin, and West Berlin could probably have used a visit from a popular president to generate revenue, neither Choice (A) nor Choice (C) is a correct answer. The speech contradicts Choice (D).

43. **A. West Berliners have become a strong symbol of free people's struggle against communism.** Kennedy's visit to West Berlin came at the height of the cold war. If you've read up on history, you likely know that Berlin was one focal point where communist forces were confronting the western Allies. The other choices may have an element of truth, but none is the most complete answer choice.

44. **D. 18 to 24 years old.** The least engaged group of eligible voters is the 18-to-24-year-old group. Appealing to that group is most likely to create change simply because so many in that group haven't voted in the past. The graph also shows that voter participation increases with age.

45. **D. Voter participation of all age groups increased in 1992.** The graph very clearly shows an upswing in voter participation in all age groups in 1992. That is in contrast to the general decline in voter participation between 1964 and 2012. Your best answer is Choice (D). Choices (A) and (B) are partially true but not the best answers.

46. **C. both Choice (A) and Choice (B).** FDR's statement certainly contains some irony. Black Americans were generally assigned to service troops, not combat units, and most Japanese Americans had been rounded up and placed in internment camps. In both cases, decisions had been based on a matter of race and ancestry.

47. **D. Congress did not have the power to create a federal income tax until the passage of the 16th Amendment.** Though Choices (A), (B), and (C) are all partially true, they're not complete answers. As the passage states, Congress needed a Constitutional amendment to get the right to pass an income tax. Congress had passed an income tax act earlier that had been overruled by the U.S. Supreme Court. The issue isn't that Congress couldn't or didn't pass such legislation, but that it took the amendment to make it legal.

48. **A. There was no comprehensive plan to rebuild Iraq after the war.** The key point is the lack of a comprehensive rebuilding plan. Choices (B) and (C) may have an element of truth, but they're certainly not the complete answer.

49. **C. FDR was talking about it in 1941, and it's still a major debate today.** None of the other options is correct. FDR certainly didn't solve the issue, nor did he state that it was needed to strengthen the American economy. He wasn't proposing that the government create such a plan, only that it should be considered.

50. **A. interventionism versus isolationism.** In the United States, those favoring interventionism and those preferring isolationism have engaged in an ongoing debate. On the one hand, some people are in favor of America taking part in United Nations activities, various military stabilization and peacekeeping activities, and other forms of international intervention. Others in America prefer to stay out of all international matters, arguing that the country has enough problems at home and that America has no vital interest in other parts of the world. Though Choice (C) is partially correct, it's not the complete answer, and the other choices are wrong.

Scoring Your Extended Response

Knowing how to score an essay teaches you how to write one by showing you the parameters that are evaluated. Here is a scheme that will help you evaluate your own answer.

Feature	Criteria	Possible Points	Points Awarded
Thesis statement	Thesis stated clearly in opening paragraph.	2	
Organization	Essay presents ideas in logical order that follows a clear outline.	1	
Paragraphs	Content broken into paragraphs rather than one solid block.	3	
Transitions	One point for initial use of each transition word or phrase (repeats don't count).	3	

continued

(continued)

Feature	Criteria	Possible Points	Points Awarded
Premise	One point for each premise or main point supporting the thesis.	3	
Evidence from stimulus	One point for each piece of evidence from stimulus material.	4	
Evidence from own knowledge	One point for each piece of evidence from own knowledge.	3	
Sentence variety	One for each of the following: compound, complex, and compound-complex sentence.	3	
Focus	Essay doesn't wander off topic.	1	
Conclusion/ thesis	Conclusion restates the thesis.	1	
Conclusion/ evidence	Conclusion summarizes evidence.	1	
Spelling, grammar, usage, and punctuation	Deduct one point for each error over a three-error allotment.	–3	
Total Score		25 max	

Checking Out a Sample Response

Use the chart in the preceding section to evaluate the following essay. It isn't perfect, nor is it intended to be. It's an example of what a high-school student could produce in 25 minutes as a first-draft essay. Remember that you aren't expected to produce a perfect essay. You have neither the time nor the access to research to do that. But you must produce a reasonable, well-written essay.

A founding principle of America was equality for all. That meant not just equality before the law, but equality of opportunity. However, the equality of opportunity has not always been evident. In fact, income inequality has been an enduring issue in American history. Presidents from Lincoln to Franklin Roosevelt and Obama have all had to deal with the issue. Some took direct steps to help the poor, through land grants or expanded education, while others, like FDR, gave the working class the tools to fight for improvements. Unfortunately, since the 1970s, this inequality is once again an issue, and Congress and presidents have done little to deal with the issue.

Many presidents have taken steps to alleviate the problem, but it comes back in new ways. Lincoln started the land grant colleges to help people get an education. That solved part of the problem. However, by Teddy Roosevelt's time, large monopolies conspired to keep prices high and wages low. He responded by regulating working hours and "busting monopolies". FDR took that further during the Great Depression, by regulating banks, providing unemployment insurance, and empowering unions. They in turn helped workers improve their standard of living, and created a more egalitarian society.

Other presidents took addressed different issues. Johnson's Great Society program introduced Medicaid, Medicare, expanded social security and federal education funding. Obama addressed healthcare issues with the Affordable Care Act.

However, since the 1970s, the graph shows the share of America's wealth in the hands of the poorest 20% has barely changed, while that of the top 20% has risen almost eightfold. Presidents from Reagan on have reduced individual and corporate tax rates, which has benefited mainly the wealthiest at the expense of services for the rest of the population. The president's speech shows the effects of this income disparity on the poor. Social mobility is minimal: "A child born in the top 20 percent has about a 2-in-3 chance of staying at or near the top. A child born into the bottom 20 percent has a less than 1-in-20 shot at making it to the top".

Unfortunately, the conservative mood in Congress makes any effective measures to deal with this issue unlikely. The President states that this (income inequality) should not be a partisan issue, but sadly, it is. This is an enduring issue, and is likely to continue to be so.

Answer Key

1. C	14. D	27. C	40. D
2. A	15. A	28. C	41. B
3. C	16. C	29. B	42. B
4. B	17. D	30. A	43. A
5. C	18. A	31. B	44. D
6. A	19. B	32. A	45. D
7. D	20. D	33. D	46. C
8. D	21. C	34. D	47. D
9. C	22. A	35. D	48. A
10. A	23. B	36. D	49. C
11. C	24. C	37. A	50. A
12. A	25. A	38. C	
13. D	26. A	39. A	

Part V
The Part of Tens

For a list of ten bonus tips and tricks to pump up your score on the GED Social Studies test, check out www.dummies.com/extras/gedsocialstudiestest.

In this part . . .

✔ Take a look at ten study techniques and tactics to train for the test, including techniques for getting and staying centered, where to focus your efforts, and what to read to broaden your knowledge of government, civics, history, economics, and geography.

✔ Focus on ten crucial skills to master prior to test day, including reading comprehension, summarizing information, citing sources, detecting bias and propaganda, reading maps and graphs, and interpreting political cartoons.

Chapter 15

Ten More Ways to Prep for the GED Social Studies Test

In This Chapter
▶ Allocating time and taking practice tests
▶ Being mentally prepared
▶ Delving into civics, history, economics, and geography

By reading this book and answering the practice questions, you're doing exactly what you should be doing to prepare yourself for the GED Social Studies test. If you prefer being overprepared to being underprepared (the kind of person who heads out on a weekend camping trip with two of everything just in case), then you may be wondering what more you can do to improve your score. In this chapter, we answer that question by presenting ten more ways to prepare for the test.

Don't burn yourself out. For every hour you spend preparing for the test, spend a couple of hours resting or engaging in recreational activities. Your brain needs downtime to process the massive amounts of information it's absorbing.

Blocking Out Test Prep Time

You have a million other things to do, and at least a couple of them are probably more enjoyable than preparing for a standardized test. But if you're committed to performing well on the test, you need to set aside some time. Most time-management experts suggest that instead of finding the time (something you're unlikely to do), you should make the time. Devote a daily time slot to your GED studies. If your day is already overcrowded with activities, look to the beginning or end of the day to find at least one hour to set aside. If weekdays are out, you may have to sacrifice a portion of your precious weekend. If you don't schedule a time, you're very unlikely to do what's necessary to perform well on the test.

Choose a test day that's far enough in the future to give you sufficient time to prepare, but not so far that you run out of steam (and interest) prior to test day. Schedule the test so you have a day to work toward; knowing this date will help keep you motivated.

Team up with someone. You're more likely to remain on task if you team up with someone who's also preparing to take the test. You can hold each other accountable for honoring your commitments to test-prep time. Having a teammate also comes in handy when you need someone to look over your Extended Response.

Taking the Diagnostic Test Before the Practice Test

Prior to devoting huge amounts of time and energy to test prep, take the diagnostic test in Chapter 3 to identify your strengths and weaknesses. Don't waste time on skills you already have. Focus your time and effort on your weakest areas. After taking the diagnostic test, review the answers carefully; they explain what's required to answer each question correctly. If you struggle with certain types of questions, give those extra attention when you review for the final test.

After addressing your areas of weakness, take the practice test to make sure you "get it" and to get your head in the game for the actual test. The practice test familiarizes you with the test format, the types of questions you'll be asked, and the subject areas covered on the test while simulating the actual test-taking experience. If you mark the answers on a separate sheet of paper, you can redo the test as often as you want. Between retakes, carefully check the answers you missed and the ones you answered correctly. Both help you understand how the test works, and the questions you miss help identify areas where you need to pay some special review attention.

Take the diagnostic and practice tests under the same conditions as the actual test: in a quiet room, with no interruptions (including your phone), no music, no snacks, and no breaks. And most important, be sure to set and adhere to the time limit.

Trying Computer-Simulated Tests

If you have the social studies skills and knowledge needed to answer the questions and write the Extended Response, the format of the test (paper or computer) shouldn't make a huge difference in how well you do. However, you can shave precious seconds off your response time to each question and avoid making careless mistakes on the computerized version of the test by answering a few questions on the computer.

At www.gedtestingservice.com/educators/freepracticetest, you can find links to view sample tests online or download and take the tests on your computer (a Mac or PC). You can purchase additional (complete) practice tests online for less than $10. Questions are presented exactly as you'll see them on the actual test so you can get a better feel for how to navigate the test and answer questions. For example, some reading passages have tabs you must click to access all the text. You want to discover this quirk before, not during, the test.

When taking a computer-simulated test, look at everything on the screen and practice accessing different features. Click to move to the next question and then click to move to the previous question. Get comfortable "driving" the test so you don't have to think about it on test day; you can focus on answering questions. Also practice writing your Extended Response using the online text editor. Use the cut, copy, paste, undo, and redo features to get a feel for those, too.

Finding and Answering More Questions

The GED Testing Service website is the best place to find sample questions, but the selection of questions is limited. The free practice test, for example, contains a measly ten questions. Fortunately, you can find tons of social studies questions online. They may not be in the form of GED test computer-simulated questions, but they still provide valuable practice and expand your breadth of knowledge.

Using your favorite online search engine, search for "GED Social Studies sample questions," "high-school social studies questions," "GED Social Studies sample test," or some other clever phrase that's likely to pull up a list of links to web pages with sample questions. To dig a little deeper, you may want to conduct searches in a specific social studies subject area, such as geography, civics, or economics. Use your imagination. You're likely to find copies of complete high-school social studies exams that serve as a gold mine of knowledge and practice. You can buy additional sample practice tests from the GED Testing Service at www.gedmarketplace.com.

Getting Schooled in Civics

About half the GED Social Studies test consists of questions on civics (the rights and duties of citizens) and government. Reading and understanding some of the founding documents of this nation is important. The GED examiners expect a general familiarity, enough that you understand the questions and content on the test. Here are some specific topics for you to review; for more about U.S. history, civics, and economics, turn to Chapters 8, 9, and 10:

- **The structure of the federal government:** You need to know in general terms what each branch of the federal government does. You need to know the role of Congress and each *chamber* of Congress: the Senate and House of Representatives. Compare the powers of the Congress, the executive branch (the president and cabinet), and the judiciary (the Supreme Court). When you study the three branches of government, you should know how someone becomes a member of each branch, and in general terms, what each branch does. For details, visit www.whitehouse.gov/our-government.

- **Checks and balances and separation of powers:** One of the features of the U.S. government is that each branch of the federal government has some control over the actions of the other two, but each has very specific roles and areas of responsibility. Having different branches of government prevents any one branch from becoming too powerful. Review how that works and why that system was established. For details, visit www.whitehouse.gov/our-government.

- **Types of governance systems:** The U.S. government is only one of several types of governments established around the world. Review the differences between the American congressional (presidential) system of government and the parliamentary system, the two most common forms of democratic government. For details, visit www.scholastic.com/teachers/article/forms-government.

- **Election rules and procedures:** You need to know what the qualifications are for someone to run for office, how often elections take place, and how election campaigns are funded. Review who gets to vote for which candidates and how they're elected. Find out more at www.usa.gov/Citizen/Topics/Voting/Learn.shtml.

- **Political parties:** The United States has two main parties, the Republicans and the Democrats. Review how these parties are different and how they're similar. What policies separate them? For the Republican Party platform, visit www.gop.com/platform. To find out more about Democrats, visit www.democrats.org.

- **Key documents from U.S. history:** Read the Declaration of Independence, the Constitution of the United States, and the Bill of Rights. Although these documents aren't exactly light reading, they're not very long. Every citizen, especially any citizen taking the GED Social Studies test, should read them and at least have a general idea of what's in them. You can find complete transcripts of these documents online.

- **Government and economic philosophies:** Brush up on the three main economic systems used around the world: capitalism, socialism, and communism. You should also know a little about Keynesian economics and how it has influenced the way governments respond to recessions and depressions.

✔ **Contemporary issues:** The best way to familiarize yourself with the many issues in U.S. civics and politics is to read newspapers and news magazines, look at political and news websites, and watch television news and current events programs — especially the Sunday morning talk shows, where politicians and pundits make their weekly rounds.

For additional info, check out the following sources (all published by Wiley):

✔ *GED Test For Dummies* by Murray Shukyn, Dale Shuttleworth, and Achim Krull

✔ *Congress For Dummies* by David Silverberg

✔ *Politics For Dummies* by Ann DeLaney

✔ *U.S. History For Dummies* by Steve Wiegand

✔ *World History For Dummies* by Peter Haugan

To gain additional knowledge and insight into history, politics, economics, and geography, check out these resources, many of which are free and easily accessible:

✔ Your daily newspaper or monthly news magazine

✔ Local and national television news

✔ Other television news channels

✔ Online newspapers, blogs, and news sites

✔ Any history or civics textbook

If you're taking the Canadian version of the GED Social Studies test, brush up on Canadian history and civics along with a smattering of U.S. history.

Reading History for Fun

Reading history may not be everyone's idea of fun, but it's interesting. U.S. history covers about 20 percent of the GED Social Studies test. The topics covered fall into two major categories: key documents and people and events. Among the documents you want to be familiar with, or at least be able to read at first glance, are extracts from documents such as the Magna Carta, the Declaration of Independence, and the U.S. Constitution. The importance of having looked at these documents at some point in your studies is that they're written in much older English. The Magna Carta was originally written in Latin, but the translations are also mostly in old English. Reading that can be a challenge.

The history topics will be familiar to anyone who's ever looked at an American history textbook. Pick up any high school American history book at your local library or used bookstore as part of your review. Start with the colonial period, the American Revolution, and the early republic. Major topics after that include the Civil War and Reconstruction, civil rights issues, the World Wars and cold war, the Vietnam War, and American foreign policy since 9/11.

This book presents highlights from these periods in Chapter 9. A great and delightfully easy-to-read resource is *U.S. History For Dummies* by Steve Wiegand (Wiley).

The best advice for this section is in the heading: Read. The advice is always the same: The more you read, the more you know, and the better you understand the questions on the test.

Studying Economics for Fun and Profit

Economics topics make up about 15 percent of the GED Social Studies test. These topics include fundamental economic concepts such as markets, labor and capital, comparative advantage, and others. The second set of economics topics are micro- and macroeconomics. Microeconomics studies how businesses and consumers operate on a local and national level, while macroeconomics studies how economic activity works on a global scale. Examine the role of government, institutions, and the effect of government regulation on economic activity.

Some sections of the economics part of the test do overlap with history. For example, economics has an impact both on rivalry among nations and on the level of development of any economy. Scientific, agricultural, and industrial revolutions all changed the way people live and had an impact on everything from religion to governance, wealth, and international rivalries.

Chapter 10 of this book provides an excellent introduction to economics. For deeper and broader coverage, check out *Economics For Dummies* by Sean Flynn (Wiley).

Reading Geography, Just Because

Geography is a fascinating subject because it combines so many areas of study. It accounts for 15 percent of the content on the GED Social Studies test. You can break the geography coverage into three general areas: the relationship between the environment and societal development, borders and their effects, and human migration. From your own general knowledge of these topics, you know that includes a large helping of history and economics. Altogether, that creates an interesting buffet.

The environmental portion of the geography component includes the effects of the environment and resource base on national development, the effect of technology on sustainability, and an examination of how humans change the environment and how the environment affects human development. The sections on borders and migration look at what borders are, how they function, and some of the problems they create. It looks at why people migrate and the effects migration has on both national and cultural development and rivalries.

Chapter 11 covers much of this material. If you need more information, or maybe want to read more just because, search the web for any of the key terms in that chapter to find a great deal of really interesting material. A visit to your local bookstore will yield several interesting used high school textbooks.

Keeping Calm under Pressure

You know that some people choke under pressure. However, you can reduce the risk. You're already taking the most important step to deal with test anxiety and the pressure of actually taking the test — you're preparing for it. The next step is to take practice tests under conditions similar to those on test day.

Simulate the test-taking experience. Astronauts and pilots do it, and so should you. We're not suggesting that you build your own testing center, but you can certainly find a quiet place with fluorescent lights, a desk, an uncomfortable chair, and perhaps even a computer. Your local library may be the perfect place. If not, find a quiet room in your home and take the practice test in Chapter 13.

To make the simulation even more realistic, do the following:

- ✔ Turn off your music, TV, smartphone, and any other digital distractions.

- ✔ Lose the drinks and snacks. They're not allowed in the testing room.

- ✔ Set a timer. The biggest source of pressure for most test-takers is the limited amount of time they have to complete the test.

- ✔ Don't take bathroom breaks. They waste time during the test.

Psyching Yourself for the Test

Any athlete can tell you that mental preparation is as important as physical practice. Studies show that athletes who visualize playing a successful game do as well as those who spend a great deal of time on physical practice. The same applies to taking an academic test. You need to understand and know inside yourself that you're ready. You can accomplish this mindset two ways. Retake the practice test just to show yourself how well you can do. Turn the questions into flash cards and practice with a friend. Work toward a deadline, but don't schedule the actual GED test until you can do well on the practice test. And when you've done well, keep reminding yourself of that fact. Knowing that you have the skills, that you've done the reading, and that you've developed the understanding is the best way to build the confidence you need to perform well on this test.

Maintaining Focus

When you take the actual GED tests, you're under time pressure as well as the pressure you put on yourself to succeed. Clearing your mind of everything other than the test is easier said than done. After all, you have a life with responsibilities and worries.

As you're sitting in front of the real GED test, or even the practice test in this book, take a few deep breaths. Breathe in, hold, and breathe out. Repeat three or four times. Deep breathing keeps you from hyperventilating and getting flustered. As you breathe, think of a time when you were successful and happy in your achievement. Think of how completing the GED successfully will improve your life. Tell yourself, "I can do this. I am prepared." Center yourself with deep breathing and positive affirmations before the test, as you get started, and during the test. If you feel distracted or your attention wavers, repeat the breathing exercises. They really do help you focus.

Chapter 16

Ten Skills to Master for the GED Social Studies Test

In This Chapter

▶ Getting the most out of your reading

▶ Recognizing propaganda and bias when you see it

▶ Interpreting maps, graphs, tables, and cartoons

You don't need to know a lot about social studies to perform well on the test, but you do need skills. Most of the skills required involve extracting information and insight that's presented in various formats, including text, graphs, tables, maps, illustrations, and even political cartoons. Other skills, such as the ability to spot propaganda and bias, are also useful when you're called on to analyze a passage. In this chapter, we explain ten valuable skills required to do well on the GED Social Studies test so you can start developing these skills during the lead-up to test day.

Nailing Down the Lingo

Social studies relies on some very specific terminology that you may not be accustomed to. If you can't determine the meaning of a term from the context in which it's used, you may not fully understand a passage or the question-and-answer choices that accompany it. As a result, you may struggle to identify the correct answer. Here are a few key terms and concepts you should be familiar with:

✔ **Budget deficit:** A situation in which the government's expenditures exceed its revenue for a given period of time; in other words, the government spends more than it collects in taxes and other funds. (Don't confuse the budget deficit with the *national debt,* discussed later in this list.) *Deficit reduction* focuses on cutting expenditures and/or raising revenues so the government doesn't have to continue to borrow so much money.

✔ **Civil rights:** The rights the Constitution guarantees to each individual living in the United States, whether citizen or resident. In a social studies context, this term usually refers to either minority rights or equal rights for women and other groups who feel disadvantaged.

✔ **Consumer price index (CPI):** The overall measurement of prices consumers pay for a specific basket of goods, such as food, tobacco and alcohol, housing costs, leisure goods, and other common purchases. The CPI is often used to calculate inflation and becomes a subject of debate over which items are included in the basket of goods and what their estimated prices are.

- ✔ **Deflation:** A rare occurrence when prices of consumer goods and services fall. Economists often warn of the threat of deflation because it can slow down an economy. People are less willing to buy products when they know that tomorrow the products will be cheaper. They're also more reluctant to borrow money because the money they borrow will be worth less the next day. Bankers don't like when people stop borrowing money from them.

- ✔ **Due process:** Protections enshrined in the Bill of Rights and the Constitution, which guarantee all citizens and residents of the United States protection against arbitrary action by the government or state authorities. Due process helps ensure that suspects receive a speedy and fair trial.

- ✔ **Ideology:** A system of beliefs, values, and ideals of the individuals who make up a society. For the GED Social Studies test, ideology is important as a reference to the set of core values that guide leaders in their decision making. For example, President Wilson wanted Americans to abandon the tradition of isolationism and become actively involved in world politics. This desire was based on his ideology. Similarly, FDR's ideology led him to use government intervention to alleviate the harm caused by the Great Depression.

- ✔ **Globalization:** A feature of the modern economy, where the production of goods and services has been distributed to countries around the world. One important side effect for the American economy has been the loss of high-paid blue-collar work as those jobs are transferred to low-wage economies. At the same time, the United States has experienced an expansion of both high-tech jobs and service industry jobs. Globalization has also led to investment by individuals and companies in countries around the world.

- ✔ **Inflation:** Increased prices for consumer goods and services. Inflation isn't necessarily a bad thing if it's managed well. After all, if you borrow money to purchase a home, the inflated money you use to pay back the loan is worth less than the money you borrowed. Most governments try to regulate their economy in such a way that the inflation rate stays around 2 percent annually. You should also be familiar with these two related terms:

  - **Hyperinflation:** Inflation at a very high rate. Hyperinflation occurred in the Weimar Republic, post–World War I Germany, when the value of the German currency dropped so steeply it was virtually worthless.

  - **Stagflation:** High prices along with high unemployment and little to no increase in wages. A combination of deficit spending, a poor economy, and high oil prices has resulted in stagflation.

- ✔ **National debt:** The total amount of money a country's government owes. Not to be confused with the *budget deficit* (see the definition earlier in this list).

- ✔ **Speculation:** High-risk investments. Investor speculation was one cause of the market crash in 1929 that started the Great Depression. So many people were buying so much stock that prices rose dramatically, and people believed that those prices would never stop rising. It created what economists refer to as a bubble, when stock prices far exceed their real value. Like a bubble, these prices can burst, destroying all the investments. Government regulation on investment banks was an important part of FDR's New Deal.

These are just a few of the terms you should understand for the GED Social Studies test. Create your own list as a study aide as you read all those used textbooks you obtain. A list of terms and definitions is a simple way of amassing a great deal of information.

Reading for Meaning

People commonly zone out when they read, especially when reading dry material such as social studies content. They read the words, but nothing registers; they can read an entire chapter of a book and be unable to describe what they just read. To avoid zoning out when you read, become a more active reader. Here are some techniques to try:

- **When you finish reading a paragraph, ask yourself what it actually means.** If you can summarize the content in your own words, you probably understood.

- **Highlight any vocabulary you don't know and make a point of looking it up.** It seems obvious, but knowing the meaning of vocabulary is essential to understanding what you're actually reading. If you're uncertain of a word's meaning, look it up; don't dismiss your doubt. (Check out the preceding section for a list of terms you may want to start with.)

- **If you're a visual learner, illustrate the passage.** You can use a flow chart approach like Figure 16-1 to show relationships among ideas or even to trace a series of events. Start by placing the central idea in a circle somewhere on a piece of paper. Draw an arrow that connects it to a circle containing the next important idea. If one idea supports another, write them down and draw arrows to where they connect.

- **Explain what you've read to someone else.** Somehow, explaining the concept you're trying to learn to someone else focuses your mind. Focusing on the details so you can tell them to someone else organizes those details in your mind and helps you remember and understand them.

- **Make flash cards.** You can use ordinary index cards. Write a term or concept on one side and explain it on the other. If you're a tactile learner, the process of writing reinforces and clarifies the info, and you end up with a stack of cards you can use to review the information.

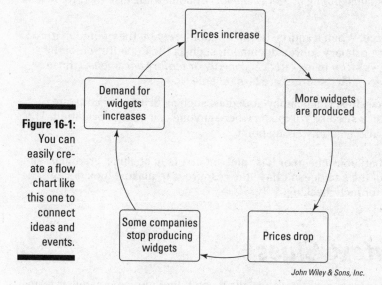

Figure 16-1: You can easily create a flow chart like this one to connect ideas and events.

John Wiley & Sons, Inc.

Summarizing Information

Summarizing information when you're taking notes is a key skill. Practice by following these steps:

1. **Read the document from beginning to end.**

2. **Go back and highlight the points that strike you as important.**

3. **Look for bold, italicized, or highlighted words.**

4. **Go through your points and divide them into two groups: interesting and important.**

5. **Now look for and note any information that elaborates on those key points.**

You can test how good your notes are by using them to rewrite the document. When you compare your version to the original document, look for points you missed. Use these results as a guideline for taking better notes next time.

Identifying Appropriate Sources

Textbooks are pretty reliable sources, but when you start using the Internet to add to that store of information, you need to be both careful and discriminating. Just because it's on the Internet doesn't mean the information is valid or free of bias. So how do you decide what's worthwhile? Follow these suggestions:

- **Check the author's credentials.** If the person has written books or articles in the same academic field, she's probably a credible expert.

- **Click the About Us link.** Find out who's behind a particular website. Knowing the purpose of the site and any of its sponsors can help you determine whether the information is unbiased.

- **Check the domain ending.** If the domain of a site ends in .gov (short for *government*), it probably contains accurate, impartial information. Domains ending in .edu *(education)* and those with .lib *(library)* are generally reliable, as are many sites ending in .com *(commercial)*. Domains ending in .net *(network)* or something else tend to be less reliable.

- **Go to the primary source.** When a source is quoted, don't rely on the quoted material to be accurate; go to the primary source document, such as the Constitution of the United States or the news story being cited. *Secondary* or *tertiary documents* (those quoting a primary or secondary source) are less reliable.

- **Use reputable reference sites.** Online encyclopedias, such as Britannica.com, are much more reliable than a site like Wikipedia where anyone can post information. The CIA World Factbook is also a good starting point.

Steer clear of any website that looks cheap or has rampant errors in spelling, grammar, and punctuation. If the creator of the site doesn't have the resources to make it look decent, the person lacks the resources for fact-checking.

Picking Up on Context Clues

You can often derive meaning from context, especially if you bump into an unfamiliar term. Look for clues in the context to determine the general meaning of the word and then look it up in the dictionary to find out whether you were right. In many cases, authors define a term's meaning right after introducing the term for the first time. They may not give the dictionary definition, but they give you enough to understand the word's meaning in the context in which it's used. Here's an example:

Acidification of lakes is a serious problem. As the pH of a lake drops, the acid in the water creates more damage.

Here, the author introduces the term "acidification" and immediately provides a functional definition of the term — a drop in pH that makes the water more acidic.

Recognizing Propaganda

Propaganda is biased or misleading information intended to sway the audience's opinion or convince the audience to pursue a course of action that they'd be disinclined to follow if they knew the truth. Here are some propaganda warning signs to watch for:

✔ **Name calling:** This approach can be blatant or subtle. Nothing is subtle about describing someone as a redneck, but that term immediately creates an image in the listener's mind of someone who may not be quite as intelligent or cultured as someone else. A more subtle approach is to refer to groups as "special interest groups," "ultra-conservatives," "extremists," or even "card-carrying liberals." In each case, attaching one of these terms creates a negative image. Fortunately, these terms are relatively easy to spot.

✔ **Testimonials:** Before bans on cigarette advertising, ads commonly featured the phrase "three out of four doctors recommend brand Y." Attaching a respected name or group to a product or point you're trying to make can transfer some of the credibility to the product.

✔ **Gross generalizations:** Whenever you see the words *always, never, everyone, nobody,* and so on, proceed with caution. The writer is probably making a gross generalization and discounting any evidence that may cause doubt.

✔ **Selective, one-sided information:** If you're not sure about the legitimacy of something you're reading, look at what the article is telling you and then ask yourself, "What's omitted?" Selecting only favorable information is a great way authors can make sure text supports a particular point and ignores or dismisses opposing points.

✔ **Repetition, especially in speeches:** Politicians especially may use repetition to whip a crowd into a frenzy. Repetition can serve as a chant to lull listeners into accepting the message without questioning it.

Most of the passages you read in preparation for the GED Social Studies test will be relatively factual. If you see any of these techniques used, you know to scrutinize that source more skeptically. Beyond the test, this life skill will certainly help you when dealing with politicians or advertisers.

Detecting Bias

Bias is prejudice for or against something or someone. If all people were perfect, this world would be a very dull place. People have biases, some tiny and insignificant; some major enough to control their world view and how they act and react. People write books, magazines, and newspapers. People create blogs and websites. It is only when their personal world view is presented as "truth" that bias becomes a problem, and you have to learn to spot it and go a little but further to see the broader picture.

A great place to check your bias meter is the nightly national news. You may notice that some networks favor liberal views over conservative ones, for example. Such bias in itself isn't particularly a problem if you know which direction a particular news outlet or broadcaster leans. The world has become very partisan, and many in the media have taken sides.

Here are a few suggestions for becoming more sensitive to bias:

- **Check the newspapers for placement of a particular story.** Which stories an outlet gives front-page coverage with a large headline and photograph and which ones it hides in a small story on the back page are sure signs of its biases.

- **Look for repetition of or a long-term focus on a story.** Repetition of a story long after the event has passed without any new revelation can be a clue to bias.

- **Watch for omissions.** Compare stories from different news outlets to look for information in one report that's been omitted from others. Try to get the entire story and find out which news outlets are more apt to provide unbiased coverage. Omissions may occur in photos, video, and interviews as well.

- **Compare coverage of politicians.** All media do stories about politicians. You can detect a bias by considering how flattering the image of the politician used is. Compare photos in the different media of the same politician. You may find signs of bias.

Textbooks try very hard to screen for bias, but issues arise when politicians shape curriculum; history is one subject where such interventions happen. Religion, culture, political views, even nationalism, all shape the way people see the world. One controversial issue has been the treatment of Native Americans. Some state boards of education have changed the curriculum to minimize discussion of such issues, sweeping them under the rug, and presenting a "patriotic" interpretation of American history. The curriculum can stress some events while ignoring others, shaping how history is presented. You should be aware that some content may represent a point of view rather than a neutral presentation of facts. Whether you believe such omissions represent bias depends on your own personal views. The best advice is never to rely on only one source.

Reading a Map

Nowadays, reading maps typically involves entering your destination's address into a GPS system and then following the route to your destination. On the GED Social Studies test, however, you read a map to identify a country's or state's borders, analyze demographics (population data), extract bits of data, or evaluate a region's terrain.

Figure 16-2 shows a map that not only displays the borders of the United States and the states it comprises but also serves as a graph to present demographics related to manufacturing jobs in the different states.

To extract information from a map, begin by scanning the image. Note the title, the color/shading scheme, the *legend* (which tells you what each color/shade means), and any other printed information on the map. You can identify quickly that Figure 16-2 shows the number of manufacturing employees by state. The purpose of the map is to show you where manufacturing is more prevalent based on the number of people employed in the manufacturing sector. From that information, you can tell that manufacturing is concentrated in three main areas — California, Texas, and the states around the Great Lakes — and that each of the states with the darkest shading has more than 399,000 people employed in manufacturing. The lightest shading indicates that northwestern states represent the largest area with very little manufacturing employment.

By scanning the image further, you can also see that this data is from the year 2012 (as noted in the fine print immediately below the map) and describes the labor force in terms of educational attainment (as noted in the round graphic). For more about extracting information from maps and other images, check out Chapter 7.

The U.S. Census Bureau website's Maps and Data section at www.census.gov/geo/maps-data is a great source for additional maps for practice.

Where does manufacturing occur in the United States?

Manufacturing Employees by State

Total Number of U.S. Manufacturing Employees = 11.2 million

More than 399,000 (10 states)
100,000 to 399,000 (24 states)
Fewer than 100,000 (16 states and D.C.)

In 2012, 28.7 percent of manufacturing employees 25 and older had a bachelor's degree or higher.
Source: 2012 Current Population Survey

Source: 2012 County Business Patterns

Figure 16-2:
A map indicates borders and may be used as a graph.

Image courtesy of the U.S. Census Bureau (www.census.gov/library/infographics/ manufacturing_2014.html)

Extracting Data from Tables and Graphs

More than one question on the GED Social Studies test is likely to require that you extract data from a table or graph. A *table* arranges data in columns and rows, whereas a *graph* displays data more graphically, as its name implies, to better illustrate the big picture and perhaps trends.

Tables are relatively easy to read. After all, they're just labels and numbers arranged in rows and columns, as shown in Figure 16-3. However, the devil is in the details:

- **Title:** The table may include a title that describes the data the table contains and perhaps the year it represents.

- **Note:** One or more notes may clarify what the numbers and other data represent. In Figure 16-3, for example, the note indicates that the numbers in the table represent thousands, so to obtain the actual values, you need to multiply each number by 1,000. So, for example, the number of Hispanic women ages 15 to 50 years in the United States isn't 14,068 but rather 14,068,000.

- **Data:** The column and row labels and the values that make up the most essential part of the table are the data.

- **Details:** Details further explain the data. In Figure 16-3, for example, the details break down the number of children born per 1,000 women into percentages of women who have no children, one child, two children, or three or more. This division gives you finer details of the total number of children born.

- **Explanations/footnotes:** Below a table, you may see some "fine print" where the details are hiding. It explains what the numbers represent, how they were obtained, and other details.

Table 1.
Children Ever Born Per 1,000 Women 15 to 50 Years Old by Age, Race, and Hispanic Origin: June 2012—Con.
(Numbers in thousands)

Characteristic	Number of women	Children ever born per 1,000 women	Margin of Error[1]	Percent distribution of women by number of children ever born[2]				
				Total	None	One child	Two children	Three or more children
RACE AND HISPANIC ORIGIN—Con.								
Hispanic (any race)								
15 to 50 years	14,068	1,546	30	100.0	35.3	17.2	22.2	25.2
15 to 19 years	2,205	128	13	100.0	90.4	7.5	1.3	0.8
20 to 24 years	2,158	589	35	100.0	60.2	25.0	12.0	2.8
25 to 29 years	2,040	1,384	72	100.0	34.1	22.1	25.0	18.9
30 to 34 years	2,045	1,947	98	100.0	16.2	21.4	30.0	32.4
35 to 39 years	1,936	2,404	121	100.0	9.4	13.8	32.2	44.7
40 to 44 years	1,790	2,389	125	100.0	10.9	15.5	28.7	44.9
45 to 50 years	1,894	2,356	120	100.0	14.3	15.3	30.7	39.7

Z Represents or rounds to zero.
[1] This number, when added to or subtracted from the estimate, represents the 90 percent confidence interval around the estimate.
[2] The denominator for each of these percentages is the total number of women in the given age and race/ethnicity category. The numerator is the number of women in that age and race/ethnicity category who have the given number of children. These percentages describe the fertility patterns of a given group of women. Across the line, the percentages will sum to 100 percent.
Source: U.S. Census Bureau, Current Population Survey, June 2012.

Figure 16-3:
A typical table.

Image courtesy of the U.S. Census Bureau (www.census.gov/content/dam/Census/library/publications/2014/demo/p20-575.pdf)

To read a graph, simply look at it to get an overall idea of the data or trends it represents. Look more closely at the following components of a graph to extract additional details:

- **Chart title:** The chart title describes the data that the chart represents, sometimes including the date of the data.

- **Graph title:** A chart may include more than one graph, in which case each graph has a title describing the data it displays. In Figure 16-4, the bar graph on the left represents individual unemployment rates by education (as a percentage), while the bar graph on the right shows median weekly earnings by education (in dollars). Both graphs indicate that the data is for 2014.

- **Data:** The data are the points, bars, lines, slices of pie, and so on that represent the numerical quantities, numbers, percentages, and so on.

- **Data labels:** Graphs often include data labels to describe what the data represent. In Figure 16-4, the vertical column in the middle is the educational attainment that each bar represents. Each bar on the left is accompanied by the specific percentage the bar represents, while each bar on the right is labeled with a dollar amount.

- **Details:** Graphs often include additional details to further explain or summarize the data. Below the left graph in Figure 16-4 is the average unemployment rate. Below the graph on the right is the median weekly earnings for all workers.

This particular graph contains a great deal of information and requires relatively careful examination. Nothing is terribly difficult about reading a graph, but you must pay attention to the details.

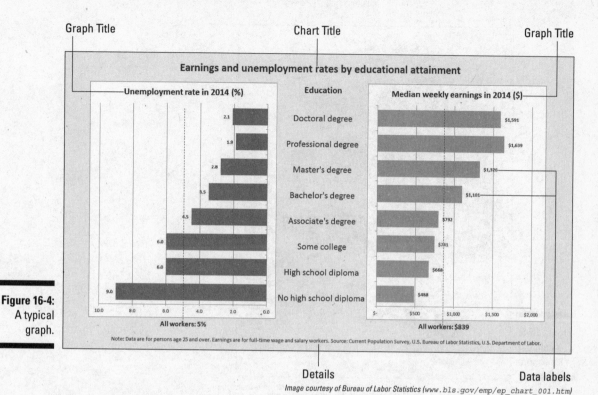

Figure 16-4:
A typical
graph.

Deciphering Political Cartoons

You may encounter political cartoons on the GED Social Studies test, but they aren't there simply to keep you from dozing off. These cartoons originally appeared in newspapers or magazines to make a political statement or illustrate the conditions at the time.

To interpret the meaning of a political cartoon, examine it closely and note the details. For example, the cartoon shown in Figure 16-5 dates back to Germany's unrestricted U-boat campaign in World War I. You can tell that by the helmet of the person steering the U-boat and by the old-fashioned appearance of the submarine itself. You can see that the artist considers the campaign an illegitimate form of warfare because the flag being flown from the ship is the Jolly Roger (commonly associated with pirates) with the skull apparently wearing a German helmet. The victim, a woman draped over the bow of the U-boat, probably represents the first woman to fall victim to the U-boat attacks — a stewardess aboard an English merchant ship sunk without warning in 1914. The woman may also represent the many murdered civilians, victims of this brutal war. She is there to arouse anger against the German navy's unrestricted submarine warfare and Germans in general.

Image courtesy of ProjectGutenberg.org from *America's Black and White Book:
One Hundred Pictured Reasons Why We Are At War, by William Allen Rogers*
(www.gutenberg.org/files/47484/47484-h/47484-h.htm).

Index

About the Authors

Achim K. Krull, BA, MAT, is a graduate of the University of Toronto with specialist qualifications in history and geography. He has taught at both the high-school and adult education levels. Achim worked for many years in the academic alternative schools of the Toronto District School Board as administrator/curriculum leader of Subway Academy One and cofounder of SOLE. He has written textbooks, teachers' guides, and a large variety of other learning materials with Murray Shukyn, including scripts for educational videos, as well as newspaper and magazine articles. Achim designed and currently teaches an academic upgrading program for young adults preparing to enter apprenticeships.

Murray Shukyn, BA, is a graduate of the University of Toronto with professional qualifications as a teacher at the elementary and secondary levels, including special education. He has taught at the elementary, secondary, and university levels and developed training programs for adult learners in the coffee and food-service industries. During his extensive career spanning more than 50 years, Murray has taught professional development programs for educators and is acknowledged as a Canadian leader in the field of alternative education. He was instrumental in the creation of such innovative programs for the Toronto Board of Education as SEED, Learnxs, Subway Academy, SOLE, and ACE. In 1995, Murray became associate director of the Training Renewal Foundation, which introduced the GED in the province of Ontario. As a consultant to government, media, and public relations companies, he has coauthored numerous textbooks and magazine and periodical articles with Achim Krull and coauthored several books to prepare adults to take the GED test with both Achim Krull and Dale Shuttleworth.

Dedication

From Achim: To my wife, Helga, and the espresso machine; both helped me through the many hours of work.

Authors' Acknowledgements

We wish to say a special word of thanks to Grace Freedson of Grace Freedson's Publishing Network for all her efforts in negotiating for these books and guiding us through the often murky waters of negotiations.

Thanks to John Wiley & Sons acquisitions editor Lindsay Lefevere for choosing us to write this workbook and for pulling together a talented team of professionals to help us produce a top-quality product. Thanks to wordsmith Joe Kraynak at joekraynak.com for teaming up with us during the early stages of the project to produce a quality manuscript and deliver it in a timely manner.

We thank Chrissy Guthrie of Guthrie Writing & Editorial, LLC, for shepherding our manuscript through the editorial process and to production and providing the guidance we needed to make a good manuscript great. Thanks also to our copy editor, Megan Knoll, for weeding out any errors in spelling, grammar, and punctuation and, more importantly, ensuring the clarity of our prose.

Special thanks to our technical editor, Sonia Chaumette, for detecting and eliminating any substantive errors and omissions that would otherwise undermine the accuracy and utility of this workbook.

Publisher's Acknowledgments

Executive Editor: Lindsay Lefevere

Editorial Project Manager and Development Editor:
Christina Guthrie

Copy Editor: Megan Knoll

Technical Editor: Sonia Chaumette

Art Coordinator: Alicia B. South

Production Editor: Kinson Raja

Cover Image: Anton Balazh/Shutterstock